S0-BAW-401

HOW TO SURVIVE OFF THE GRID

OUTDOOR LIFE

HOW TO SURVIVE OFF THE GRID

TIM MACWELCH
and the editors of
Outdoor Life

Illustrations by
TIM MCDONAGH
and Conor Buckley

weldonowen

I'D LIKE TO DEDICATE THIS BOOK TO MY FRIEND DAVE KLAUS.

I want to thank you for your tireless (and I mean TIRELESS!) support of my writing, my training and my public speaking. You have been so generous with your knowledge of human behavior, team building, planning and preparedness, and I am ever grateful for these things. If there were more people like you, providing the kind of guidance you have given me, it would be a far better world.

CONTENTS

GET THERE

LIVE THERE

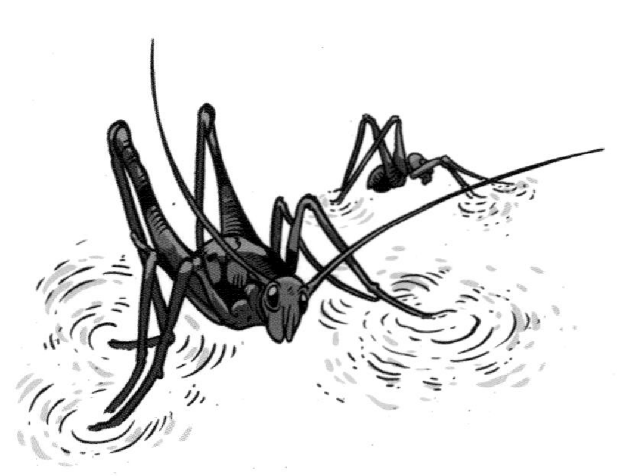

SURVIVE THERE

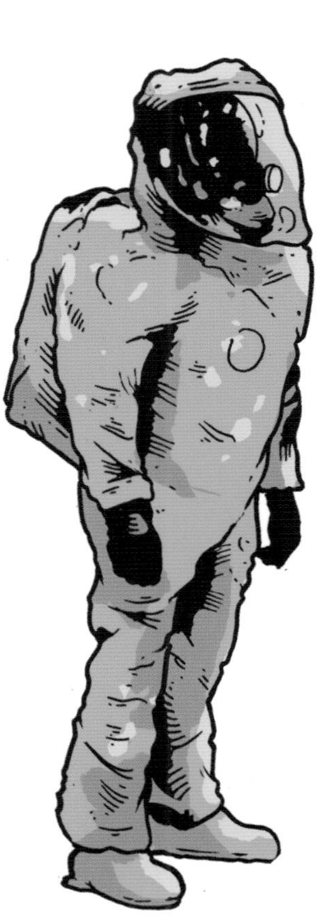

DO IT YOURSELF

Admit it. Deep down, you nurse a belief that you could survive without all the creature comforts that have grown up around your life like ivy. The on-demand electricity. The flushing toilet. The mobile phone.

You picture yourself out there with a sharp axe in your hands and a log to hew. Or maybe a rabbit to snare and a garden to grow. Or a gravity-fed water system to design and build and then share with your less resourceful neighbors. And now, you can.

You are holding in your hands a manual for surviving in post-modern times, when the lights go out and the phones go dead. But it's more than that. It's also a manifesto of hope. Humans have always been resourceful, and what author Tim MacWelch delivers on every page of this book is a reminder that you are far more capable than you think.

There's no better guide to this world of primitive (and surprisingly advanced) skills than MacWelch. He's a certified survival expert, sure, with vast and varied knowledge. But what comes through in this book is his helpful voice. He's a coach, and a friend, a colleague who has been here before and wants you to learn from his mistakes.

He's also damned funny, especially when telling . you precisely how to use your own solid waste to grow your vegetables—a self-contained food cycle if ever there was one—or to use gunpowder to test your moonshine's potency. MacWelch also offers more sober and practical guidance: how to fashion a crossbow and fix a car. How to design a safe room in case of a home invasion, and how to doctor yourself and your loved ones far from any emergency room.

Even if you never have to rely on the tips in this book, knowing and practicing them is a good idea. Read this book now, while the lights are on, so that you can take care of yourself and your loved ones when they go out for good.

ANDREW MCKEAN
Editor-in-Chief, *Outdoor Life*

GET OUT THERE

For most people, getting off the grid means specifically that you are independent of the electrical grid, and the utilities and services that accompany it. But more detailed definitions for "off-the-grid" are as diverse as the people who are choosing this self-reliant lifestyle. Maybe you have a desire to "go green" or you want to be a modern day pioneer. Perhaps you're a prepper with the goal of being independent and the drive to take your fate into your own hands. Whatever your reason for choosing to live a life "unplugged", going off the grid displays not only the American spirit of independence, but the human spirit as well.

For those who are ready to take this journey, the first step is finding a place where you can live by your own means, and building the infrastructure you'll need to live under your own power. Once you've created your new home, you'll need to gain the skills and knowledge to sustainably provide nourishment for yourself and your family. In fact, one of the biggest parts of your OTG education is learning how to raise plants and animals for your nourishment. All of these skills can be very empowering. They also put our feet squarely on the same path that our ancestors once followed. And in a perfect world, the material we'll cover in the first two chapters of this book would be enough to live off the grid indefinitely.

But it's not a perfect world. Bad luck can strike at any time. So to round out the information in this book, we've added a section to get you ready for unforeseen emergencies and take your self-reliance skills to the next level. Who knows? One major disaster, natural or man-made, could force an entire region or nation to rely on their own personal means, or perish from being unprepared and uneducated in the techniques presented here.

If you can't survive after all this? It was your time to go.

TIM MACWELCH

GET THERE

For many folks, going off the grid represents simplicity, sustainability, a life of substance, and most of all, freedom. The tiny house and tree house trend, the back-to-the-land and homesteading movements, the modern interest in sustainability—these all appeal to the childhood dream of living in trees, forts and little club houses.

As kids, we yearned to be living under our own steam and by our own rules, not the crushing yoke of our parents. And as adults, many people are rediscovering that same drive to provide for themselves and live off the grid, not under the thumb of a huge mortgage and mounting utility bills.

For those ready to take this journey, the first steps are finding a place where you can live by your own means, and building the infrastructure you'll need to live under your own power. This chapter shows you how to get started with the very basics—land, shelter, power, and water. Freedom is closer than you think!

STAKE YOUR CLAIM

LOOKING FOR YOUR OWN LITTLE SLICE OF EDEN? MAYBE IT'S A REMOTE CABIN SITE, OR A TOWN HOME WITH A GLORIOUS BACKYARD GARDEN. AT THE END OF THE DAY, YOUR HOME IS WHERE YOU MAKE IT—BUT TO MAKE IT REALLY WORK, YOU'LL NEED SKILLS IN SITE SELECTION AND PLANNING.

So you've decided to take the plunge, and make your off-the-grid dream a reality. What next? Before you spend a single dime on land, lumber, or livestock, think long and hard about the difference between your wants and your needs. For example, if you're living in a crowded city, you may want to find your own pristine parcel of land without another neighbor at all for miles around. But just how remote do you need to be in order to be at peace and off the grid? If it takes you a three-day walk to reach the nearest town, this might be a bit too much for a recent urbanite. A common knee-jerk reaction when fleeing from an unhappy situation is to go to extremes, but do you really need to isolate yourself from the world to be happy? For most people, the right location will lie somewhere in between the city and the wilderness. The real trick is finding a good balancing point between a happy, comfortable, modern life, and a romanticized back-to-the-land fantasy that can turn out to be too much work for you to sustain.

DEVELOP YOUR VISION Last year, a brilliant friend challenged me to create a vision of my future—not as a dream but as an action plan. He had me write for one hour a day, three days in a row, describing all of the things I wanted to have within a decade or two. He advised me to describe my "shining city on the hill" in great detail, as if I were standing right there and looking around right then. I had thought that I was moving toward my goals—at least, until I did this revealing exercise. Now, I challenge you to do this same exercise and define the look of your own future. It's honestly hard to know which path you should take when you don't even really know where you're going. Determining what your future should look like to you may indeed be your most important step forward.

GOOD TO KNOW

KNOW YOUR NEIGHBORS
You might flee to a rural area to live the independent dream in quiet solitude, but there will still probably be other people around. Meet them and see what they are like, before you sign papers for land. If you're going to be off-grid, your new neighbors will matter a lot more than ones you had back in the burbs. There may come a day when you need these nearby folks, and they may need your help in turn.

You might have to prove yourself as a newcomer, but virtually everyone can appreciate that there is strength in numbers. And once you are officially their new neighbor, you can break the ice by asking to borrow something, like a shovel for example. Return it soon—in better condition than you received it (metal oiled and edge sharpened)—and they'll see right away that you're worth having around.

GET THE LAY OF THE LAND All the hard work in the world may not turn a terrible site into the bastion of self-sufficiency you deserve and desire. This is why it's so important to look at all of the good points and the bad ones of a land parcel when searching for the site of your off-grid oasis.

Water Ideally, the land should have some manner of water source on it, such as a stream, pond, river frontage, or even a boggy area that could be excavated and turned into a clear pond. Find out (if you can) whether the water on the site is seasonal or is present year-round. If the property already has a modern well on it, you're lucky. If the site doesn't have a well drilled yet, ask the neighbors about their water well. How deep did they have to go to hit water? It's important to understand that drilling depth can affect the price of the well. Deeper means more expensive. But if you go cheaper and shallow, the well might go dry during the summer or a drought. A final thought about water is drainage. If it rains heavily or floods, where will the water go? (Hopefully not through your home site.)

Open Sky This means that you don't have to chop down a forest to build on the land. Either someone has done it for you, or the property is not in a woodland habitat. Whatever way you get your open sky, it means that you will have some nice open space for solar panels and wind power, if those are in your plan. My ideal amount of open sky is 50 percent open and 50 percent wooded. This can give you the best of both worlds. In the northern hemisphere, look for sites with open southern exposure for both solar power and gardening.

Access and Limitations Find out about all of the local laws that impact your use of the property. Can you even build anything there or put a road on it? Is the road maintained by the state up to your property? Do you have to take care of the road yourself with the assistance of your neighbors? What about zoning for agricultural use? Do you need building permits for anything besides the home? Will you have to travel over an easement to get to your land? If you will be planning to raise critters, are you allowed to have the ones

COMMON MISTAKE

DON'T UNDERESTIMATE THE LABOR
The worst form of estimation is underestimation. From the back-to-the-land movement of the 1960s and 1970s, to the modern tiny house movement, people have underestimated just how much labor is involved in a self-reliant lifestyle. It's a ton of work! This is why generations of people have fled the countryside and built their lives in the city—it's an easier lifestyle. This doesn't mean that one is better than the other, as they both have their merits and flaws. But it's obviously more work to crank a bucket of water up from a well than to turn the handle on a faucet. And you know it's harder to chop firewood and carry it around, than to push a button on the wall thermostat. But don't forget: Self-reliance means that you are actually relying on yourself, and not someone else. Therein lies the beauty of it. You become the architect of your life, and you build it exactly how you like, one chore at a time.

you want? I know this is a lot of questions, and there are many more you should ask. The point is to do the research before it's too late, so that nothing catches you by surprise.

Weather The weather will be greatly impacted by the geographic region you choose, but local features (such as mountains) can also create their own microclimates. Try your best to get an idea of the average rainfall numbers, high and low temperatures, wind and storms, and so on. Find out if the area is prone to flooding, tornadoes, or other extreme weather hazards. Discover whether the dirt road washes out in winter or if you're likely to get snowed in. Consider the prevailing winds in your weather calculations, too. It's great to have some kind of windbreaks (hills, trees, or both) that naturally obstruct

T/F

DOWSING REALLY WORKS

TRUE Dowsing, also called divining or water witching, has existed for at least 500 years. I've never believed in wizardry, and the average person has little success seeking buried items or resources, with or without divining rods. Yet people who do seem to have "the gift" apparently experience a lot of success locating water—one of the most important necessities of survival—so it might be worth your while to hire a celebrated dowser. Some skeptics believe that dependable dowsers are just really good at locating water through dips in the land and the types of vegetation. But supernatural or not, a professional opinion rarely hurts a situation.

storms and high winds. If the property has deciduous trees, try to scope it out in winter; when the leaves are gone, you'll get a much better view of the land.

Rent, Lease, or Buy Which makes the most sense for your plan? Renting is usually performed on a short-term basis; leasing typically refers to a longer period of occupancy. The bad part with either is that you don't own the land, and there's no guarantee that you'll get to stay there for very long. You may park a trailer or tiny house there, put in a garden, and promptly get kicked out. All your hard work would then be lost. You won't be building a home on land that you don't own (unless you have a really unusual situation going on). If you're buying land by mortgage, someone else still owns the land (the bank) but still, you can pretty much do whatever is legal to do on the property. If you pay in full with cash, then it'll just be you (and to some extent, the government) in charge of the land. My advice is simple: Rent if you must; buy if you can.

The Outside World If you're getting older or if you have some sort of health-related issue, you may not want to live too terribly far away from a hospital, or at least a small medical facility. This modern asset can be a life saver (no pun intended). Other useful elements of contemporary living can include things such as schools (if you have any children), shopping, gas stations, and restaurants. I know what you're thinking: "Restaurants? But we're going to eat all of our own food that we grow or hunt!" That's a fine goal, but here's the reality check: If you spend one too many days eating nothing but moose meat, you'll end up mounting your own head over the fire place. Trust me—you're going to need a restaurant within a few hours' drive of your homestead. So here's your homework question. How self-sufficient can you really be (especially long-term), and what can you not live without (literally and figuratively)?

Bug-Out Compatible Perhaps you're one of those people who wants a piece of land for an emergency stronghold (also known as a bug-out location). An off-the-grid property can

GOOD TO KNOW

TAKE IT EASY Your land's roads and other access points may sometimes cross over someone else's property, Bureau of Land Management territory, or other government-controlled areas. In this case, you'll probably need to obtain an easement, a common term for the right to travel, run utilities, and perform other specific things on a piece of property that is owned by someone else. Keep this issue in mind when checking out land and properties. Would you have to put up with an easement that allowed other people to travel across your land? Or would you be going across another's property to reach your own? What if that person is a jerk? These aren't deal breakers, as easements are incredibly common. It is, however, good to find out about any and all easements through, and around, your potential property.

BARE MINIMUM

TOOL UP You need lots of stuff to build a homestead from scratch and be comfortable there. Fear not; we'll show you what you need in this very book. But for now, you may be wondering: What are the bare bones you'd require? What would you need in order to prepare an area for settlement? Certainly you'd want a map of the property and a compass, to mark off distances and boundaries, lay out site features, and orient the home and gardens in the right direction (this really matters). You'd also need tools to clear the land, and basic supplies to live on while you build the homestead. Research the tools and supplies that pioneers used to establish farms, forts, and towns. Also, find out if there are any superior modern replacements for those tools (chain saw beats axe, every time). Finally, for the psychological good of your family or group, I'd recommend things to lift the spirit in challenging times or after a long hard day—a bible, some bourbon, a sack of candy, or maybe all three.

be the perfect solution, if it meets all of your group's needs. A bug-out friendly property should have great resources, such as potable water, wood, wild edible plants, and lots of game animals. The piece of property shouldn't be so far away that you couldn't reach it on foot during a crisis. If you're not living there and working from the site, about a three- or four-day walk from your home or workplace is pushing the limits. Finally, the property should also be defensible by its occupants, just in case things get really rough for a while.

SOIL QUALITY CAN VARY GREATLY EVEN ON A SINGLE PIECE OF LAND. CHECK WITH THE LOCAL AGRICULTURAL OFFICE TO GET A SOIL MAP, WHICH WILL GIVE YOU CRUCIAL INFORMATION ABOUT THE LAND'S FERTILITY.

GIMME SHELTER

SHELTER IS A CRUCIAL SURVIVAL PRIORITY—AND THE CENTER OF YOUR SELF-SUFFICIENT LIFE. WHATEVER SIZE AND SHAPE YOUR DWELLINGS MAY TAKE, AND HOWEVER YOU MAY BUILD THEM, THESE HAVENS FROM THE ELEMENTS WILL EVENTUALLY CARRY THE SAME NAME—HOME.

When you're living off the grid, you're taking full responsibility for your own shelter and protection. Depending on the climate you're in, there may be many options available. A simple turnkey approach is to buy or lease land that already has a nice home on it. This is the easiest way to get started, though it's also usually the most expensive. A cheaper alternative is to look for a fixer-upper home. You will have some work ahead of you, but if you can do all of it yourself, then you'll feel that much more accomplished, along with saving some money. A third choice is to settle on a parcel that includes structures which can be modified for living. Barns, vacated and deconsecrated churches, missile silos, and other unusual structures have all been converted into residences. A fourth option is to bring a trailer, tiny house, yurt, tent, or RV to the site with you. Any one of these could be a stepping stone or your end game. And, of course, you can build a home yourself from the ground up—a tough but fulfilling approach.

HAVE A PLAN Planning your steps is just as important as your vision of the finish line. Just ask my friend about her family's plan to live in the woods while building their dream home. In the beginning, their family lived in a tent with two parents, three sisters, two dogs, a cat, a rat in a cage—and very briefly, one grandmother who soon said "no way" and got an apartment in town. As the house-building efforts crept forward, the family moved on up to a trailer and, eventually, into their fantastic new house. Things ended well enough, but only after a couple of fairly challenging years. Remember to plan out both the small stuff and big stuff during your preparations—unless you want to spend a long winter cooped up inside a wet tent alongside several fighting kids and multiple pets.

YOUR VAN, TRUCK, OR OTHER VEHICLE CAN BE A SHELTER IN A PINCH. YOU MAY BE COLD AND CRAMPED, BUT IF YOUR TENT FLIES OFF INTO THE WINDY NIGHT SKY, YOU CAN HUNKER DOWN IN YOUR FRIENDLY VEHICLE SAFE FROM COLD, RAIN, AND PESKY CRITTERS.

READYMADE HOMES If you're not building from the ground up (at least, not right away), what options do you have for shelter and what are their benefits and drawbacks? Here are a few of the most common and why you might want to consider them.

Instant Homestead (A) Buying a piece of land with a house already built on it will be the quickest approach when you're establishing your independent lifestyle—and also the most expensive approach. Depending on the local real estate market, you may have plenty of properties for you to consider. Some of them might even be off the grid already. Try to find out the honest reason why the owners are letting the property go. Sometimes they really just wanted to move back to the big city; other times, though, the land or shelter may have real problems, so do your due diligence!

Your Home, Only Tinier (B) The growing tiny homes trend has inspired plenty of books, lots of television shows, and

BARE MINIMUM

GO NOMADIC WITH TIPIS The tipi is a marvel of design, capable of withstanding winds that would knock down a square structure. The secret is the round cone shape, which allows the wind to pass around it and the rain to efficiently run off of it. This portable shelter can even be set up or taken down by one person. Buy a higher-tech fabric version or craft your own from skins and poles.

loads of people worldwide who want to simplify their lifestyles. The inductees into this way of life are reducing their footprints, their utility bills, and their own burdens, to live in compact homes—many of which are also portable. For singles, couples, and small families without a shred of claustrophobia, this might be right for you.

Mobile Homes and Trailers (C) Plenty of folks already reside in trailer parks and mobile home neighborhoods, so either of these can be a good option for folks on a budget, especially if you can find a used trailer that's still in good condition. Getting a new trailer can be just like buying a new car: once it's been driven off the lot, its value will take a big hit. You may choose to live in a trailer while you're constructing a more permanent home on-site; the mobile home itself could also be the end-all be-all. If the latter is the case for you, why not get the upgrade, such as a double-wide with a deck and carport?

Yurts (D) For a tent, a yurt isn't actually all that cheap. But these Mongolian-inspired dwellings are quickly gaining traction within the DIY community. Yurts are round tents with an expandable wooden frame. Most modern versions include a skylight dome on the top, a woodstove pipe vent, and functional doors and windows. If you can't swing the cost of a yurt, then see about picking up a large military style tent that's woodstove compatible.

TRUE STORY

UPCYCLED HOUSING
Tiny homes and yurts aren't the only options for living under your own power in a creative and meaningful way. All across the globe, people are taking shipping containers, metal grain bins, straw bales and other unconventional items and turning them into homes. And this creativity is nothing new. In the mid-1970s, a college professor in California was able to build an entirely recycled cabin using castoff lumber, windows and cardboard boxes. No, this paper palace didn't disintegrate in the first rainstorm; the cardboard was the heavy waxed stuff used for boxes that ship vegetables, and it was cut into squares for use as siding material and shingles. After being treated with a fire retardant material (as waxed cardboard is quite flammable), the cabin was cleared for residency.

ESSENTIAL SKILL

FELLING A TREE Believe it or not, cutting down a tree is one of the most dangerous activities that we'll be discussing in this book. You need to use all due caution and don't try it alone. Take a friend who can go for help if something bad happens. Now that you're scared, here's how to do it.

STEP 1 Clear all the brush and saplings around the tree you intend to drop. This will give you a clear area for working and remove trip hazards that would throw you down into the path of a falling tree.

STEP 2 Pick a path that you want your tree to take so that it falls between other trees instead of hanging up on them.

STEP 3 Cut a notch on the back side of the tree with axe or chain saw not quite halfway through the trunk.

STEP 4 Carefully cut the front side, watching out for tree movement. As soon as you see the trunk start to lean, get out of the way.

CLEARING THE LAND Before you can start to build that dream home, you're going to need to find or create the right spot to put it on. Some properties have natural clearings, but in many cases, you'll need to do some work to get it ready. It's hard and messy work clearing the land for a home, farm or any other fixture of off grid living. You may even feel a bit bad about tearing up the landscape with any vehicles, machinery, and heavy equipment. But know this: Nature can be forgiving, and the natural world heals quickly in most areas. Follow these tips for clearing the land, and you'll help it heal even faster.

Leave Some Trees If you need to collect some logs, for any purpose, a great strategy is to do a select cut. This is quite different from the wholesale butchery of a clear cut. Select cuts take out some trees, leaving the others with more open space, light, and water. This can enhance a forest in the long run, rather than harm it. You may select the trees to take by their species, their heath, their location or any other factors. But in the end, you are being a good steward, not just a consumer.

Don't Get Stumped It's common for beginners to want to cut down a tree as close to the ground as possible. This gives you longer logs to work with if you're building a log cabin, but it makes stump removal unnecessarily difficult. Fell your trees leaving a 3-foot- (1-m-) tall stump. This will provide some much-needed leverage when pulling out the stumps with machinery or Babe the blue ox.

Beat the Bushes Shrubs, vines and other low vegetation can difficult to remove, especially if you are allergic to poison oak, poison ivy and poison sumac—and it's present on the property. But there is a low tech solution that works like a charm, if you can afford a little fencing and a livestock purchase. Goats are voracious eaters, indiscriminate in their diet, and the bane of all vegetation. Fence in a herd of goats and in a couple of weeks, they'll clear all the vegetation and vines, even poison ivy. Then all you need to do is cut down the woody growth that was too thick for them to eat.

COMMON MISTAKE

PUT YOUR BEST FACE FORWARD Most of today's home builders aren't in touch with the seasons and the environment like builders were a few centuries ago. As a consequence, most rectangular houses are oriented against the street or main road. Nowadays, the long axis of the floor plan is always parallel to the street, presumably to make the house look bigger. In fact, rather than worrying about where the street is located in regards to the house, take the time to consider the importance of sun's position and prevailing winds.

Early Americans and many other groups knew that building on an east-west axis provided great advantages. Passive solar heating can be achieved in the winter by using more windows on the south side of the home, than on the colder north side.

If you simply use the windows that were meant for the north side of the house on the south side, it won't cost anything extra—and prevailing winds could be used to cool a home by opening the eastern and western windows for a breeze in the summer. Before you decide on the blueprints for your home—and its orientation on the property—do an in-depth study of passive solar heating and other energy saving techniques. Then, work as many of these techniques as you can into your building plans.

T/F

YOU NEED LOTS OF LAND TO GROW FOOD.

FALSE The truth is, you really can get by with a lot less land than you think. A single intensive gardening plan can actually feed one person for an entire year on little more than 1,000 square feet (92.9 sq m) of garden space. Add in a small house, and you could fit every bit of this single-person paradise onto a quarter-acre (0.1-hectare) lot. With some similar—but not so extreme—gardening techniques, and a little bit of careful planning of available natural resources, you could get your property requirements down to a couple of acres (approximately 1 hectare), and a little more can even give you room for a few cattle or horses.

BUILD A LOG CABIN

Heroes of the colonial American frontier, such as Daniel Boone, Simon Kenton, and pretty much every other settler of European descent, built their own cabins from logs in the eastern woodlands. All you needed was a strong back, an axe, a few other hand tools, and a pocket full of nails to build a small home for very little money (FYI, most settlers were flat broke). If logs are an abundant resource in your area, you can follow in this great American building tradition by creating a small shed or even a small home from locally harvested logs. Here are a few key factors.

FOUNDATION Some early cabins were built right on the bare ground (not a great idea in wet or termite-infested areas). More sophisticated techniques came later, such as stone walls for perimeter foundations and stone blocks for piers under the structure. Today, we could use any number of foundation methods on a modern cabin, including concrete slabs with integrated hot water heating.

CHIMNEY For traditional log homes with fireplaces (or more modern builds with a woodstove insert), you'll need to build a sturdy chimney. Original frontier cabins had chimneys of wood that were covered in mud as a partial fire-proofing. This is incredibly dangerous and should be avoided at all cost. Mortar and local stone are a more durable and far safer set of building materials.

DOORS & WINDOWS It's tempting to try to create doors and windows by leaving openings while building the walls. This is very unsteady and dangerous. Door and window openings should be cut in with a chain saw and braced for strength if necessary—only after the walls are complete.

WALL CONSTRUCTION Every log has a thick end and a thin one. When building your walls, alternate these ends to avoid building a crooked or lopsided cabin. Otherwise you'll be the laughingstock of your woodland community.

WHAT YOU'LL NEED

Here's a list of the supplies for building a log cabin:

- Axe
- Draw knife
- Chain saw or hand saws
- Framing square
- Ropes
- Block and tackle set
- Post hole digger
- Concrete
- Level
- String
- Plywood and lumber
- Hammer and nails
- Screws
- Doors and windows
- Shingles or other roofing material

GOOD TO KNOW

FLASHING Caps of metal flashing are a great way to block moisture from wicking into your log walls from posts and piers below. They also interfere with the travel of termites, a major concern for someone in an all-wood house.

JOIN TOGETHER At the end of the day, your log cabin will be cozy and sturdy . . . or rickety and breezy, depending on how well you fit all of the pieces together. Here are some crucial things you need to know about notching. What's that, you ask? If you've ever played with a toy-log building set as a child, then you already have a good handle on the way that log notching works. It's a series of interlocking connections that keep the logs in place, each supporting its neighbors. Here are four popular notching styles that you could use.

The Round Notch (A) The round notch is simple, but efficient. Use a scribing tool to mark the shape of the lower log on the top one, cut away the wood, and roll it into place.

The Square Notch (B) If you've taken the time to square your logs, then a square notch is the next logical step. Cut halfway through each log with a saw and then pop out the chunk with an axe or froe.

The V Notch (C) This one can be done with the same axe you used to fell the tree, but a chain saw is far quicker. Create a 90 degree angle on the top of the log end, and a matching notch to connect them.

The Chamfer and Notch (D) Another notching style best suited for square logs, the chamfer and notch is a little tricky to cut but far stronger than any other method of notching.

COOL TOOL

THE SPLITTING MAUL
If I had to name one essential tool for the modern-day pioneer, this might well be it. Here are just a few of its multiple uses: axe, sledge hammer, log splitter, shingle maker, cow killer (yes, people used to kill livestock with a headshot from a maul when bullets were in short supply) and beer bottle opener (for when you work up a thirst killing cows). My favorite maul is an 8-pound- (3.6-kg-) head Snow and Nealley that I've had for over a decade. The teardrop shape is very effective at splitting common firewood species. It's like Kryptonite against stubborn logs.

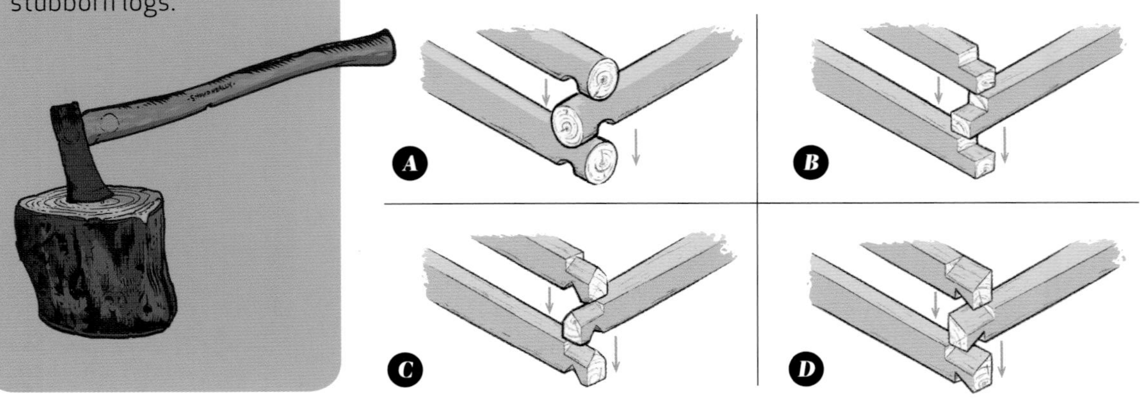

GOOD TO KNOW

STACK IT UP Dead air space inside dry logs was the original form of insulation in cabins and similar structures. Later, interior wall framing and insulation added more warmth. Do your research and pick the best fit for the walls and roof of your off the grid home. It's better to over-insulate than under-insulate.

Here are some popular options. In the first three, the wall is anchored with a sill log; each log atop it has caulking and insulation to seal up your living space. The final one, which uses no insulation, sill log, or reshaping of the logs, is truly old-school.

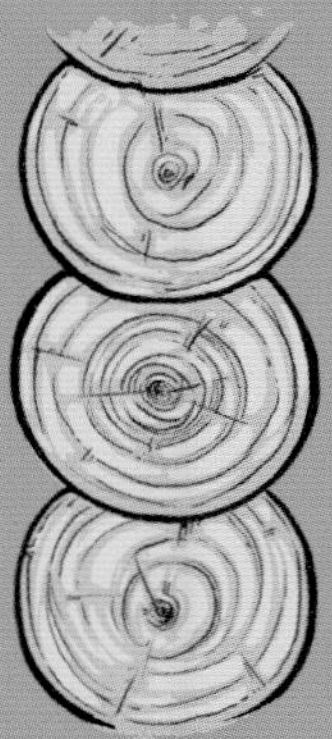

Round Logs, Scandinavian-Style Fit In this method, based on an old Scandinavian building technique, a round channel is cut underneath each log, and then the channel is filled up with insulation.

Two-Sided Logs, Flush Fit With a portable saw mill—or by undertaking some careful work with a chainsaw—you could cut two sides of each log flat so that they will fit flush above and below.

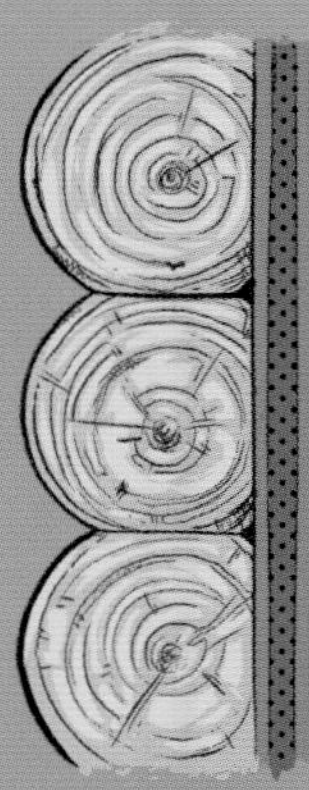

Extra-Insulated Interior Wall For greater insulation in cold climates, or a more finished interior, work down three sides of the log and then line it with interior walls made from some other material.

Round Logs, Chinking in Between If rustic is what you're after, leave the logs round and use chinking (a kind of caulk) in between them. You'll need to re-chink as the years go by, so keep an eye on them.

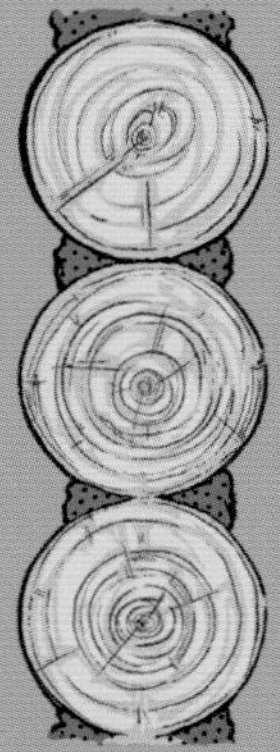

GOOD TO KNOW

CAT ON A HOT TIN ROOF
Some folks just skip the whole shingling portion of their building project and go for an old-school tin roof of the sort that is still seen on barns around the country. "Barn tin" is corrugated or grooved in any one of a number of patterns, and you just nail it down with washered nails. There are some people who greatly enjoy the retro Depression-era look, while others simply find it, well, depressing. Metal roofs have been known to rust away, although today's metallic roofing materials are much more sturdy and longer-lasting. If you've got the money to burn, a copper-panel roof can be a good decorative and protective choice: it's long-lasting and will age to a beautiful dark greenish patina . . . but, on the other hand, if you have *plenty* of money to burn, then you are probably not one of the people reading this book right now!

RAISE THE ROOF So your brand new home's walls are in place. The doors and windows have been cut in and finished, and the chimney's completed. Now the roof construction can begin. A roof over your head is arguably the most important aspect of your shelter. It's got to be very sturdy and able to withstand the elements. And, if you're doing the work yourself, it also must be easy to build. You don't want a roof that'll take a 12-man crew or a crane to install. Here are two of the chief roofing systems that you could use to put a roof over your cabin.

Post-and-Beam This is an ancient building technique that involves using a long (and often heavy) wooden beam which is supported by vertical posts or sometimes other supports. It's a very strong roofing system, though it is definitely challenging to build with a small crew and with no crane to lift the great beam.

Trusses A more modern style of roofing, trusses are triangular sections of roof framing that are built on the ground and then lifted into position to form a modular roof support system. Truss by truss, they are combined and connected, then covered with sheathing, and finally the roof covering.

FINISH THE JOB The roof is sheathed in plywood or boards cut on site with a portable sawmill. Tar paper or some other waterproof material should be placed next. Finally, shingles or shakes are nailed in place, starting at the bottom edge of the roof and working up to the peak.

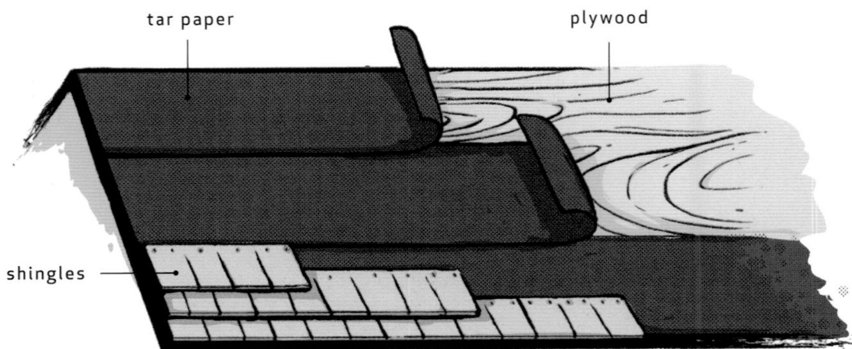

ESSENTIAL SKILL

SHAKE IT OFF Roofing shakes and shingles protect your home from the elements, and help to keep you warm and cozy by shedding the rain, holding off the snow, and helping to keep heat from escaping. So, what are they and how do you use them? The terms "shake" and "shingle" are often used interchangeably, though shingles are typically sawn into regular dimensions, while shakes are split, giving them a more rustic appearance and irregular dimensions. Both shakes and shingles are typically used for roofing, but they can also be used for a house's siding.

By using nothing more than a wooden mallet and a tool known as a froe, you can split your own shingles on-site. Cedar and cypress are excellent wood choices for shakes, as these two wood types are easy to split and highly rot-resistant. Select short logs that are about a foot and a half long (45 cm). These are called bolts and the wood should be free of any knots, which would not only interfere with splitting the wood, but leave some of the wood with knot holes, and thus unsuitable for shingling. The thickest end (the "butt") of a shake or shingle should be about ½ inch (1.25 cm). The width can be any dimension, but narrower shakes and shingles will be much less likely to warp than wider pieces of wood.

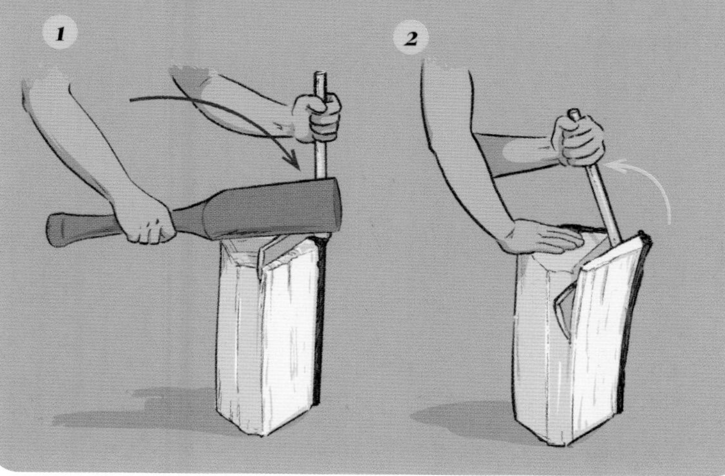

IF AVAILABLE ON SITE OR NEARBY, SLATE ROCK CAN BE TURNED INTO BEAUTIFUL GREY SHINGLES THAT ARE EASY TO INSTALL AND CAPABLE OF OUTLASTING THE DWELLING (SEVERAL TIMES OVER!).

WATER OF LIFE

WATER EQUALS SURVIVAL; WITHOUT IT, WE WON'T LAST LONG. WHETHER ON THE GRID OR OFF IT, WE RELY ON WATER FOR HYDRATION, COOKING, HYGIENE, ELECTRICAL POWER, AND MORE. WATER IS THE LIFEBLOOD OF ANY SELF-RELIANT HOME. WITHOUT IT, THERE IS NO LIFE OFF THE GRID.

Imagine a severe and prolonged drought. The earth has become scorched by the heat. Plants are dead, all the local wildlife has fled for greener territory, and the only remaining water comes from aquifers deep beneath the surface. How important would that water be to you and your family in this situation? It might be the most important thing you have, right?

Now, imagine bestowing this level of importance on all of the water that you are using right now. Would you take hour-long showers every day and wash your car every week? Doubtful. Water can be an extremely precious commodity, and you will finally realize it when you have to supply all of your own water to your off the grid household for drinking, bathing, watering the garden, and laundry. Fresh water sources will rarely give you unlimited supplies of clean water throughout the whole year. This is why we learn to manage our water use. In this section, we will see several different ways to collect and store water and—even more importantly—some options to use it wisely.

WATER, WATER EVERYWHERE Many modern people live their lives without ever really thinking about where their water comes from (besides "out of the faucet"). Can you live without a municipal water supply piped in to your home? Of course you can! Not long ago, folks cranked water up out of a well with a wooden bucket and rope, and they survived. Modern people in the developing world carry heavy jugs full of dirty river water home to their family on a daily basis. It's hard work, but they still manage. If a disaster knocked out all the utilities in your house today, you could still provide your most basic water needs if you truly had to. If you can afford to choose an off-grid lifestyle, you can afford the tools and technology to provide the clean, safe water you need.

ALWAYS KEEP EXTRA WATER ON HAND IN CASE YOU HAVE DIFFICULTIES WITH YOUR SYSTEM. FACTORY-SEALED BOTTLED WATER OR WATER-COOLER JUGS ARE HANDY AND LAST INDEFINITELY.

GET THE WET STUFF Your prospective water source is a big deal when you are looking for a place to call home, one of the biggest in fact. After all, a person can go weeks without food (not fun weeks, but you can go a surprisingly long time on very, very short rations). But without water? You won't last half a week. So, consider your options carefully. In a best-case scenario, you'll have a few to choose from—or perhaps combine more than one of the following.

Use Municipal Plumbing Wait—what happened to going off the grid? Yes, that's the goal, but the cheap and quick solution is to get connected to municipal water and sewage. If the property has this option, it can be a good way to get started. Then later, you can cut yourself loose.

Get It Delivered Another option for folks without springs and wells is to get your water delivered. A truck full of water comes to your homestead, dumps water into a large holding tank, and you use it as you see fit.

Drill Your Own Well With a small investment in the right equipment, you can actually drill your own water well to get supplied from the local water table. These wells can be productive and clear or they may be muddy and go dry if overused. For a lot more money, like thousands and thousands of dollars, you can have a professional company drill you a proper well.

Use the Local Watershed Spending your days going back and forth from the river with a bucket isn't the only option here. You may be able to create the gravity-fed water system we'll explain later in this chapter.

Grab Some Rain Catching rain water is an old practice that still makes sense. The average roof on a single family home is 1,500 square feet (111 sq m), and one inch (2.5 cm) of rain falling upon one square foot (929 sq cm) of surface area will yield over half a gallon (1.9 l) of water. This means that even a small shower can yield several hundred gallons (1,000+ l) of water (but read on for factors to consider).

ON THE GRID

COLLECTING RAINWATER The rain can be a great source of water for homes, gardens, livestock and many other uses—but you do have to do your homework before you aim a downspout into the kitchen sink. First and foremost, the rain (like any other natural resource) can be unpredictable. This means that living off rain water alone is problematic. Another issue is contamination. The birds, bugs, and other beasts that do their business on your roof or other collection surface are contaminating the water with bacteria, viruses, and many other pathogens. This means that effective filtration and/or disinfection are needed before you use the water for drinking or bathing. Finally, you'll have to research the local legal issues with rain collection. In some areas, you could be technically committing an "unlawful diversion of rainwater." Even though rain collection makes a lot of sense, it can still be considered a violation of water rights if it's happening on a large scale and without the proper permits. But don't worry, the SWAT team isn't coming to get you because you have a water barrel under your rain gutter.

GOOD TO KNOW

SAVE EVERY DROP How much water does an OTG home need? According to the USGS, the average American citizen uses 80 to 100 gallons (303–379 l) of water a day. This may seem impossible, but if you take a shower, wash clothes, and flush the toilet a bunch of times, it all adds up quickly. The worst culprit in water usage is the toilet (26 percent of average household water consumption), followed by laundry (21 percent), and showering (17 percent). If your OTG home has a composting toilet system, outhouse, or other water-free septic system, the biggest water hog is gone! Hand wash clothes and our water needs drop again. Cut your showers a little shorter, don't let the faucet run freely, and you could drop your daily water use to something like 20 to 30 gallons (75-114 l) per person per day—a water-thrifty footprint indeed!

COMMON MISTAKE

LOWBALLING YOUR NEEDS One big mistake that people often make with a water supply is underestimating their real water usage and building a plan around an amount per day that is way too low. On paper, a conservative number looks good and we feel good about it. People going OTG for an environmentally friendly lifestyle might try to wiggle that number even lower than they know it should be. But then, when you try living off a system that won't provide enough water, you're in for a shock! Your arbitrary number is not nearly enough. Before you say goodbye to your municipal water bill, take your time to figure the actual number of gallons (or liters) you use per day, ideally across seasons. This honest average will give you the numbers you need to make the right choice when it comes to managing your water and finding the right source.

GRAVITY-FED WATER SYSTEMS People around the world are setting up simple water supplies with pipe, a receptacle for water, and the free energy of gravity to bring the water to their homes and farms. This is very far from some new prepper technology; in fact it's ancient. The Romans used aqueducts to deliver massive quantities of freshwater to their bustling cities, nearly 2,000 years ago. The only thing that has changed is the conduit. Rather than using beautiful stone masonry work, we can now use cheap plastic pipe.

Find Your Source An uphill spring is an ideal source for gravity fed water, especially if it's potable and drought resistant. Search for a year-round spring during a summer drought. If it's still running in dry conditions, you have a champion. You could also collect from a creek, river, or pond that lies above your demand point. These should always be filtered for household use, due to the greater likelihood of contamination.

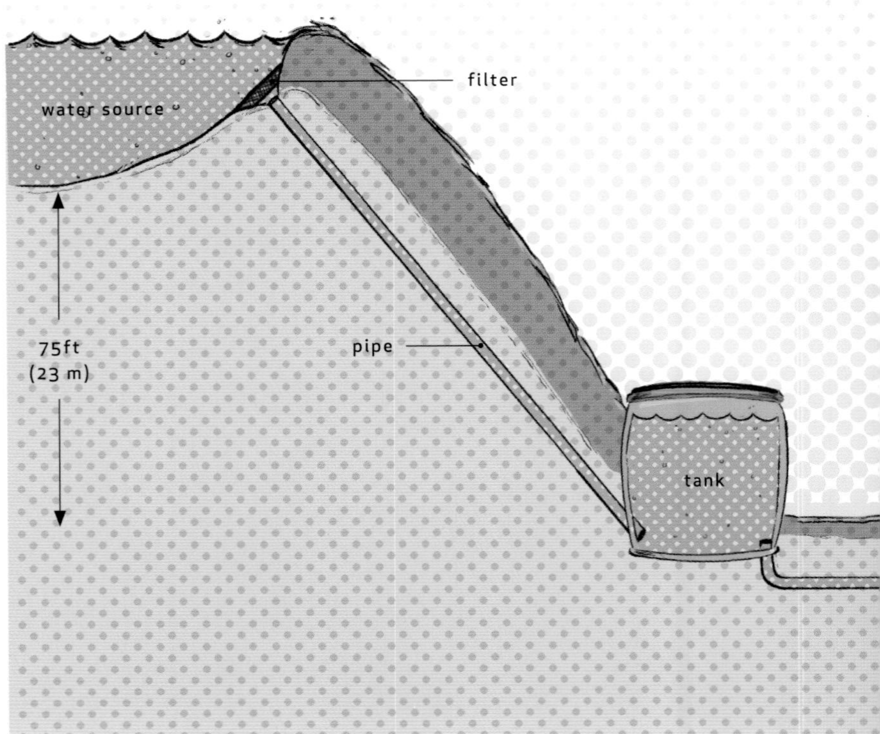

Create a Receptacle The water receptacle can be made from almost anything. Plastic tanks and in-ground concrete boxes are common containers. Just make sure that there's a sturdy cover over your receptacle, along with some kind of screen in front of the water line, to keep little frogs from clogging up the flow. The receptacle also needs an overflow, as you'll only be using a fraction of the water entering the box.

Pipe It Out Plastic piping that is safe for water supplies is your best bet for a water line. Attach it to your receptacle and then bury the piping below your frost line to prevent winter freezing. Once the line has reached your demand point, pipe it out to your needs. Most municipal supplies and independent homes operate on standard pressure of about 35 psi (2.5 kg/sq cm, or 2.4 bar). To get this from gravity alone, the source should be about 75 feet (23 m) above your outlet.

TRUE STORY

WATER EVERYWHERE, AND ONLY A PINT TO DRINK Sometimes we can learn from survival stories and tales of ingenuity that don't exactly line up with OTG living. For example, oceanic survival is one of those genuinely ironic circumstances, where you can die of thirst while surrounded with water. Take the story of Steven Callahan as inspiration. This young man was adrift in a raft in the Atlantic Ocean for 76 days in 1981. He survived by collecting rain water and rationing it carefully. During the month before his rescue, he survived on just one pint per day. While this isn't exactly a model for your survival plans, it does illustrate just how tough the human body can be – and how the will to survive can allow for miraculous endurance. But again, it's better if you don't use Callahan as a role model. Make sure to account for enough water in your survival plans.

COOL TOOL

UV DISINFECTION UNIT

If you have electricity at your homestead, either self-generated or purchased through a utility provider, you can virtually guarantee the safety of your drinking water by using an ultraviolet light disinfection unit. These small devices are installed in your water line and emit ultraviolet light at the proper wavelength and intensity to destroy bacteria, protozoa, mold spores, viruses, and other pathogens that you may encounter in untreated water. The actual device is a small cylinder with an ultraviolet fluorescent lamp in the center. As water passes through the narrow opening between light and the inner wall of the cylinder, it receives a dose of intense light that is fatal to all known water-borne pathogens. And should your home lose power, there are even small battery powered models available.

FILTRATION AND DISINFECTION All living things on Earth require water in order to survive. That includes us, but there are no shortage of microbes in the water too. Waterborne pathogens have been (and will continue to be) a huge threat to the safety and health of anyone who is providing their own water supply, especially from surface water sources. Dysentery and other similar water related ailments have been killing kings and commoners alike for millennia, and it's still happening right now. The World

	CARBON*	SAND
USED FOR	INORGANIC CONTAMINANTS (aluminum, arsenic, cadmium, calcium, chlorine, chromium, iron, lead, mercury, nickel) ORGANIC MATERIAL (e.g. algae) MICROORGANISMS (e.g. bacteria, fungi) PESTICIDES; OTHER ORGANIC POLLUTANTS	ORGANIC MATERIAL MICROORGANISMS SOME HEAVY METALS SOME PESTICIDES
LESS EFFECTIVE FOR	VIRUSES SOME HEAVY METALS FLUORIDES, NITRATES, AND SODIUM RADIATION	VIRUSES HEAVY METALS RADIATION
NOTES	KDF is a chemical compound that greatly increases the effectiveness of carbon filters in removing heavy metals and other toxins. Replace the filter before the recommended date for best safety.	These are vessels of sand that catch and hold particulates. These are an excellent first step in your system, especially if you occasionally have sediment in your water which would hopelessly clog a finer filter.

*** use filters impregnated with KDF**

Health Organization has estimated that waterborne pathogens kill as many as 3.4 million people a year worldwide. Whether you get your water off of your roof, from a spring, or out of a tank, you should be sure that you're using the necessary equipment so that you and your family don't fall victim to this global epidemic.

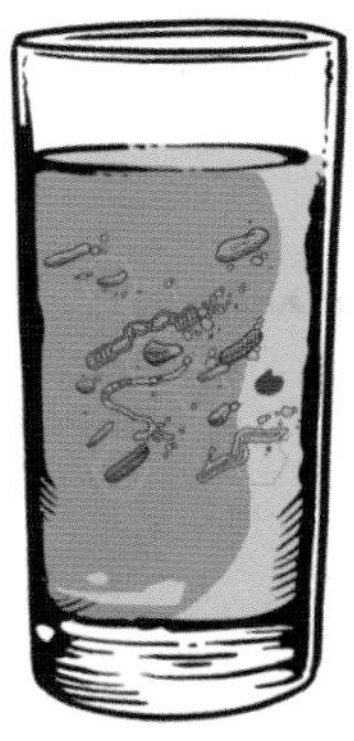

	CERAMIC	REVERSE OSMOSIS
USED FOR	ORGANIC MATERIAL MICROORGANISMS	ALMOST EVERYTHING (this very effective type of filter is marketed as being able to remove biological agents, pesticides, asbestos, arsenic, some radioactive particles, and more)
LESS EFFECTIVE FOR	VIRUSES HEAVY METALS RADIATION PESTICIDES; OTHER ORGANIC POLLUTANTS	SOME DISSOLVED GASES (including a number of potentially carcinogenic radioactive pollutants)
NOTES	I'd trust my life to these. The best ceramic filters have silver embedded in them. The ceramic screens out the larger pathogens, and the silver kills the little ones (such as viruses).	Nothing larger than a water molecule can fit through, but this filter type can clog the fastest (a carbon pre-filter may help), and may also require "normal range" water pressure, something you might not have on a gravity-fed system.

GOOD TO KNOW

DOUBLE UP ON FILTERS

If you're getting water from rainwater tanks, a well, or a local creek or river, consider a whole-house filtration system.

Flushing your toilet with contaminated water might be okay—unless your dog uses it as a fountain, and gets sick from giardia or other pathogens. As for the shower, rinsing off with microscopic particles of algae, pesticides, and arsenic is anything but refreshing. Doing your laundry with high mineral content water gets less clean, looks dingy, and wears out sooner.

Getting pure water means a very fine filter not designed for high-volume flow. Installing a high-flow filter on the main water pipes into your home will do fine for the laundry, bathroom, and the like. Water used for drinking and cooking can pass through a second filtration system designed to catch anything that the first system missed.

T/F

I CAN JUST "GO" IN THE WOODS AT MY PROPERTY WITHOUT ANY PROBLEMS

FALSE Human waste is loaded with organisms that are better contained than tracked all over your homestead, possibly contaminating your waterways. While a few single-use "cat holes" in the topsoil aren't going to be an ecological disaster, a lot of them (or a bunch of unburied waste) can become a real health hazard. If you're still building that off-the-grid paradise, or there's been some emergency, you should at the very least create a sanitary latrine rather than making like a bear in the woods.

WHEN YOU GOTTA GO You never really think about how crucial bathroom facilities are until you're forced to make do with something inconvenient, stinky, or unsanitary. Luckily, there are a number of options for the off-the-grid facilities.

Composting Toilets These crafty inventions use no water, but rather a dry process whereby human waste is broken down into dry, non-stinky matter that can be used as actual compost or disposed of without worrying about contaminating groundwater. Electric and non-electric versions of the composting toilet abound. If you can, spring for the electric version. This has a fan to fight odor, and a heater to break down the waste quicker. Either way, this system requires no water and it can be legal in areas where an outhouse is not.

Outhouses Old-school outhouses are still "in service" in areas where a traditional septic system or municipal sewage hookup isn't an option. The outhouse contains human waste and allows it to break down naturally. It's not a perfect system, as bacteria can leach into the ground water or contaminate a wide area during a flood. But it can be a quick off-the-grid solution, or for emergency sanitation. Dig a deep yet narrow hole, downwind and downhill from your cabin, camp, or home. Make sure you are at least 50 yards (46 m) away from shallow wells, waterways and other water sources. In areas with a high water table, such as bogs or wetland areas, strive to keep the hole shallow. The hole's bottom must be at least 6 feet (1.8 m) above the water table. Once your hole is done, build a seat or an entire outhouse building. The most basic build is a wooden box with an open top and open bottom, with a toilet seat attached. This is placed over the hole in a secure manner (with

BARE MINIMUM

A BASIC LATRINE Here's how to create the most basic form of outhouse, when you have no other sanitary options. First, dig a trench into the topsoil, one foot (30 cm) wide, one foot (30 cm) deep, and several feet (1+ m) long. It should always be downwind and downhill from home or camp. Leave the dirt piled nearby for waste coverage. When nature calls, straddle the trench (with careful footing), make a deposit, clean up, and bury the evidence with a sprinkling from the loose soil pile. This keeps down the fly population and helps to cover the odor as well. Keep your latrine area private by stringing up tarps, or select an area that offers natural cover, such as boulders or brush. I like to keep toilet paper in a coffee can, a little trowel, and some hand sanitizer at my latrines.

tarps around it for privacy) and you're done. You can also construct a little building to cover the hole, as long as you have the skills and materials to do so. Whichever way you go, just sprinkle a bit of dirt, wood ash, or lime down into the hole when it gets too stinky. When the hole is looking full, move the whole setup. Bury the old outhouse holes under a mound of dirt, and it all goes back to the soil.

GOOD TO KNOW

FUNNY PAPERS Back in the day, when the outhouse was the average family's primary potty option in rural areas, the Sears and Roebuck catalog did double duty. After the family had made its annual order of everything from school clothes to farm implements, the bulky tome was quickly repurposed as surprisingly effective toilet tissue. The trick is to crumple a page into a tight ball, then flatten it back out. Repeat this "crumple and flatten" technique a few times and your page becomes quite soft and absorbent. (The remaining pages gave you some reading material.) Today, various grades of pulpy paper can be given the Sears catalog treatment and repurposed for use in your outhouse or composting toilet. Just don't flush them down a standard toilet, as they may clog the line.

BARE MINIMUM

BATH TIME For some of us, a soapy rag on a stick and a bucket of warm water are all the things that we need to stay clean. For most, though, that's not going to cut it, so you'll probably want to spend some effort (and money) designing your hygiene setup.

Shower Bag One step up from that rag on a stick is a solar shower bag suspended from a tree branch. You can give yourself a rinse off, but it's not very much like a real shower. And it's definitely no fun at all in the winter.

Low-Flow Many OTG homes get by with a solar water heater running into a low-flow shower and draining into a greywater leach bed. This is much closer to a regular shower, while still using very little water or energy. But it's not exactly luxurious and it's still an outdoor option that may not work year-round in some climates.

SHOWER AND BATH PLANNING For those wanting modern (but independent) comfort, there are options in plumbing for a self-reliant home. A small shower is often the best answer; those wanting tub baths need more room (and more water). These can all be options for you, if you plan ahead when designing your home. Be sure it's a plan you can live with—remodels are messy and expensive.

Tankless Water Heaters A great option for OTG living is an on-demand water heater. These devices don't waste energy heating water when no one is using it, doing so only as needed. Electric units and gas units may heat up to 5 gallons (18.9 l) per minute, and take up very little space.

Solar Versus Wood Fired Solar water heating systems can be very economical for heating water, if you live in a sunny area. You'll still get some heat on cloudy days, but it can't compare to full sunshine. A wood-heated water supply is another option, and it works day or night. You need a supply of firewood to produce heat, but if this resource is plentiful in your area, it's certainly an option. Further along, we'll even show you how to make an inexpensive DIY wood-fired water heater from a barrel and steel pipe.

LAUNDRY DAY Clean clothes may seem low on the list of issues if you're living in off-the-grid emergency situations. Shelter, security, water, and other topics take priority. But there are reasons for this task: The oils and dirt that build up in clothing tend to destroy fibers quickly (not to mention smelling bad). Dirty clothes can harbor fungi and bacteria, causing skin rashes, infections, or other maladies.

Options for Scrubbing The old-fashioned washboard and tub have been employed since the 19th century, and they still do a fine job of laundering clothes to this very day. The method uses little water and no electricity—great for the OTG lifestyle. The method is also gentle on clothing, increasing its longevity. A wringer often accompanies this setup: rollers that squeeze the water from clothing to speed drying. Modern manual washing equipment

RECIPE FOR SUCCESS

DIY LAUNDRY SOAP Virtually any soap will pass for laundry soap in a pinch. You can dump dish soap into the wash water, or rub bar soap directly on wet clothing. You can even shave off small pieces of soap and allow them to dissolve in the water before laundering clothes. You already know that your normal laundry detergents are great performers, but you could also make your own effective and natural laundry soap (and you'll actually know what goes into it). An added bonus: this mix is a fraction of the price of your normal detergent.

STEP 1 Assemble your supplies. You'll need bar soap (any will do), borax (a naturally occurring mineral), and washing soda (very similar to baking soda). Use a cheese grater to grate the bar soap into fine shavings.

STEP 2 In a big bowl, blend together 1 part of your grated soap, 2 parts of washing soda, and 2 parts borax.

STEP 3 Store your powder blend in an airtight container such as a large-mouth jar.

STEP 4 Measure out approximately 1 to 2 ounces (25—50 g) per load of laundry.

If soap is lacking, use hot water and scrub the clothes anyway. This will remove some dirt and oil, which is better than removing none.

includes the pressure hand-washer. A small drum holds dirty clothes and a small amount of hot water with a touch of soap. The hot water naturally pressurizes the vessel, which you hand crank to agitate the load. This takes no electricity, just elbow grease.

Bye-Bye Greywater When you're done, dump soapy water and rinse water (or other grey water) into the top soil, 200 yards (183 m) or farther from any water source. If you only use a little soap, you can dump greywater around plants.

COOL TOOL

GET MEDIEVAL ON STAINS Medieval Europeans had soap for bathing and laundering clothes; they also had a great technique for literally slapping the filth out of their old-school garb. A large paddle called a "beetle" was used to beat the dirt out of the soapy wet clothing. Carve your "beetle" out of a plank of lumber, so that it resembles an oversized paddle for an errant child or a small paddle for a canoe. Ball up your soapy wet clothes on a board leaning into your washtub, and spank them with the beetle. The slap creates water pressure and water movement that removes dirt and oil. Lather, rinse, and repeat the merciless beatings as needed.

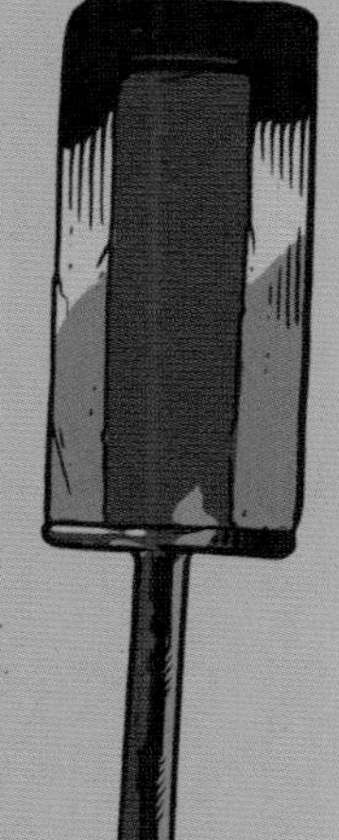

THE HEAT IS ON

IN THE DAYS OF OLD, A WARM STONE HEARTH WAS THE CENTER OF EVERY HOME. EVEN IN HOT CLIMATES, CHILLY NIGHTS WOULD BRING THE FAMILY TOGETHER BESIDE ITS GLOW. OUR NEED FOR HEAT HASN'T CHANGED, BUT MODERN METHODS FOR STAYING WARM ARE AMAZINGLY DIVERSE.

Your off-the-grid home will need a heating system that suits your local resources and your overall plan for the home site—and a backup system as well. Unless you have an entire farm of solar panels, and more batteries than a big-box store, electric heat won't be a reasonable option. This means that wood, gas, heating oil, or the sun itself will be heating your home. Passive and active solar heating systems work great, if well designed and used in the appropriate location. Natural gas or LP gas could be a good fit for those in treeless terrain with intermittent sun. Heating oil could work (and double as off-road diesel fuel in a pinch). Even wood pellet stoves could find their way into an OTG home. But, for most folks, the self-reliant fuel of choice would be the incredibly warm glow of burning wood. Woodstoves can work day or night, without electricity, and in spite of bad weather. If your homestead site is wooded or partially wooded, you could even create your own timber management plan and burn only the wood you harvest onsite.

LOOK FOR LEAKS However you decide to heat your self-reliant home, the best system money can buy won't do much good if all of that precious heat leaks out through cheap windows, gaping cracks around doors, and paper-thin walls. Insulation and draft reduction are major players in the efficiency (and comfort) of your off-grid residence. Do it right and invest in well-constructed windows, a layer of thick insulation in your walls, and some tight seals throughout the home to avoid wasting all your hard-earned heat. Stop your warmth from escaping by maintaining the weather strips on the sides of every exterior door. You can also press rope caulking into any window joints that are leaking. If your OTG home has a fireplace of its own, make sure your chimney flue damper seals up tightly.

GOOD TO KNOW

HARD OR SOFT WOOD
All tree wood is similar, but density makes all the difference. Hardwood has releases more heat per unit than softwood, and creates a longer burning coal bed in your wood stove. The most common hardwood species in the Northern Hemisphere are oak, hickory, elm, maple, and beech. Softwoods such as pine, tamarack, basswood, hemlock, birch, and poplar weigh less per unit and store less energy. Softer wood species burn quickly and their coal bed doesn't have the same longevity as hardwood. This doesn't mean that you can't use softwood. In fact, it's the only choice you'll have in some areas. In the coldest parts of North America, it's pine, spruce, birch, aspen—or nothing. Folks there stay warm burning softwood during the longer colder winter. But they have to cut a lot more wood, and feed the fire more often, than those in the south.

BUILDING YOUR WOODPILE In the spirit of independence, you may decide to cut your own firewood–but if that's not an option, you can always buy it. Depending on the fire wood suppliers, predicted winter weather, and other factors, the price can vary wildly. Wood is commonly sold in units called "cords," a stack typically 4 feet wide, 4 feet tall, and 8 feet long (1.2 × 1.2 × 2.4 m). A true legal cord is a stack of 128 cubic feet (3.6 cubic m) of wood, or a loose pile totaling 180 cubic feet (5.1 cubic m). The price of a cord can vary widely, from about a hundred bucks to three times that, depending on the season and availability.

Keep It Dry Freshly cut wood may be up to 50% moisture by weight, compared to dry seasoned firewood at 15-20% moisture. Whether you are storing fresh-cut or seasoned wood, it should never be stacked on bare ground; the wood wicks up moisture, and rot sets in quickly. Wood can be stacked on rails, wooden pallets, or other supports to allow air flow. If you don't have a woodshed (an open building for wood drying), cover the stack with a tarp, leaving the sides open for ventilation. This keeps the rain off your wood, while allowing the air rising up from underneath to dry it.

Check for Dryness Say you've cut your own wood, split it, and stacked it–but you're not sure it's ready to burn. How can you tell? Cut wood typically develops cracks (called checks) in the cut end of each piece when it is dry. It will also have changed color since being cut, turning more yellowish if dried in the shade or greyish if dried in the sun.

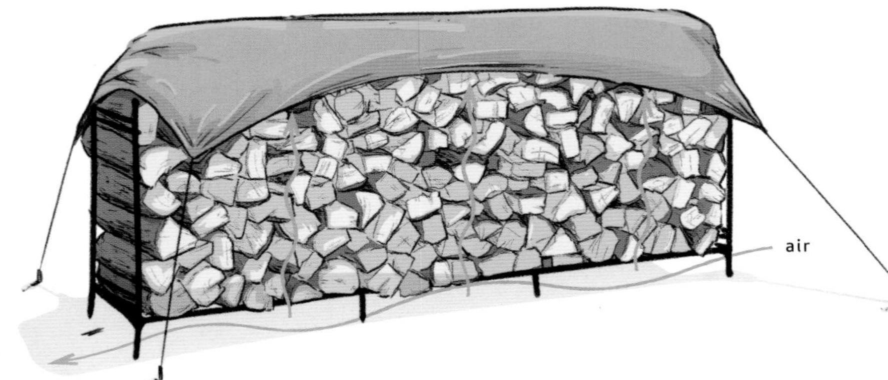

ESSENTIAL SKILL

FIRE STARTER Lighting your fire in a stove or fireplace is an art; everyone seems to have their own little tricks. Matches and lighters (especially long-necked ones) are common methods of ignition. But the really important part is your material selection and your "fire lay". My basic setup is quite simple: I sift through the cold ashes of the previous fire, remove the ashes for disposal, and then set the charcoal aside. In the clean fire box, I'll place crumpled balls of scrap paper and the charcoal chunks, between two small pieces of split firewood. I'll lay dry twigs or split kindling pieces on top of the paper and charcoal, and then set another small split firewood piece atop it all, at an angle. From overhead, the three small firewood pieces look like an "H" with a crooked crossbar. Then I light the paper with the chimney flue or stove draft open. The materials light quickly with this open and airy fire lay design, the charcoal catches too—creating the beginning of a coal bed—and the fire takes off.

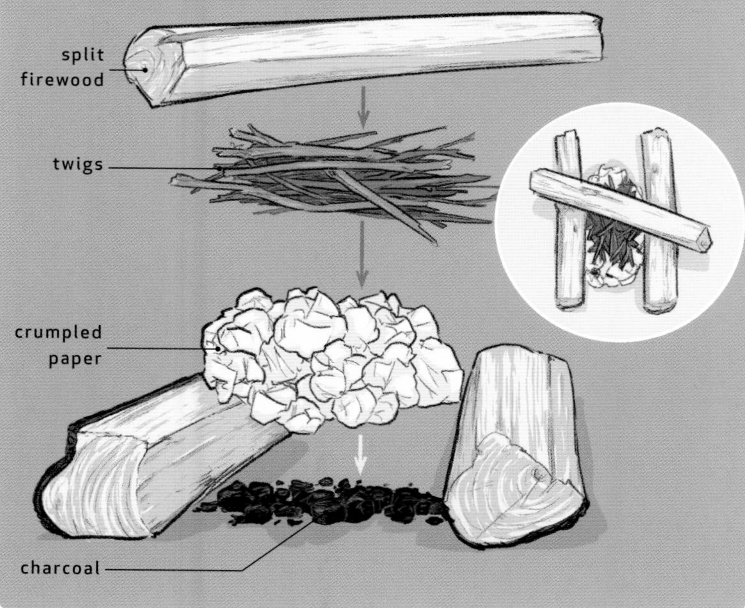

COOL TOOL

PUT IT OUT One of the most important items for those with a fireplace is a way to put out a chimney fire. Soot, creosote, and other flammables can ignite when the stove runs hot, starting a fire in the pipe or flue liner. If this gets hot enough, heat transfers through the wall or ceiling, lighting adjacent materials and starting a house fire. The solution? A Chimfex extinguisher. This looks like a common red road flare; you strike the end to light it just like a road flare. Once lit, you toss it into the fire, to one side, not on the flame. Close the stove door or fireplace covers tightly, and close the draft. The Chimfex creates a thick volume of non-flammable smoke, replacing the oxygen, and suppressing a fire in about 22 seconds. Keep two on hand for each stove or fireplace, since chimney fires can reignite and larger flues may need more than one Chimfex.

T/F

IT'S OKAY TO BURN FRESH-CUT WOOD

TRUE For all our talk about dry, seasoned firewood, you'd think it's the only thing that will catch fire. Nope! Fresh-cut wood will burn too; you just need an established bed of coals to get green wood to ignite. Wet or green wood needs plenty of heat to evaporate the higher water content before the wood can burn effectively. Many people, myself included, will cut some live wood over the winter, particularly on nicer days. This wood is then blended with dry wood to extend its burn time. You may not want to do this trick every night: Wet or green fire wood is smoky and can create excess creosote, a sooty, tarry substance that collects on chimney walls and is highly flammable.

MAKE YOUR CHOICE Wood stoves offer certain advantages and are the best choice for off-grid applications. But pellet stoves do have their own appeal. Here are some of the points for and against these two popular stove types.

	WOOD STOVE	PELLET STOVE
PROS	THE BEST HEAT OUTPUT NEEDS NO ELECTRICITY YOU CAN COOK ON FLAT-TOPPED STOVES YOU CAN CUT YOUR OWN FUEL	SELF-SUSTAINING, SO LONG AS THE PELLET HOPPER IS LOADED GOOD HEAT OUTPUT EASY CLEAN UP LOW SMOKE OUTPUT SOME UNITS ARE ABLE TO RUN ON FUEL OTHER THAN PELLETS (LIKE DRIED CORN)
CONS	MESSY; NEEDS MONITORING THE FUEL CAN BE LABORIOUS TO CUT, SPLIT, AND HANDLE MORE OF A FIRE HAZARD	REQUIRES ELECTRICAL POWER USELESS DURING A POWER OUTAGE WITH NO BACKUP ELECTRIC SOURCE PELLETS MAY BE HARD TO GET DURING EMERGENCIES

Install Your Own The most significant issue is finding a safe place to set up the stove and pipe in your home. An improperly installed stove or pipe puts you at serious risk for causing a house fire. But installed right, your risks are greatly reduced. The safest stove installation involves the use of an existing fireplace and chimney. The stove sits on your fireproof hearth and the stove pipe goes up the chimney, passing through a shield which also seals up the chimney flue. You can also run a stove pipe out through a ceiling or wall, with careful fire- and water-proofing measures in place. Wood stoves also need to sit on a fireproof area. The bare concrete slab of your basement is great, but it could even have tile, stone, or brick over the slab. Any other flooring will need an insulated stove mat, or an area with ceramic tile, stone, or slate installed on top of cement underlayment board.

Heat Safely House fires are the most obvious threat here, but carbon monoxide poisoning is also highly dangerous. Many folks aren't aware of this deadly hazard, which can be caused by an obstructed chimney on a fireplace or blocked stove pipe on a woodstove. Poisoning occurs when carbon monoxide (CO) gas builds up in the bloodstream. As the level rises, the body replaces the oxygen in red blood cells with CO molecules. This robs the body of oxygen, which can cause serious tissue and organ damage—even death.

My family experienced CO poisoning firsthand several years ago when the mesh screen over our woodstove pipe became clogged with soot. We were all getting irritable, nauseated, and very tired. Then the CO alarm went off and it all made sense. We went outside, aired out the house, and didn't run the woodstove again until the stove pipe and screen were thoroughly cleaned. We were lucky—without the alarm this story might have had a tragic ending. If you're going to use any form of fire to heat your home, clean and inspect your chimneys and stove pipes often.

WOOD STOVES CAN BURN ALMOST ANY WOOD—BUT THERE ARE A FEW THINGS THAT AREN'T A GOOD IDEA. VERY DENSE AND HOT BURNING WOODS MAY BE A FIRE HAZARD, AND PAINTED OR PRESSURE TREATED WOODS ARE NOT SAFE TO BURN IN A HOME.

MAKE A WOODSTOVE

With a purchased kit or some crafty home metalwork you can turn an ordinary steel drum into a simple and affordable wood stove to heat your off-the-grid home or outbuildings. Barrel stove kits are inexpensive and they come with the stove legs, a hinged metal door, and a damper collar you'll need to create this simple stove (you supply the barrel and some tools). They are made to work with new or used 30- or 55-gallon (114- or 208-liter) barrels with closed heads.

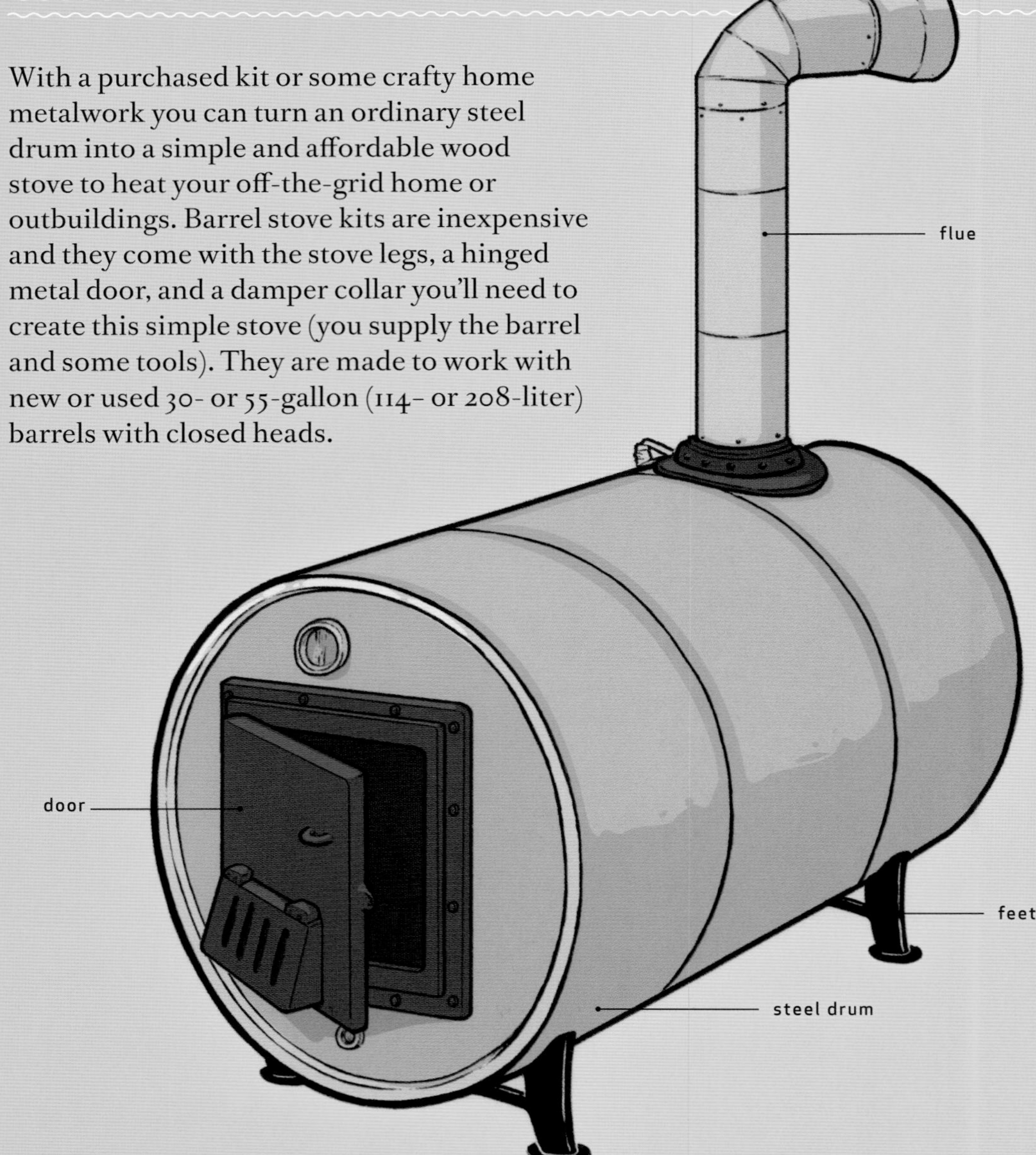

Step 1 Choose an appropriate spot for your stove. It needs to be on a fireproof surface, like a concrete floor, brick or stone hearth, or a stove mat. Also, keep the stove a proper distance from walls, with a fireproof barrier as needed.

Step 2 Trace and cut the door and stovepipe openings using the manufacturer's instructions. This can be done with a cutting torch or by drilling a pilot hole to insert a jigsaw blade, and making the cuts with a jigsaw power tool (reciprocating saw).

Step 3 Drill holes around these openings, per the instructions.

Step 4 Install the barrel stove legs, door and damper collar by bolting them in place through the holes.

Step 5 Attach your stove pipe and run it to your ceiling, exterior wall, or other safe venting point.

Step 6 Finally, line the bottom of the stove with fire bricks.

Step 7 Light your first fire and enjoy the warmth.

To capture even more heat, opt for the double-decker "two barrel" kit, which allows you to delay the heat going up the stove pipe and get more warmth from every stick of firewood.

WHAT YOU'LL NEED

To make your steel-barrel stove, get the following:

- 30- or 55-gallon (114- or 208-liter) steel barrel or drum with closed head
- Barrel stove kit, with legs, hinged door, and damper collar with flue
- Stove pipe
- Fire bricks
- Cutting torch, or drill and reciprocating saw
- Pliers
- Ratchet or socket wrench
- Screwdriver
- Long-sleeve shirt, gloves, goggles

GOOD TO KNOW

ROLL UP Some places that sell steel barrel stove kits also will sell the barrels themselves, but you can make do with any steel barrel so long as it has a closed head. Empty beer kegs are a good choice: They're built to withstand internal pressure, they have solid walls, and the only thing they contained previously was, well, beer.

GOOD TO KNOW

USE A WINDSCREEN One of the best items to use with a camp stove is a windscreen. Not only does it keep the wind from interfering with the flame of your cookstove stove, but it keeps the heat underneath the pot, right where you want it to be. You can purchase a windscreen made of high-tech materials, or make one from several layers of aluminum foil. To get the perfect fit with your foil, set up the stove and your biggest camp cooking vessel (without lighting the stove). Measure the height from the ground to the bottom of the container, and the distance around the stove and container. Fold the foil 4 layers thick, and cut to match your dimensions. This foil screen can be coiled around your cook set when you're using it, to speed up cooking and save fuel. It can be stored flat for transport, and even double as a pot lid.

CAMP OUT AT HOME If you are thinking about cooking your dinner on the porch of your tiny home or during a campout, you will have plenty of different choices of stove that you can use to boil water and cook food when you're living off the grid, short- or long-term. These choices are basically divided by what manner of fuel they use (which may also relate to their efficiency and the availability of fuel—depending on your location or situation—as well as their price). Here is a comparison of some of your most common cooking options.

FUEL TYPE		PROS	CONS
SOLID	compressed fuel cubes, woody materials	Inexpensive Readily available fuel Some sophisticated models can provide electricity from heat	Cannot be "turned off" like other stoves May produce sooty smoke
UNPRESSURIZED LIQUID	kerosene, methanol, alcohol gel	Inexpensive Readily available fuel	Slowest to boil water and cook food May produce sooty smoke
PRESSURIZED LIQUID	naphtha ("white gas"), methanol, ethanol, kerosene, automotive or aviation fuels	Easy to operate and clean	Mid to high priced to match effectiveness
PRESSURIZED GAS	butane, propane	Very efficient Easy to operate and clean	High priced (some butane stoves can be found cheaply) May be difficult to find fuel canisters in remote area or after a crisis

FIRE UP A ROCKET STOVE Long beloved of backpackers and campers, this insulated stove makes lots of heat from small pieces of wood and lets you boil water or cook food without any need of electricity or gas. You can make one using just a few 12-ounce (355-ml) soup cans, a large coffee can or empty paint can, and some all-natural kitty litter with no preservatives.

STEP 1 Cut the top and bottom off one soup can to make a feeder tube (A). Then, cut the top from another soup can to make your burning chamber (B). Lastly, cut the bottom and top off of a third can, and use tin snips to cut it open.

STEP 2 Trace the feeder tube's circumference onto the chamber's side. Cut out the circle. Do the same with your coffee or paint can (C). Insert your feeder tube through the larger outer can and into the burning chamber inside it.

STEP 3 Roll up the third soup can, and slide it about half an inch (1.25 cm) into the top of the burning chamber. Fill the remaining space (D) inside the large can with kitty litter.

STEP 4 Place a cook surface (such as a cast-iron burner top from a junked stove) on top of the large can (E). Put small sticks (F) into the tube and light them with a long match or fireplace lighter. Keep feeding sticks in to keep the heat high. (Note: The first time you light the stove, do so without cooking over it—many commercial cans have a toxic coating that should be burned off before using the unit.)

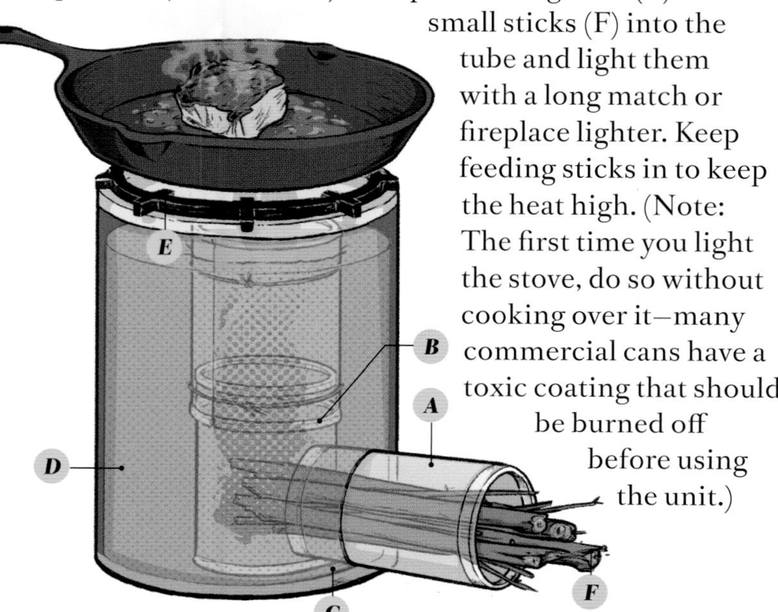

COOL TOOL

BURN YOUR BOOZE
I have used alcohol-fueled stoves for many years, while camping, backpacking, and at home during power outages. A very simple contraption, they're basically little metal cans that hold a few ounces of high-proof alcohol (methanol or rubbing alcohol work best, but you can use moonshine in a pinch). When lit, they produce a slow steady heat. One of the best features of these stoves is the ease of cleanup after a fuel spill—there isn't any cleanup! This fuel simply evaporates, and it does so quickly. You could also use the alcohol in austere conditions for wound disinfection (though it will sting painfully) or to disinfect medical equipment. The downside is that alcohol stoves are very slow to boil water. It may take more than ten minutes just to start a quart (0.9 liter) of water boiling.

POWER UP

THERE ARE MANY WAYS TO PROVIDE THE ENERGY WE NEED FOR A MODERN LIFESTYLE. IF YOU'RE TRULY INDEPENDENT, YOU CAN MAKE YOUR OWN POWER FROM THE SURROUNDING NATURAL RESOURCES. IF YOU'RE WISE, YOU'LL ALSO LEARN HOW TO CONSERVE THAT ENERGY.

There are plenty of ways to create energy for your home without being dependent on that grid we keep talking about getting off of! Exactly how you meet your need for electricity depends on a number of factors, including how much juice you're expecting to need (are you just hoping to have some lighting and maybe power up the ol' laptop for a few hours a day, or are you running a bunch of power tools every day?). Next, what kind of assist does Mother Nature offer? Is your property extra sunny? Solar looks good! High wind areas? Good news for windmills or wind turbines. Running water at a high enough volume can get you power from a waterwheel, perhaps upgraded to a mini hydroelectric project if you need a lot of power. If that water includes hot springs—bingo! You've got geothermal potential. And finally, are you going to be burning wood? Yes, you almost certainly are. That means heat, but also with the right tech, you can also generate small amounts of electricity through thermoelectric generation.

KICK IT (REALLY) OLD-SCHOOL It's not the end of all comfort if you can't provide electrical power for your self-reliant home. Although 1800s visionaries such as Thomas Edison, Alexander Graham Bell, Nikola Tesla, and George Westinghouse paved the way for electricity to transform from a scientific curiosity into the essential power source for modern life, they grew up without it. In fact, the majority of humans who have ever lived on earth never knew the glowing luminescence of a light bulb or the frostiness of a refrigerator-chilled beer. For most modern people, electricity is viewed as absolutely necessary. In truth, it's merely a luxury. You can survive in a nonelectric home, just like our ancestors and like millions of folks around the globe today.

GOOD TO KNOW

MEET YOUR DEMANDS
One of the biggest parts of setting up a power supply for an independent OTG homestead lies in figuring just how much power you'll actually need. Ideally, you are looking for the "Goldilocks" zone—not too much power or too little, but just right. And how do we do this? We calculate the power demand of every electrical draw in the proposed system. Light bulbs, well pumps, refrigerators, computers and every other demand must be tallied and detailed. Also consider high demand times, such as morning and evening, when more power may be required. Think about high demand seasonal items—for example, air conditioners in the summer. You'll need enough energy and energy storage so that you are not undersupplying any of your devices or appliances at any time—which is a sure way to burn them up.

SET UP YOUR SOLAR SYSTEM If your property gets enough sunlight, solar panels are a pretty obvious choice for your electricity-generating needs. You have a couple of options for how to do this–a standalone system or a grid-tied one–each with its benefits and downsides. You'll need to weigh cost and convenience against your desired level of self reliance. The family that's just looking to save some money on electricity and improve their property values is going to have different considerations than the folks who have decided to bunker up and prepare for the end times. Here are some basic facts and considerations to start your plan to use our friendly neighborhood star to power your home.

Standalone System As the name implies, a standalone system isn't tied to the electrical grid at all; it truly is off the grid in the purest sense of the term. The system is made up of photovoltaic (PV) solar panels, a battery bank to store the energy for nighttime use, the electronics to control the battery charging and electrical delivery, and (depending on your appliances) an inverter to turn the direct current from the batteries into alternating current that runs to your outlets. This is definitely the more expensive option, as battery banks lone can cost several thousand dollars. This is a good system if municipal utilities aren't available at your site or you absolutely don't want to be grid-tied.

Grid-Tied System This setup still uses solar panels to soak up the sun, but instead of using a battery bank for energy storage the way that a standalone system does, it's connected directly to the local electrical utility. This makes it a cheaper system, since the batteries are a major expense. It also means that you'll never run out of power, no matter how high your demand. This system is a great entry into the world of solar power, and is often adopted by those who wish to have a "greener" home. The only serious problem with this system arises when the power grid goes down. You may not have enough juice to fulfill your needs from the panels alone, and you will have no place to store excess power that your panels have produced.

COOL TOOL

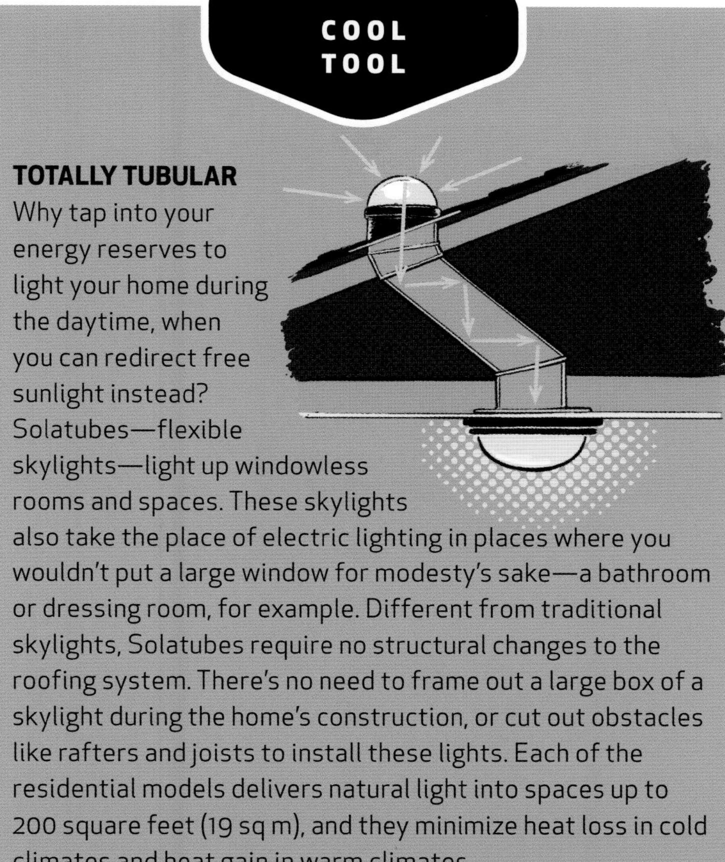

TOTALLY TUBULAR Why tap into your energy reserves to light your home during the daytime, when you can redirect free sunlight instead? Solatubes—flexible skylights—light up windowless rooms and spaces. These skylights also take the place of electric lighting in places where you wouldn't put a large window for modesty's sake—a bathroom or dressing room, for example. Different from traditional skylights, Solatubes require no structural changes to the roofing system. There's no need to frame out a large box of a skylight during the home's construction, or cut out obstacles like rafters and joists to install these lights. Each of the residential models delivers natural light into spaces up to 200 square feet (19 sq m), and they minimize heat loss in cold climates and heat gain in warm climates.

GET HOT Ever seen your cat soaking up the sun in a warm windowsill? Or, we could say, taking advantage of passive solar heating. Learn from Mittens and use the sun to warm your home, or put in a bit more investment and try an active system. A passive solar-heating strategy can be as simple as planning your home so that most of its windows are on the south side of the building, so you can maximize warmth on sunny winter days. Using dark stone flooring and walls with thick insulation is also quite effective. Active systems are more complicated, generally involving roof-mounted collectors that heat up air, water, or some other fluid, and then pump it through pipes in the walls to distribute the banked heat into the home. They're somewhat complex to set up, but require almost no power to run.

COOL TOOL

SOLAR OVENS This combination of an insulated "oven box" and reflective panels cooks food by catching sunlight and direct it into the oven, creating temperatures in excess of 400° F (204° C) under ideal conditions. A slow and steamy method of cooking, it's perfect for producing tender meats and moist baked goods. Just seal your food in the oven, align the reflectors and let the sunlight do the rest. Bake beautiful bread in four hours, cut-with-a-fork roasts and baked apples in about five, savory stews in six, and heat leftovers in about one hour. It's not as quick as a microwave, but this appliance needs no fuel or electricity at all to cook food perfectly.

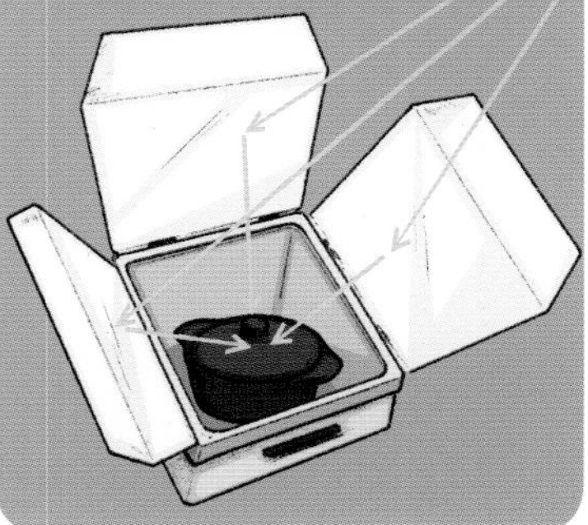

T/F

I CAN SELL MY EXCESS POWER

TRUE Many states in the US are required to buy electrical power back from you at the same price that you would have bought it from them as a customer. Elsewhere, the power companies will still pay at least something for the power you add to the grid. Companies have different interconnection standards that you will have to meet prior to selling power, so check with your local utility before you do anything. The easiest way to set this up is with net metering on a single meter. With this grid-tied system, you'll only have one utility kWh (kilowatt-hour) meter that can spin in either direction, depending on whether you are buying or selling power.

BANK YOUR POWER When it comes to power storage, you need to know about batteries. Whether you are storing electricity from solar, wind, hydroelectric, or a combination of sources, you'll need a bank of batteries tailored to your needs. Storage batteries come in different voltages that can build a 12-, 24- or 48-volt bank from modular pieces. If you aren't on a budget, glass-matt (AGM) type lead-acid batteries are virtually maintenance-free, though more expensive.

The average off-grid solar system uses open-cap deep-discharge liquid lead-acid batteries. These will lose water periodically, and should be topped off with distilled water. All batteries should be kept in an area that stays dry and maintains a stable temperature, well above freezing in cold weather. All charged batteries possess the risk of a hazardous shock and dangerous acid—be careful when working with them.

PLAY SOME AC/DC How on earth does the low-voltage direct current from your solar panels turn into the same high-voltage power that is pouring through the electrical lines to your on-the-grid home right now? It all happens in the inverter. Photovoltaic cells capture the sun's energy and convert it into direct current electricity. This is the same type of electrical energy coming from a battery. But our electrical grid and most appliances on it use alternating current, which has a much higher voltage and an electric charge that periodically reverses direction.

An inverter is designed to convert low-voltage direct current (which is a one-way flow) into high-voltage alternating current (a reciprocating flow). It does this through electronics or a combination of mechanical effects and electronic circuitry, though the original ones from the 19th century were purely mechanical. Some inverters can work in either direction, turning DC into AC, and vice versa, or even run off of your car's battery. Inverters keep showing up in new places and functions For instance, tasers have an inverter that generates tens of thousands of volts of alternating current from an ordinary 9-volt battery. Now that's electrifying!

CHOOSE A GENERATOR If you are unable to have utilities run to your home, and you can't have or don't want solar power, you could look into a generator to produce your electrical power. Here are two types of generators and why they are so different.

Portable You or your construction crew likely used one of these (or several) if you built your own off-the-grid home. These units can supply several thousand watts of electrical power, and only cost a few hundred dollars. These can be moved around, even by one person, and they are easy to transport from site to site. Most portable generators run on gasoline. The only major downsides to these affordable units is that they cannot be run full time (they'll burn up) and they are often loud (ruining the peace and quiet of your remote site). Ultra-quiet suitcase-sized units are also available, producing a surprising amount of power for their size, but these can be as much as 10 times the cost of cheaper portable units.

Whole House These units are much larger than portable units, and they are available in models that run on various fuels–including gasoline, diesel and natural gas. These units can run for longer periods than a portable generator, and supply enough power to run the average home (on-grid or off-grid). Consider buying a generator with a 220-volt option, if you have a well pump that runs on 220 volts. Generators of this size can also act as a back-up for solar systems and charge dwindling batteries after a week of gloomy skies and thick clouds.

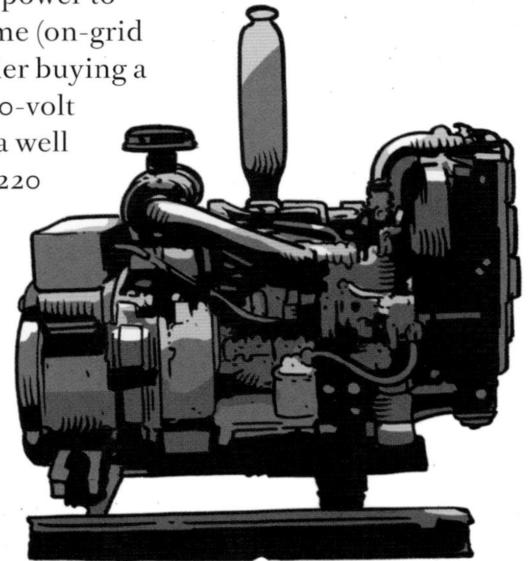

GOOD TO KNOW

POWER DOWN Once you're generating and storing your own power at home, the concept of energy efficiency will take on a whole new significance. You'll find that some appliances are real power hogs—but that doesn't mean you can't use them in your OTG home. But it does make sense to choose wisely and keep an eye on energy efficiency when shopping. If you're using an inverter to create AC power, you can use any of the energy-efficient appliances that you'd use in the average home. For those on a low voltage DC system, you can take advantage of the wide array of appliances made for RV's and motor homes. Tiny refrigerators and freezers, microwave ovens, air conditioning units, blenders, toasters and every other modern kitchen fixture exist for DC current; you just need to make sure you'll have enough power in order to run them.

LIVE THERE

Our collective ancestors lived off the land: They foraged, fished, hunted, grew crops, and bred animals. They were an integrated part of the ecosystem, not just consumers.

To renew this independent heritage, you must take an active role in producing your own food, by working with your own hands and planning carefully. Hard work is involved but, thanks to a blend of modern technology and old fashioned wisdom, it's not that hard. You don't have to own a huge farm or tame the wilderness; Even people in urban areas are taking charge of their own food security, and providing for themselves.

For stewards of fertile land, the possibilities are endless. You could raise a field of crops, an orchard of fruit, a herd of livestock, or a bit of everything. Don't think of it as taking a step backward, but taking a step on the path to a richer and more fulfilling life—and there is no life without food.

Mashed Potatoes
RICE
Turkey
Stuffing Mix
Oat BRAN
BELL'S
PASTA
Chiquita Bananas

MORE THAN MEALS

IT ALL STARTS WITH A PLAN. WHETHER PREPARING FOR THE END TIMES, OR JUST TRYING TO AVOID EXTRA TRIPS INTO TOWN, DON'T SKIP PLANNING YOUR MEALS AND STORING THE FOODSTUFFS TO MAKE THEM. OUR FOREBEARS LEARNED TO MANAGE THEIR STAPLES, AND SO SHOULD WE.

The average adult will need more than 2,000 calories per day to maintain good health and stay somewhat active. If you drop the temperature or increase the workload, they may need thousands more per day. Human beings can subsist on a diverse range of foods, but it is best if these calories come from a balance of fruits, vegetables, grains, proteins, and healthy fats. It's also best if you are storing your food in the right spot to keep it edible for as long as possible.

When you're living on the grid, storage is much less of an issue; if you happen to run out of snacks, or if you end up buying too much of something and it spoils before you can eat it, no big deal. The grocery store is not too far away or too hard to reach. Off the grid, however, planning and particularly storage become much more important. To get the maximum lifespan out of your stored food, you'll want to keep all of your supplies in a cool, dry, dark pantry, and check frequently to be sure that everything is staying dry and remaining bug-free.

CALORIES ARE YOUR FRIEND In this modern period, when obesity is a quiet epidemic across America, it may seem as thought calories can be our collective enemy. We constantly make low-calorie choices and get exercise in order to keep our waistlines from expanding, but we also tend to ignore what calories really are to us. To put it simply, calories are the energy source that we need to keep us alive. More plainly stated: calories equal survival. Without the fuel of food burning in our bodies and providing us with those calories, we would quickly grow weak and die. Yes, the food we eat should be pleasant to put in our mouths if at all possible—but at the end of the day, survival merely requires consuming something edible and safe, and it's really just about the calories.

EVEN IF YOU'RE NOT GOING OFF THE GRID, SENSIBLE PLANNING MEANS HAVING AT LEAST A FEW DAYS WORTH OF FOOD STORED IN CASE OF EMERGENCY.

STOCK YOUR PANTRY So, how should you set up that ideal off-the-grid pantry? First off, you will need to plan for your meals and efficiently store all the various foodstuffs in order to avoid running short, or having to discard or eat expired foods.

Plan Your Menus Stocking a food storage pantry can be a daunting task. However, you can make it more manageable by starting off with a solid plan. In planning out all your future menus—and, hence, what you will need to buy and stockpile—you will need to pay great attention to calorie content, various food preparation methods, your storage conditions, and any important dietary restrictions and food allergies that you or your family may have. Canned meats, fruits, and vegetables, along with a varied assortment of dry goods, can give you all the ingredients to make wholesome and familiar meals for your family, whether you're on the grid or off it.

Pack It Right Dry goods and some other foodstuffs can be safely stored for a long time in a variety of containers, when packaged with the appropriate desiccant or oxygen absorbers. My favorite containers are 5-gallon (18.9-l) food-grade storage buckets. If possible, buy new buckets with lids, although recycled ones will still work. Next up, order enough Mylar storage bags and oxygen absorbers to go with the buckets that you have. You can do small bags for rationing purposes and modular storage, or you can use large bags that line each container. You don't need the O2 absorbers in everything. Sugar, honey, and salt will never need them, but grain, powdered milk, and other foods will. 100cc oxygen absorbers are a great choice, as you can parcel out the right amount of the product for different jar sizes. You will need one 100cc packet for a 1-quart (0.95-l) jar, and 4 packets each for 1-gallon (3.79-l) jars and containers. 5-gallon (18.9-l) buckets will usually take the equivalent of 1,500cc to 2,000cc of oxygen absorbing product. Desiccant packs may also be placed in foods that have some residual moisture, such as dried fruit and jerky, to help avoid any spoilage or mold.

GOOD TO KNOW

STABLE STAPLES If you store food in a cool, dry, dark place, it should last its full shelf life in ideal conditions. Here are the shelf lives of some common foodstuffs.

WHAT IT IS	HOW LONG IT LASTS
CHOCOLATE CHIPS, SEMI-SWEET	2 YEARS
COCOA	1 YEAR
HONEY	INDEFINITELY
NUTS, SHELLED	4 MONTHS
OLIVE OIL	6 MONTHS
DRY SPICES	2-3 YEARS
CEREAL (UNOPENED)	6-12 MONTHS
DRIED FRUIT (RAISINS, APRICOTS, ETC.)	6-12 MONTHS
JERKY, COMMERCIAL PACKAGED	12 MONTHS
COOKIES, PACKAGED	2 MONTHS
CRACKERS	8 MONTHS
RICE, BROWN	6 MONTHS
HOT SAUCE	5 YEARS UNOPENED
JAM	2 YEARS

T/F

DRY RICE CAN BE STORED FOR UP TO 30 YEARS

TRUE Studies at Brigham Young University tested numerous low-moisture foods' shelf lives: whole wheat, white rice, corn meal, pinto beans, macaroni, rolled oats, potato flakes, and powdered milk. These foods stayed edible for 30 years, and kept their taste, texture, appearance, and nutrition, if properly packaged and stored. Low oxygen levels and cool temperatures aided their longevity, as did the natural low fat content. But fats, oils, shortening, and fatty foods must be rotated annually, or at least every few years, before they go rancid.

GOOD TO KNOW

FOREVER FOODS When you think about long term food supplies, it's easy to think of a pallet of MREs, or cases of canned food. But these items will only last so long. What if you wanted to put together food supplies that will last a very long time and do it cheap? Whether you're anticipating a pandemic or economic trouble, or just making practical preparations for your remote home site, these basic food supplies have a lot in common with our ancestors' annual stockpiles. Sugar, salt, and a few other key ingredients can provide nutrition, just as they did for our ancestors, without breaking the bank today. You can add these staples to your emergency food supply, all of which have a 20-plus year shelf life.

honey • white sugar • brown sugar • salt • soy sauce • vinegar • flavoring extracts • baking soda

STOCK UP ON STAPLES Dry goods are the cheapest way to go if you want to build your own emergency food supply on a limited budget. Dry pasta, rice, flour, dried beans, sugar, and plenty of other staple foods can be stored for up to 30 years with negligible nutrient loss when properly packaged and stored safely.

Flour This ingredient can be put to a variety of uses, such as fresh bread—delicious and very sustaining. It can also be used to make gravy, cookies, dumplings, and plenty of other tasty items.

Oats Most oats are rolled or milled in order to facilitate their transformation into oatmeal. This is a fine staple food as it is, but you can also use rolled oats for bread, oatmeal cookies, or granola.

Rice A global staple, rice can be boiled in water using 2 cups (473 ml) of water for each cup (200 g) of dry rice. You could also break out your flour mill to grind up some rice flour. This can be used along with wheat flour, or can replace it entirely.

Sugar Not that sugar is particularly nutritious, but it does make a great staple due to its calories and indefinite shelf life. You can add sugar to virtually anything for a flavor upgrade and calorie enhancement.

Beans Protein-packed and long-lasting, beans and other legumes can give us plenty of energy and fill up our bellies. Sure, some gas is to be expected, but still, this is another boil-only food that's just too good to miss out on. (Just be sure to soak and cook your beans thoroughly in order to avoid an upset stomach.)

Corn Dried corn can be ground into cornmeal, or boiled to rehydrate it. Some varieties can be fried until they pop (just like popcorn) or ground into a porridge similar to grits. Cornmeal can also be baked and made into cornbread, muffins, tortillas, and plenty of other foods.

Salt You don't need too much salt in your diet, but a little bit is necessary. Add salt to your dishes, both savory and sweet, to enhance their taste. It's also quite handy for food preservation and many other tasks.

Powdered Milk This chalky beverage choice doesn't have to be used as a beverage. You can add the dry mix to virtually any food to increase the protein and calories.

Pasta Your basic noodle is one of the most calorie packed dry foods out there. At roughly 1,600 calories per pound (450 g), it makes sense to stock up on this easy-to-cook staple. Just boil some in water, improvise a sauce to go with it (using canned goods or fresh produce), and you'll be eating like a king in no time.

Potato Flakes This versatile product can be prepared in a variety of ways as well—made into mashed potatoes, potato soup, potato bread, or little fried potato cakes like mom used to make. Although they can be a bit bulky (just like rolled oats), they're still very nutritious and adaptable.

MANAGE YOUR PANTRY LIKE A GROCERY STORE. PUT NEW ITEMS IN THE BACK AND PULL OLDER ONES FORWARD. THIS KEEPS YOUR FOODSTUFFS IN ROTATION AND CYCLES OUT OLDER SUPPLIES BEFORE THEY SPOIL.

VEGGIES FOR ALL

GROWING PLANTS FOR FOOD WAS A GAME CHANGER IN TIMES GONE BY. THIS PLAN OF ACTION TURNED OUR ROAMING, SCAVENGING PREDECESSORS FROM HUNTER-GATHERERS INTO HAPPIER, SETTLED, AND MORE FORWARD-THINKING PEOPLE. AND IT'S LIKELY TO HAVE THE SAME EFFECT ON YOU.

What's the most important thing to know when you're getting started in OTG gardening? There are lots of pieces to the puzzle. You'll need to know the frost dates for your area and respect them, or your tender young plants may be killed by the cold. You'll also need to know about soil fertility and how much water to use. You'll need the right seeds or seedlings for your climate and season. And you'd better learn about local pests and diseases, which can turn your gorgeous garden into a wasteland in a matter of weeks or days. These are all important, but the fundamental basis of gardening is simpler than all that. The basic tenet that I garden by is that I am a helper to the plants. I am not the one in charge; it's the plants who are really calling the shots. They want to grow and reproduce. They want to prosper. Each little seed is a tiny slumbering plant that waits until the right combination of moisture and temperature awaken it. You're just there to help them to have the right growing conditions; in exchange, they'll feed your family.

IN PRAISE OF TOPSOIL Dirt may not seem glorious, but it's the heart and soul of agriculture. Whether in a container garden on a high-rise terrace, or a rich floodplain of farmland by a lazy river, one important task is the managing of your soil and its ability to support food production. Soil fertility is the dirt's ability to grow vegetation. if enough moisture is present, plants will grow well in fertile soil and grow poorly in infertile soil. The difference between the two can be very slight and can also change quickly. The most important factors of soil fertility are the presence of essential nutrients (nitrogen, potassium, and phosphorus, along with other elements) stable moisture content, good aeration for root growth, agreeable pH, and no toxic substances, such as various salts.

COMMON MISTAKE

BE CAREFUL WITH COMPOST Composting is pretty easy, but there are a few ways we can screw up. One risk is potentially dangerous dung added to compost heaps. Canine, feline, and even human "leavings" should only be composted in the hottest piles to avoid disease-causing pathogens in your garden. If your pile isn't screaming hot, put droppings in a moderately warm pile and let it age one year before applying. Another worry is moisture—the organisms that turn trash to dirt need water! A pile should be as wet as a wrung-out sponge; check periodically and spray it with a hose if needed. Finally, don't compost anything that could harm the organisms or draw scavengers. Black walnut hulls, citrus rinds, and treated lumber or sawdust can kill beneficial organisms in your pile, while meat, dairy, or cooking oil will just draw rats and other pests.

BUILD A COMPOST PILE Keeping your soil healthy enough to sustain crops requires fertilization; for the self-reliant gardener, this means compost. Here's an easy way to maintain a compost system for your OTG home.

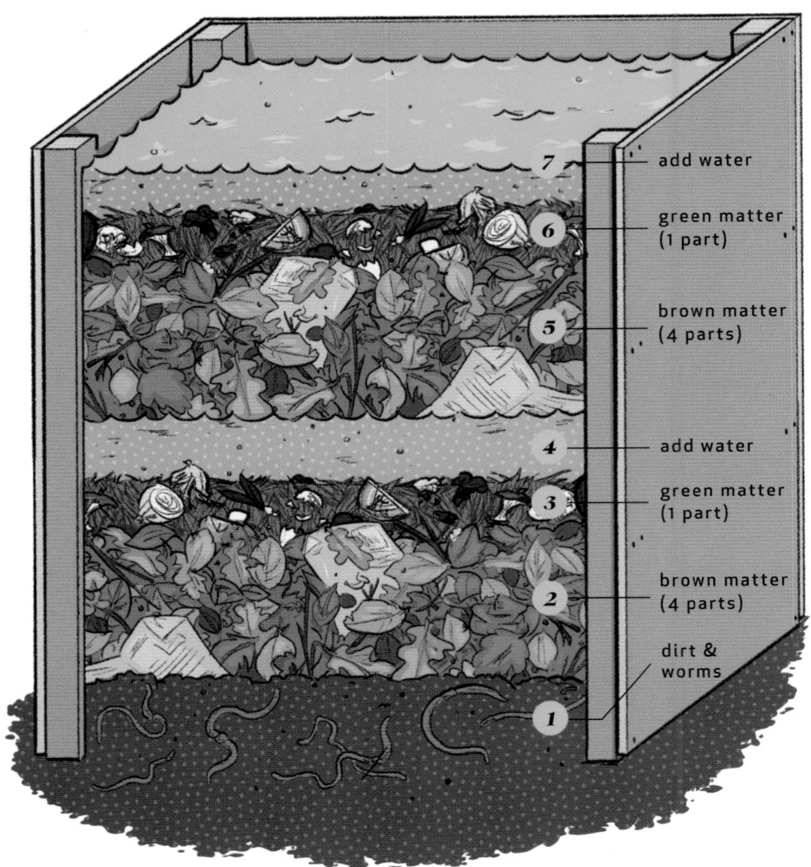

Compost is partially decomposed organic matter, and it is your garden's best friend. Through the tireless labors of earthworms, insects, fungi, microorganisms, and enzymes, all sorts of organic matter can be converted into dark nutrient-rich compost in as little as two weeks, under ideal conditions. Compost can be beneficial to any patch of earth as it helps to improve the soil structure, provides more nutrients to living plants, moderates any pH and fertility problems, and stimulates beneficial organisms in the dirt. Since compost almost literally makes itself, all you have to do is pile up the right materials in a heap. For the best possible results, you will need carbon-rich to nitrogen-rich organic materials in about a 25:1 ratio. The larger amount of the high-carbon "brown" organic materials (such as straw, wood chips, and dead leaves) along with a lesser amount of "green" materials with a high nitrogen content (including grass clippings and kitchen scraps) can be blended and watered until they have the moisture content of a wrung-out sponge. It's important to keep in mind that compost-producing organisms will need a lot of oxygen to do their work. There will be plenty of it available when the compost pile is first built, but you should take time to stir the pile thoroughly once a week to help keep it all properly oxygenated. You'll know that your pile is working efficiently if the compost starts getting hot. Heat is a byproduct of high levels of microbe activity, but even a cool pile of compost is still decomposing. It just takes a lot longer, up to a year or more.

INVITE YOUR PLANTS TO TEA Are your precious veggies looking a little bit sad? Maybe they could use a good drink—of compost tea, that is. Despite its name, this strange brown fluid isn't really tea, and it can't exactly be called compost either, but nonetheless, it is definitely an invigorating beverage for your plants. In order to make your own tea, you will need a heaping helping of some quality compost, an aquarium air pump with a set of tubing and a few air stones, an ounce (30 ml) of organic unsulfured molasses, a 5-gallon (18.9-l) bucket, and 3 gallons (11.4 l) of rainwater. Combine the water and molasses in the bucket, and then stir in several shovels of compost, being sure to leave some room at the top of the bucket to prevent it from bubbling over. Connect the air stones and tubing to the aquarium pump and let it run for three days, then turn off the pump and let the bucket settle. Strain off the water and use it immediately as a soil drench, or spray it on your plants within one hour of stopping the aeration. When sprayed onto plant leaves, compost tea provides nutrients, helps suppress disease, and may even enhance the nutrients and taste of your home-grown vegetables.

T/F

YOU CAN USE HUMAN WASTE AS FERTILIZER

TRUE It sounds gross, but night soil (or humanure) has been an indispensable tool for agriculture in some parts of Asia for millennia. This practice is fading in favor of modern (and, let's be honest, less odorous) fertilizers, but night soil kept many nations fed for thousands of years, while other farming practices around the world drained the soil. Aged solid waste and mineral-rich silt from local waterways allowed ancient farmers to grow up to four crops per year in the same dirt farmed by their great-grandfathers. It doesn't hurt that Asia's monsoon rains provide ample moisture in late summer, while the rest of the world's farmland is drying up—but still, four crops a year is amazing!

COOL TOOL

FORK IT UP Whether you hate the idea of running a noisy rototiller, or you simply want to aerate your garden soils deeper than a tiller can go, then a broad fork may be the tool you've been seeking. This two-handled tool looks like a massive pitchfork, but it's actually used for deep soil aeration and garden bed preparation, and it runs on body weight and leverage instead of fuel. Just place the fork where you want to turn over the soil, stand on it to drive the steel tines into the soil, and lean backward, pulling on the two handles to pry the loosened soil upward. Larger versions of a broad fork can reach to 18 inches (46 cm) or deeper, thus allowing nutrients and water to penetrate more deeply, and creating openings for easy root growth. Use this tool when preparing garden beds in spring or fall, and watch all of the veggies pile up.

PLAN YOUR PLOT If you're a newcomer to growing some or all of your food yourself, the planning process can feel somewhat daunting. But with a solid plan in place, and with the right land and supplies, even the total newbie can reap great (and tasty!) rewards. At the most basic level, you will need a dirt patch to grow your veggies, some seeds or seedlings to plant in the ground, a shovel, a rake, a hoe, some compost or fertilizer, and, last but not least, a way for you to water the plants.

Maximize Space So, just how big does that dirt patch of yours have to be? The answer is, "surprisingly small." If you're planning on going fully off the grid, then you will probably have some room to spare, but I would still recommend planting as though your gardening space was at a premium. That's my own personal strategy: a fairly large gardening bed, but one that utilizes tight spacing methods that have been designed for smaller plots. By following the strategies developed by gardening wizard Mel Bartholomew for his square-foot method, for example, you could grow a lot of vegetables in no more than a single square foot (0.09 sq m) of soil and a whole lot more than that in just 10 square feet (0.9 sq m). For most of us who choose to live off the grid, your space isn't likely to be so limited. I still like to use the tight spacing that's been recommended by Bartholomew, John Jeavons, and other space-savvy gardeners, but I also like to use large gardening beds. Combining these two concepts can be a bit of work over such a densely-grown area, but there can also be a similarly high yield.

Spend the Time It's been said that the best fertilizer in the world is the sweat of a gardener. Of course, that's not a literal fertilizer product, but there is actually a strong relationship between the amount of time and effort you spend on a garden and what you get out of it. You should plan on visiting your plot daily, from the beginning of your gardening endeavors to the end. This will allow you time to weed, inspect for pests and disease, water if necessary, and plan ahead for the next season.

GOOD TO KNOW

GO DEEP Poor soil need not be a garden-killer, thanks to deep soil preparation. It's said that this technique dates back to antiquity when early farmers noticed that plants tended to grow very large and healthy in the loose soil turned up by a landslide. This story may be more fairy tale than fact, but the results are real enough. A century ago, the French intensive-gardening method popularized deeply-worked soil and, in more recent times, garden guru John Jeavons has carried the torch to a new generation of green thumb hopefuls. It's a fair bit of manual labor, but the technique has proven its value time and again. Dig a 1-foot (30-cm) deep trench in your garden bed, moving the dirt out of the way. Chop or loosen the bottom of the trench the same distance down. Dig an adjacent trench and dump your loose dirt into the first trench. Repeat the process until the entire bed is worked to a depth of 2 feet (60 cm).

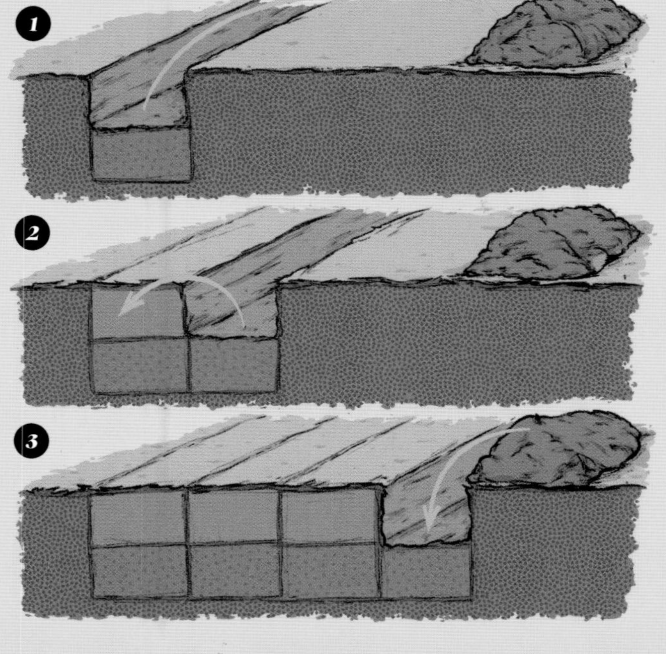

WHEN PLANNING YOUR GARDEN BEDS AND ROWS, YOU'LL WANT TO ORIENT THEM ON A NORTH-SOUTH AXIS TO MAKE BEST USE OF SUNLIGHT.

PLAN YOUR PLANTS

Learning to grow your own food is a big part of self-sufficient living when you're in an off-the-grid situation. This chart lists some common veggies for your own garden, and which make good neighbors (or not) depending on factors such as growing periods, or competition for resources, when planted next to each other.

PLANT	FRIEND	FOE
BEANS	CORN, CABBAGE, CUCUMBERS	GARLIC/ONIONS
CARROTS	LETTUCE, PEAS	STRAWBERRIES, CABBAGE
CELERY	BEANS, CABBAGE FAMILY, SPINACH, TOMATOES	POTATOES
CORN	BEANS, CUCUMBERS, MELONS, PEAS, PUMPKINS, SQUASH	CABBAGE, TOMATOES, CELERY
CABBAGE FAMILY	POTATOES, BEETS, CELERY, GARLIC/ONIONS	TOMATOES, BEANS, PEPPERS, STRAWBERRIES
GARLIC/ONIONS	CARROTS, BEETS, STRAWBERRIES, TOMATOES, LETTUCE, CABBAGE	PEAS, BEANS
POTATOES	BEANS, CORN, CABBAGE, EGGPLANT	PUMPKIN, CUCUMBER, SQUASH, MELONS, SUNFLOWER
SQUASH	CORN	POTATOES
TOMATOES	ONION, CARROTS, CELERY	CABBAGE FAMILY, POTATOES

GROW A SQUARE MEAL What's known as "square foot" gardening is really popular in small spaces such as suburban back yards, but can also make a great kitchen garden anywhere. Start by building a garden box to hold your soil. This plan is for a 4 foot by 4 foot (1.2 x 1.2 m) box. The walls should be at least 8 inches (20 cm) high, to hold your dirt in. Lay some string over it in squares to map out what to plant where, and then follow the handy guide below as to how many seeds to plant in each square of your grid.

trellis (should face north)

TOMATO 1	CUCUMBERS 2	POLE BEANS 8	CORN 4
SWEET PEPPER 1	PEAS 8	RADISH 16	SQUASH 1
CARROTS 16	BEETS 9	SPINACH 9	LETTUCE 4
BROCCOLI 1	ONIONS 16	CABBAGE 1	POTATOES 4

COMMON MISTAKE

START OUT SIMPLE Being able to raise your very own garden full of vegetables is a necessity of survival for some, and it's a fascinating skillset to learn regardless. But don't go wild planting every single thing you can think of. Begin with a few crops that help each other grow. If you have the opportunity, you could even start with one single variety of plant, and learn about how to properly take care of it. Once you've mastered one or a few vegetables, go from there.

GOOD TO KNOW

MORE THAN CABBAGES
The cabbage family is made of cole crops, also called Brassicas, or cruciferous vegetables (after their four-petaled flowers). Broccoli, cabbage, Brussels sprouts, kale, bok choy, and cauliflower are just a few of the literal dozens of varieties—all of which are high in fiber, vitamin C, and plenty of other nutrients.

RECIPE FOR SUCCESS

NATURAL PEST CONTROL

Insect pests have plagued farmers since the very first patch of crops were planted. It often feels like you have a choice between eating poison-covered food or losing crops to hungry pests. But you can take a third option with this nontoxic, DIY pest-control spray.

ORGANIC ORANGE SUPER SPRAY

Ingredients:

3 tablespoons (44 ml) of liquid organic castile soap

1 ounce (30 ml) of organic orange oil

1 gallon (3.8 l) jug of water

1 spray bottle

Directions:

Mix the three liquids in a 1-gallon (3.8-l) jug. Shake well, and pour into your spray bottle. Spray hard-shelled insect pests with extreme prejudice. You can also add one cup (237 ml) of diatomaceous earth to the mix for soft-bodied invaders, such as slugs and caterpillars.

GO SMALL A container garden is a great way to grow your own food in an apartment or other small space, bringing some self-sufficiency into you life even if you can't fulfill your off-the-grid plans quite yet. And even once you get out to your own land, a container garden can be a way to have a little garden right up on your porch, so herbs and salad veggies are only a few steps from the kitchen.

Contain Yourself When it comes to the growing containers themselves, you can get really creative. Consider using pots, plastic bins, 5-gallon (18.9-l) buckets, or even some big plastic garbage cans. Whatever you choose, drill or cut holes in the bottom for water drainage, if there aren't any. For more predictable plant growth, you can purchase (or build) self-watering containers. Window boxes are an option if you don't have any room at all.

Get Dirty Once your containers are chosen, fill each with topsoil or potting soil. The latter is the best choice, and it may be available with fertilizer included. For lightning-fast container gardens, lay out a bag of potting soil in your proposed container garden spot. Cut one or two holes in it. Plant your seeds or seedlings right in the dirt bag and keep it watered. Potting mix may lack some soil nutrients and beneficial microorganisms, but it's ready to go, and reusable for years.

Tend Your Tiny Garden Make sure you take good care of your container plants, since they are much more dependent on you than plants in the ground. Place the containers in a spot with at least 8 hours of direct, uninterrupted sunlight every day. Otherwise, you'll have slow growth and stunted plants. A south-facing yard or balcony will be your best bet for their location. Plan to water your containers regularly and deeply. Rainwater is best for plants, but you could also fill a bucket with tap water and let the chlorine evaporate off for several days before watering your vegetables. Finally, choose varieties of vegetables and greens that are meant for containers. Look for descriptions such as "patio" or "miniature" on the label. These won't take up as much room as full-sized veggies.

GOOD TO KNOW

CONTAINER-FRIENDLY PLANTS Some plants need lots of room underground in order to develop their massive root systems, while others just don't need that much footprint. In general, you should skip tall vegetables such as corn and those with trailing vines, such as pumpkins. Focus on herbs, tough perennials, root crops, and salad plants for the best results in your urban Eden.

WHAT YOU PLANT	WHAT THEY NEED
CILANTRO, CHIVES, BASIL, AND PARSLEY	HAVE TO BE REPLANTED EACH YEAR
ROSEMARY, MINT, THYME, AND SAGE	PERENNIALS THAT LAST FOR YEARS IN THE SAME POT
POTATOES, BEETS, AND RADISHES	DO BETTER IN COOL CONDITIONS
SWEET POTATOES	IDEAL FOR VERY WARM AREAS
LETTUCE AND SPINACH	CAN HANDLE SHORT DAY LENGTH OR LOW LIGHT
CUCUMBER AND CHERRY TOMATOES	DO WELL IF THEY HAVE ENOUGH SPACE AND LIGHT
GREEN BEANS AND PEPPERS	CAN HANDLE HEAT AND DRY CONDITIONS
PEAS AND KALE	CAN HANDLE VERY COLD WEATHER

DON'T FEEL LIKE YOU HAVE A GREEN THUMB? TRY SOMETHING THAT'S VIRTUALLY IMPOSSIBLE TO KILL, SUCH AS MINT, AND THEN LEARN TO CHECK ON IT EVERY FEW DAYS. PLANTS WANT TO GROW. ALL THEY NEED IS WATER, LIGHT, AND A LITTLE HELP.

COMMON MISTAKE

COUNT YOUR CALORIES Whether planning a survival garden on your skyscraper balcony or at your undisclosed bug-out location, don't just grab a bunch of seed packets based on their attractive marketing. One big consideration when buying the seeds to grow a self-reliant or survival garden is the caloric value of the plants. There simply aren't enough calories in leafy veggies alone. Growing greens is good, but your main focus should be the higher calorie vegetables. You can buy "survival garden" seed assortments, but be warned before you buy that prepackaged bucket. Are there enough high-calorie plants in there, and do those vegetable plants grow well in your area? You may be better prepared by selecting your own seeds for each plant type, taking into account the soil, weather, pests, rainfall, and frost dates of your area.

TAKE IT INDOORS In many locations, it's near impossible to grow any vegetables in the colder months—without a greenhouse, that is. A greenhouse can be a game-changer, especially when you combine the heat from sunlight with another heat source such as a propane heater or warmth from underground. We generally think of greenhouses as big, sturdy structures of glass or plastic. And they certainly can be that. But you can also do something a lot easier to implement and more reasonably priced, and still get great results for winter growing.

Organic gardener, writer, and plant whisperer Elliot Coleman has been using a simple geothermal technique to grow food in the winter in an unheated greenhouse in the northerly state of Maine for years. His revolutionary greenhouse-within-a-greenhouse technique (which is combined with a geothermal trench in the ground) has spawned plenty of variations, most of which are suited for off-grid use.

For a simplified version of this cold-weather gardening trick, dig a trench in your greenhouse 1 yard (1 m) deep and as long as your beds. Plant your beds with cold-tolerant veggies, and cover the row tightly with a polyethylene grow tunnel. Warmer air then rises from the trench at night, keeping your plants from feeling the chill.

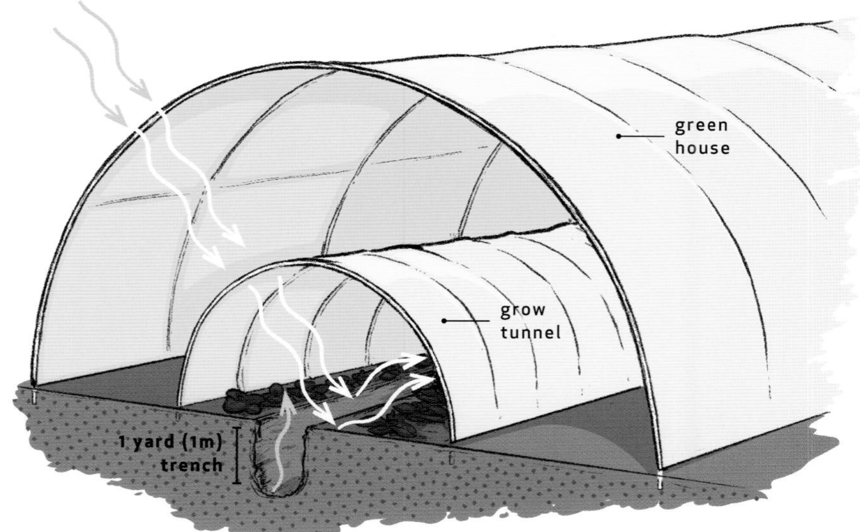

GOOD TO KNOW

COLD-HARDY CROPS

While most plants require warm weather to grow, some veggies can move the water out of their vulnerable cells as the temperature approaches freezing. The ice crystals form in open spaces between cells, then melt and reabsorb into the plant cells when the temperatures rise again. Only a prolonged deep freeze can kill the sturdiest of these cool-weather crops. Agriculturalists divide veggies into categories depending on how well that crop is likely to hold up when the mercury drops. Here are terms you're likely to see, followed by a nice selection of veggies that should get you through even a very chilly winter.

LIGHT FROST TOLERANT 28–32 °F (-2 TO 0 °C)	HARD FROST TOLERANT TO BELOW 28 °F (-2 °C)
ARTICHOKES	BROCCOLI
ARUGULA	BRUSSELS SPROUTS
BEETS	CABBAGE
BOK CHOY	COLLARDS
CARROTS	GARLIC
CAULIFLOWER	KALE
CELERY	KOHLRABI
CHINESE CABBAGE	LEEKS
ENDIVE	MUSTARD
PARSNIPS	ONIONS
PEAS	RADISHES
RADICCHIO	SPINACH
SWISS CHARD	TURNIPS

POPEYE THE SAILOR MAN MAY BE FICTITIOUS, BUT THE MIGHT OF SPINACH IS REAL! PLANT THIS COOL-WEATHER CROP AND ENJOY HEALTHY GREENS EVEN IN COLD WEATHER.

BARE MINIMUM

DIY COLD FRAME One of the quickest ways to build a cold frame is with just a few bales of straw and an old storm window. Set up the straw bales to make a square with an open center. This square should match the size of the window that you will be using. The open space inside the bales is where your dirt and plants will go. (First make sure that you're using straw rather than hay. The latter is full of grass and weed seeds which can fall out into your soil and take over.) For best results, keep the glass on the window clean, and set up your quickie cold frame on a south-facing hill, so that plenty of light will stream into the growing space. Make sure that you open the glass a little on the morning of sunny days (or else your plants can cook in there). And close it up completely in late afternoon if the weather forecast predicts a frosty or freezing night.

IT'S A FRAME-UP Cold frames can be a handy gardening option if you aren't yet sure that you want to go all the way with erecting a full-size greenhouse. These small growing enclosures are often made using a wooden frame with a large, clear cover or a recycled window with a sash attached. The frames can then be placed over garden beds or outside of the garden. Orient your frames to face south to catch the sunlight (if you're in the northern hemisphere), then place them in a sheltered spot (up against a wall or with a hedge to the north) that will offer some protection from chilly winter winds. You can even sink the frame into the ground to provide additional insulation and warmth from the earth itself.

The cold frame works by trapping the heat of the sun during the day, then transferring it into the soil where it will then be radiated out again during the nighttime. Cold frames also trap moisture, which can be important in arid climates, and can also cut down on your watering chores in any climate. Remember that cold frames can extend your growing season into winter, but they can't work miracles—you'll still need to grow frost tolerant plants.

The best trick these frames can do is to protect tender plants in winter, but they're versatile and can perform other chores as well.

COOL TOOL

AUTOMATIC VENT OPENER In cold weather, temperatures can drop quickly in a cold frame when clouds cover the sun, and the temperature can double when the sun comes back out. Without some kind of temperature regulator, your plants can alternately freeze or get cooked. Your best solution is to build in vents that let air in as necessary, so that the temperature inside the frame remains consistent. But how do you manage that without paying your teenager to stand around inside the greenhouse all day, opening and closing the vents as needed? Automatic greenhouse vent openers are small armatures that open and close your vents based on air temperature. These vent openers can be the perfect solution for an off-grid growing system because they do not require electricity. The opener operates due to a metal cylinder full of wax which expands when heated. This expansion pushes a small piston to open the vent. When the temperature decreases, the wax contracts, the vent closes, and the piston resets.

Protect Spring Seedlings In the early part of spring, a cold frame is particularly useful for hardening-off any seedlings that have been started out indoors or inside a greenhouse. Without this hardening-off period, the tender young plants can be burned by the sunlight or have their stems broken by strong spring breezes. The cold frame provides a great transition period to allow young plants to gradually adjust to the outdoor weather.

Start Summer Slips During the spring and summer, you can also use your cold frame to assist in the propagation of many types of plants. Start your white potato and sweet potato slips in sand, peat moss, or potting mix inside the cold frame in order to keep them warm and moist as they develop their roots.

IF THE COLD SEASON ISN'T TOO HARSH IN YOUR AREA, YOU MAY WELL BE ABLE TO USE YOUR FRAMES TO KEEP GROWING FRESH GREENS, HERBS AND ROOT CROPS THROUGHOUT THE LATE FALL AND INTO EARLY SPRING.

GOOD TO KNOW

THE CUCUMBER TREE

Lots of garden plants, trees, or shrubs can form symbiotic relationships mirroring natural ecosystems if you use skillful intercropping techniques. A few years ago, I planted an apple tree in the north end of my garden (so it wouldn't shade any vegetables). After it grew for a few years, I trained several cucumber vines to grow up into the young tree's branches. Soon after, I had beautiful straight green cucumbers hanging all over the tree's lower branches. A few months after that, we picked our first few apples from the juvenile tree. This system of sturdy "trellis" trees and shrubs, planted with various climbing fruits and vegetables, can be combined in countless ways. Grow green beans on a cherry tree. Have grapes hanging from your pear tree. Train hops (for beer) to climb up a peach tree. It's all up to you.

UNDERSTAND INTERCROPPING There is a long list of reasons that people have historically grown a number of carefully selected plants together as a smart agricultural strategy. It's an efficient way for plants with different nutritional needs to share the same soil for maximum efficiency. Tall plants can provide shade for shorter ones, helping with weed control, or serve as a kind of living trellis. Space that would otherwise be underutilized can be filled with smaller, less resource-intensive crops . . . and the list goes on.

Traditional Three Sisters Gardening The Three Sisters—corn, beans, and squash—have been planted together by Native Americans for centuries. Native nations and tribes throughout North America adopted this ancient gardening technique, built by intercropping companion vegetables to create a thriving community of plants. In this system, each of the three plants provides food for their gardener, and each plant also provides something that helps the other plants. The corn stalks provide a strong vertical "pole" for the climbing beans. The beans provide nitrogen to the hungry corn plants. The running squash relatives (such as pumpkin) naturally fill any open spaces, becoming a shady ground cover that helps to retain moisture and chokes out weeds. It's a great gardening system, and an important part of our world heritage.

Add a Fourth Sister There's no law that says that you have to stop at three sisters! A fourth member of the happy family can be sunflowers, grown on the north side of garden beds so they don't shade out shorter plants. These plants aren't just pretty, their seeds are high in healthy calories and provide a wide variety of important dietary minerals.

An African Variation The Three Sisters technique can also be successfully done with other vegetable plants. I have had good luck with a trio of vegetables from the other side of the world. Okra, black-eyed peas, and watermelons are plants native to Africa, that I have grown together for an African Three Sisters garden. I use okra as my corn substitute, planting it here and there. Black-eyed peas are sown loosely around the okra and the melons are planted in any openings. The black-eyed peas are the champion of the system, providing nitrogen to the other plants and shading the soil to help prevent water loss. The okra is much taller than the bush-type peas, so it receives plenty of light. The melons may not grow to huge sizes in this system, but small and sweet is fine by me.

GOOD TO KNOW

FERTILIZE WITH FISH

Many American school children learn about the New England Plymouth settlement and how a Native American man named Squanto taught colonists to use fish heads as fertilizer. The problem with the story is that fish parts were not a traditional Native fertilizer at that time. It's true, though, that fish parts provide nitrogen and phosphorus, supporting a plant's green growth, flowers, and fruiting. The catch: foxes or other scavengers will be drawn to the fish graveyard, and dig it up, killing young plants and exposing unsprouted seeds to the birds. If you use this technique, do it in a tightly fenced garden or keep a watchdog nearby. For those with a strong gag reflex, fish can also be placed in a bucket of water to decompose into a "broth" that can be used as a soil drench for garden vegetables.

COOL TOOLS

AUTOMATIC WATERING SYSTEM Most gardens are happier when watered regularly and in the early morning. But who has time for that when there are so many other chores to do at your off-grid ranch? This is where timers and other automatic devices can come in handy, when attached to soaker hoses or drip lines for watering. These can be programmed for specific times, on daily or multi-day schedules. Morning is best since water droplets at midday can act like magnifying lenses, actually burning the leaves. The a.m. shower is also better for disease prevention. Evening watering can promote fungal disease in plants susceptible to these ailments. To conserve water, set up your self-watering garden with soaker hoses or drip lines. This wastes less water than sprinkler systems, and delivers the water right where it's needed—at the roots.

THE SECRET GARDEN Obviously, tomatoes, peppers, and sweet corn taste great, but they are low in calories and are obviously food to anyone wandering by. In a time of crisis, it would be easy for almost anyone to justify stealing the fruits of your hard labor. One solution is to grow a secret garden of just root crops. Only a savvy gardener will know what these plants look like above ground, and root crops are a relatively high-calorie food that can be stored in the ground where they grow. This can be a great benefit, if you feel that break-ins, robbery, or home lootings are likely in your area during an emergency, as your food will be safely hidden in the ground.

Hide a Suburban Food Plot One of the best ways of hiding your garden in a suburban or urban backyard is to grow some food that won't even look like food to the casual passerby—and don't just plant them inside a traditional garden plot. Plant your crops in flower beds, containers, and other places throughout your property that look like ornamental plantings rather than proper garden beds. Avoid rows and orderly planting. Make it look random and weedy for some camouflage. You can even scatter them on property edges to blend in with local weeds and brush. Another added benefit to using this dispersed planting strategy: By avoiding a dense concentration of the same plant type, the unique scent of those plants is dispersed. This may make individual plants harder for pests to find, and act as a natural, pesticide-free tactic for bug control.

Leave It in Plain Sight What should your top-secret garden include? Here are some stealthy suggestions. Plant some of each of the following for diversity:

- White potatoes and sweet potatoes
- Peanuts (in warm climates with sandy soil)
- Turnips and rutabaga
- Parsnips
- Carrots and radishes (lower calorie, but good for variety)
- Jerusalem artichoke (looks like a tall flower, with edible tubers underground)

Start planting your sweet potato slips and peanuts in mid-spring, once the last frost is gone. The other plants are hardier, and can be planted in early spring. Plant these hidden crops in places with at least eight hours of uninterrupted sunlight each day. Water the veggies regularly if rain is scarce and monitor them for pests.

Eat Your Weeds Many common garden weeds are actually perfectly edible wild plants. Chickweed, purslane, lamb's quarters, dandelion, curly dock, amaranth, wild onion, plantain, and plenty of other wild edibles pop up in my garden beds throughout the growing season each year. Those weeds have parts that are edible raw or cooked, and each are packed with nutrition. When appropriately prepared, many are even delicious. Dandelion flowers that are battered and deep-fried are one of my favorite wild treats, and they are loaded with vitamin A. Chickweed and purslane are excellent in salads and full of important minerals. You might start to wonder why you're not just growing weeds since they are so wholesome and prolific. And once you learn to positively identify these persistent weeds, you'll see them throughout the year in your garden and virtually everywhere else.

ESSENTIAL SKILL

LEARN TO FORAGE

You'll start to see food everywhere when learning to identify wild edible plants. This fascinating—and savory—field of study is a great companion to your gardening skills, since so many garden weeds are actually food too. In its most basic form, learning to forage is learning how you can identify safe foods, differentiate them from common lookalikes, and prepare them as food. Of course, you'd need to pay attention to details and have 100-percent positive identification of the plant. This is usually safest when done with a good field guide. These books often contain "keys" which group and differentiate plants by flower color, leaf patterns, or branch patterns. They may also be grouped by season. Whatever you do, be sure that the plant is the species you believe it to be. If you have any doubts, don't eat it!

FRUITS AND NUTS

TREES PROVIDE OXYGEN FOR US TO BREATHE, AND THE MATERIALS TO BUILD OUR HOMES. THEY WERE USED TO BUILD THE FIRST BOATS AND SHIPS THAT ALLOWED HUMANITY TO COVER THE GLOBE. AND THE RIGHT TREES CAN PROVIDE US WITH FOOD, YEAR AFTER YEAR.

Growing plants for fruits and nuts is very different from raising a bed full of vegetables. These particular plants may live for decades or even a century. During that time, those trees, vines, and shrubs can bear food for your future self, as well as for future generations. But it's not an overnight success; it will take some time for all these slow growers to get productive. Whether it's just a tree or two, or a full-scale orchard or vineyard, the plants that produce fruits and nuts provide us with important calorie sources and delicious seasonal food. Few things will taste better in the dead of winter than the homemade preserves you made from your home grown cherries. It's like eating a jar full of summer, and it's one of my favorite foods of all time. Tree nuts, meanwhile, provide us with the highest calories we'll get from the plant kingdom, not to mention plenty of great flavors. This group of hardy plants gives us the means to make jelly, jam, wine, and a host of other beloved foods and beverages that we'll be talking about in later sections.

THE PEANUT GALLERY Peanuts don't quite belong in this section, though many think they are a nut. The peanut—also called a goober pea or groundnut—is a legume. The part that we eat is known as a leguminous bean pod (which forms underground), not an actual nut (defined as a fruit with a hard ovary wall, typically growing aboveground). Peanuts are native to South America, where they were first cultivated for food centuries ago. Since then, they have spread around the world as a food, grain, oil source, and seasoning. Today, peanut growers produce an annual crop of roughly 46 million tons (42 million metric tons) per year. You can grow your own by planting the seeds in sandy soil after all danger of frost has passed, and digging them up 4 or 5 months later.

T/F

WILD TREES CAN'T HURT YOUR ORCHARD

FALSE Most wild trees out there won't have any relationship with the orchard trees you'll plant, but a few are a bad influence on your impressionable young trees. Some red cedar trees host a fungus known as cedar-apple rust. If infected cedars are nearby upwind of apple trees, spores can infect the apple trees, damaging leaves and ruining fruits. Wild cherry trees can carry "cherry X" or cherry buckskin disease, which causes deformed cherries. One of the worst tree diseases, fire blight, can kill your pear trees when spread from infected wild trees by pollinating insects.

NURTURE YOUR ORCHARD There are a few guidelines and truths that apply to most or all fruit trees, but in a category this big, there's still a fair amount of variation in what will make your trees happy. Do your research carefully so you'll be sure you're picking the right trees for your region, and know how to care for them. Here are some big-picture tips to get you started.

Pay Attention to Pollen Some trees are more sociable than others, and they may need a variety of companions to do well. When planning your orchard, pay close attention to the trees that require other pollinating trees to be fruitful. Certain tree cultivars require a closely related, yet different tree variety for cross-pollination. Most tree catalogs and nurseries are happy to suggest companion trees for your fruit and nut tree purchases.

Bury Some Treasure Many natural materials can provide long lasting fertilization to your fruit trees – all you have to do is bury them when you are planting the tree. Hair, fur, and feathers are all great sources of phosphorus, a key nutrient for flower and fruit development. These are slow to decay, and provide years of nourishment. My favorite is crushed oyster shells. These provide calcium and other minerals that can sweeten the taste of your fruit.

Plant Comfrey *Symphytum officinale*, or common comfrey, is a member of the borage family and a great plant to grow around the base of fruit trees. The plant has large, hairy leaves and pretty, bluebell-like flowers. Commonly used to make salves and other healing remedies, comfrey puts down deep roots which are excellent at pulling up minerals. These minerals end up in the leaves, which then decompose at the base of the fruit tree. The net result of the relationship is that the comfrey acts as a miner, digging minerals from deep underground and dropping them at the base of the tree as a natural fertilizer.

Try Dwarf Trees Looking for maximum fruit yield inside a smaller growing area? Then dwarf tree varieties are

RECIPE FOR SUCCESS

BANISH BUGS NATURALLY As enticing as ripe fruit can be to a person, it must be even more heavenly to a bug—but how do we block these enthusiastic insects from destroying our long awaited fruit crop (and without using poisons that you'd need to wear a HAZMAT suit to apply)? The answer is diatomaceous earth—DE for short. This ancient substance is actually the fossilized remains of microscopic single-celled plants called diatoms. These living things were once phytoplankton that lived in the primordial oceans of the world. Today, they are mined and ground into powder to make an exceedingly safe and effective control for insects and parasites. The broken fossils have razor-sharp edges, which cut up the skin of larvae and the exoskeleton of adult insects, killing them by dehydration. The dust needs to be dry to work, but it can be easily spread as a liquid spray, becoming effective once it fully dries into a silver-white coating.

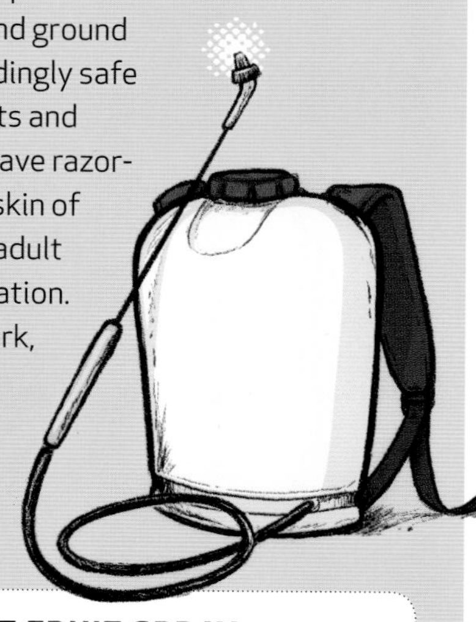

SILVER BULLET FRUIT SPRAY

Ingredients

½ cup (118 ml) of DE

1 gallon (3.8-l) of water

1 backpack sprayer

Directions

Mix the DE and water thoroughly in the sprayer. Walk through your orchard and coat every piece of fruit. Reapply after heavy rains.

for you. These diminutive trees can be hybridized and/or grafted trees capable of producing high yields while taking up very little space. If you have a small backyard or if you just want to grow a fruit tree in a large pot, then dwarf varieties are the answer.

KEEP IT LOCAL. FIND OUT WHICH TREE VARIETIES DO BEST IN YOUR CLIMATE, AND AVOID PLANTING TREES THAT WON'T PROSPER. THERE'S NO POINT IN GROWING TREES THAT WON'T PERFORM WHERE YOU LIVE.

DON'T FORGET TO HARVEST YOUR LOCAL WILD TREE NUTS. HICKORY NUTS, ACORNS, BEECH NUTS, AND MANY OTHER WILD NUTS OFFER HIGH CALORIES AND UNIQUE TASTES!

GO NUTS Planting nut trees in your orchard will add beauty to your homestead—and healthy fats and protein to your diet. Pay close attention to the maximum size these trees can reach, and plant accordingly to avoid crowding them. This is a common rookie mistake, as some of them want to be planted 60 feet (18.2 m) from their neighbors, which is easy to mess up when they're young and seem so small.

NUT TREE	MAX SIZE TREE CAN REACH	CALORIES PER OUNCE (28G) & NUTRIENTS
PECAN	131 FT (39.9 M) TALL PLANT 60 FT (18.2 M) APART	196 CALORIES, SOME POTASSIUM, AND A LITTLE IRON
ENGLISH WALNUT	114 FT (34.7 M) TALL PLANT 60 FT (18.2 M) APART	185 CALORIES, SOME POTASSIUM, CALCIUM, AND IRON
BLACK WALNUT	131 FT (39.9 M) TALL PLANT 60 FT (18.2 M) APART	175 CALORIES,HIGH POTASSIUM, AND PROTEIN
ALMOND	33 FT (10.1 M) TALL PLANT 22 FT (6.7 M) APART	164 CALORIES, POTASSIUM, CALCIUM, B VITAMINS, AND IRON
CHESTNUT	98 FT (29.8 M) TALL PLANT 24 FT (7.3 M) APART	64 CALORIES, POTASSIUM, AND VITAMIN C
HAZELNUT	49 FT (14.9 M) TALL PLANT 30 FT (9.1 M) APART	178 CALORIES, POTASSIUM, AND IRON

RECIPE FOR SUCCESS

DIY DEER REPELLENT White-tail deer are remarkable creatures, but they can do serious damage to young trees and fruit. Deer just can't seem to resist munching on the leaves and rubbing their antlers on the bark of saplings. But there is a way to make them keep their distance, with a safe and sustainable spray. When you have an abundance of eggs from your OTG flock, you can use egg yolks and water to create a spray for the leaves and tree trunks—even the young fruits. Douse this stinky mix all over your trees, and repeat after rains wash it off.

BENEFITS	PROBLEMS
EASY TO SHELL, AS NUTS ARE LARGE AND SWEET. WOOD IS NICE FOR SMOKING FOOD. TAP FOR SYRUP LIKE MAPLE.	THEY DON'T DO WELL IN COLD CLIMATE. MOST VARIETIES NEED A POLLINATOR TREE.
VERY COLD-TOLERANT TREES WITH HARDWOOD THAT MAKES BEAUTIFUL LUMBER.	SOME VARIETIES MAY NEED A POLLINATOR TREE.
HAS PRETTY DARK LUMBER AND CAN BE TAPPED FOR SYRUP LIKE A MAPLE.	SECRETES A HORMONE INTO THE SOIL THAT MAY KILL OTHER PLANTS GROWING NEARBY.
MAKES ALMOND MILK AND GLUTEN-FREE ALMOND FLOUR FOR BAKING.	DOESN'T DO WELL IN COLD CLIMATES.
THE WOOD MAKES VERY DURABLE, ROT-RESISTANT LUMBER.	IT'S A LOW-FAT TREE NUT WITH NEEDLE SHARP SPINES ON ITS HUSK.
SMALL TREES THAT CAN BE PRUNED INTO SHRUBS.	CAN CONTRACT EASTERN FILBERT BLIGHT, WHICH KILLS THE TREE IF UNTREATED.

COOL TOOLS

Fruit Picking Pole If you haven't been blessed with great height, you can still reach the ripe fruit on your trees with a little help, namely a fruit picking pole. If you're crafty with wire or sewing, you can make one yourself or you can just order one from a catalog. These can be all-wire baskets or a wire rim with a soft cloth bag attached. They are commonly used with soft padding in the bottom, to protect vulnerable fruits from bruising. This little basket on a stick lets you reach up into your tree's canopy to grab the perfect apple or pear and bring it safely down. No more standing on wobbly ladders or falling out of trees.

GOOD TO KNOW

TRAIN YOUR GRAPES
Most grapevine species are covered in tendrils, which grab onto things, letting the vine climb toward sunlight. When training grapes to grow laterally (for example, on a trellis), wrap a vine around a wire or post several times and the tendrils will soon lock it in place. On a grape vine that you'll be running in two directions, prune all but the two strongest, fastest-growing shoots. Tie these in place if they aren't long enough to wrap around, or they won't stay. Next year, remove additional shoots from the main vine, and side branches from your two main branches. During the second winter, prune those two horizontal vines down to five buds on each cane and get ready for the grapes!

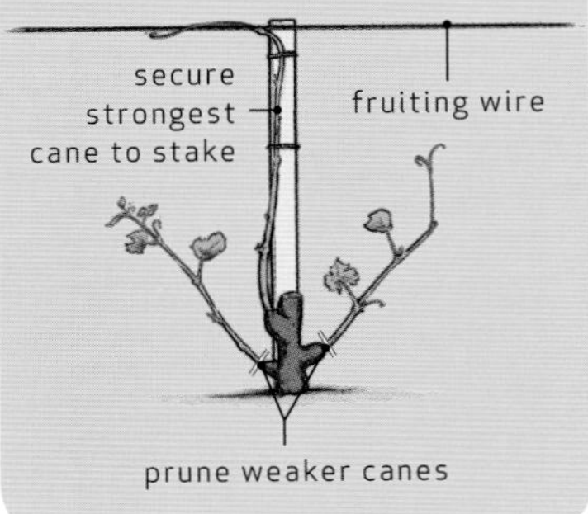

ADD MORE FRUITS TO THE MENU While they require more care and pruning than many trees and shrubs, grapevines and berry bushes have a rightful place in your garden or orchard, as they are not only delicious, but also versatile and healthful in many ways. Here are some of the benefits to these sweet fruits.

Know Your Grapes There are more than 20 species of wild grape in the United States and Canada, and many grapes which we enjoy today have these wild parents in their lineage. You could grow these wild grape species yourself for their intense flavors, or you could grow some tried-and-true varieties used for table grapes or wine. Some great wine grape varieties include Concord, Niagara, Delaware, Reliance, and Canadice; all of these are disease-resistant and quite cold-hardy. Tasty table grape varieties include Catawba, Muscadine, Steuben, Bluebell, and Vanessa. You can also take your pruned vine cuttings and weave them into useful baskets or beautiful wreaths.

Binge on Berries Raspberries, blackberries, dewberries, and thimble berries are all part of the genus *Rubus* and often referred to as brambles. There are many species and varieties of species to choose from, offering fruits that are red, purple, black, and even golden. Find out which varieties grow well in your area or transplant some wild ones into your garden. These make excellent preserves, juices, wines, and table fruit. Blueberries are another flavorful option to consider. Some species are tall and others are small, but they all produce nutrient-rich berries that make great jam or jelly. Dried blueberries are also a helpful snack when combating diarrhea. Aside from bushes and brambles, berries can also grow on trees. Red, white, and black mulberries are sweet fruits that grow on medium-sized trees. They can be eaten the same way as blackberries, and the fruits have a similar look, but with no thorns. Just avoid eating unripe mulberries, as they can cause indigestion and vomiting. For OTG utility, the inner bark of mulberry is also a great source for strong fiber, and the leaves are also the only food eaten by silkworms.

ESSENTIAL SKILL

PROPER PRUNING Since woody plants live for many years, it's easy for them to become overgrown and wild. This can mean the plant devotes too much energy toward getting big, and less energy into fruiting. The solution is learning how to properly prune your trees, bushes, grapevines, and berry bushes. Most pruning is done in late winter or spring with very sharp pruning shears or snips (A). For trees and shrubs, cut off branches that grow toward the trunk or cross each other. For vines and bushes, cut them back more severely to inspire fruiting (B), rather than branch growth.

COOL TOOL

KEEP CRITTERS AWAY Bird netting and deer fences are both kinds of mesh that is used to form a barrier between your food and all of the wildlife (or stray livestock) that would like to devour all of your fruits, veggies, and other produce. For best effect, the netting should be tented up around the berry bushes and garden beds you intend to protect, so they cannot eat anything near the mesh openings. You should also have the mesh well supported, so hungry animals cannot push the mesh toward their prize and eat through the gaps. I once had a groundhog eat an entire bed of 100 cabbage seedlings in under an hour, through an intact grow tunnel covered in mesh. The tunnel was attached securely to the ground, but the hoops were floppy. The animal simply pushed down the mesh and ate his fill, and it sprang back up when he left.

THE KEY TO SUCCESS A keyhole garden is a simple layout that uses a keyhole- or horseshoe-shaped layout with a semi-circle of trees or shrubs on the north side, creating a natural windbreak and a warm microclimate within. Berry bushes and vines can be used as an understory, with edible or medicinal plants placed inside them. If each plant that you use is perennial (living for more than two years), you could build these gardens once and enjoy them for many years to come.

AMBER WAVES

A MAJOR PLAYER IN THE SHIFT FROM HUNTING AND GATHERING TO AGRARIAN SOCIETIES WAS THE ABILITY TO GROW GRAINS FOR STAPLE FOODS. FROM BARLEY TO WHEAT, THESE GRAINS FED OUR FOREBEARS FOR MILLENNIA, AND THEY CAN CONTINUE TO FEED OUR FAMILIES TODAY.

From the simple farming techniques of the Old World's Fertile Crescent to the high-tech corporate mega-farms of modern times, we as a species have depended on the production of grains for food, trade, and utilitarian purposes. A range of diverse crops have come and gone over the ages, but some have stood the test of time. Corn and rice are the most commonly eaten foods on the planet, supplying a great deal of the calories consumed by a hungry world. Indeed, corn is the primary "cereal" crop for animal and human consumption, worldwide. Cereal crops (grass species with edible seed) and pseudo-cereal (non-grass species) are diverse groups of plants that grow in many different climates, but they do share a common life cycle. The seeds are planted in fertile soils. The seedlings emerge and grow into adult plants. The new seeds then form and the plant begins to die. These seeds are harvested after they have fully formed, and they are then used for food or saved to be planted in the next growing season.

ANCIENT AGRICULTURE In the Xihuatoxtla rock shelter in Mexico, archeologists have found stone grain grinding tools—many with corn residue still clinging to them after 8,700 years. This find is amazing, but the most important part is that by complex selective breeding, ancient people turned a simple grass with lots of unfriendly traits into a high-yield, easily harvested staple. It may have happened in stages over centuries: many independent features of the plant and its seeds were altered. Over time, a plant named teosinte (with just a few seed kernels in stony cases) became maize (a seed head with rows of free kernels on a cob). These early farmers selected and regrew seeds from plants until they had something resembling an ear of modern popcorn.

FLAX CAN BE GROWN AS A CROP FOR UTILITY AND FOOD DUE TO ITS OIL-RICH SEEDS AND THE FIBER CONTAINED IN THE STEM. FLAX FIBER HAS BEEN USED FOR FABRIC (LINEN), TINDER, AND ROPE FOR AT LEAST 8,000 YEARS.

KNOW YOUR GRAINS Much of the earth lacks the warm, wet climate required to grow rice, so corn and wheat tend to be the best and easiest crops to grow in small-scale, off-grid fields and large-scale farming operations. Both require tilled earth and minimal weed competition, and both need appropriate amounts of rain or irrigation to grow. Sweet corn requires 60 to 100 days to reach maturity, while "dry" corn for grain will take several weeks longer to

CROP	IDEAL CLIMATE	HUMAN FOOD USES	OTHER USES
CORN	TEMPERATE REGIONS	GRAIN, OIL, AND FLOUR	LIVESTOCK FEED AND FODDER, MOONSHINE
RICE	TROPICAL AND SOME TEMPERATE REGIONS	GRAIN AND FLOUR	STRAW, RICE WINE
WHEAT	TEMPERATE REGIONS	GRAIN AND FLOUR	STRAW, PAPER, VODKA
BARLEY	TEMPERATE REGIONS	GRAIN, FLOUR, AND MALT	LIVESTOCK FEED, BEER
RYE	TEMPERATE TO COLD CLIMATES	GRAIN AND FLOUR	STRAW, WHISKEY
SORGHUM	WARM AND TEMPERATE CLIMATES	GRAIN, SYRUP	LIVESTOCK FEED AND FODDER, HARD LIQUOR
OATS	TEMPERATE TO COLD CLIMATES	GRAIN, PORRIDGE	LIVESTOCK FEED, STRAW

form and dry, depending upon variety and the amount of heat during the growing season. Winter wheat is planted in late fall and takes 7 to 8 months to reach harvest, while its quicker cousin—spring wheat—takes roughly 4 months to reach maturity. Whichever cereal crop you plant, there are many other uses for each besides just "cereal."

BE A SPIN DOCTOR Crop rotation is one of the most important practices to help maintain the fertility of your soils, and keep your crop yields high. It's also a practical way to discourage various diseases and pests that take advantage of the same crops planted in the same place, season after season. By planting different crops in rotation, you can deprive those diseases and pests of the host plants that they need to parasitize in order to reproduce. Part of your farm management practices should include careful record keeping, and these records should have notes about which crop was planted in which area (and when). Some farms rotate their crops on a 3-, 4-, or 5-year rotation plan, sowing light feeders, such as wheat,after growing greedy feeders, such as corn, to give the soil a rest after the significant nutrient uptake of a field of corn. And you can even use this practice on a small scale for garden beds and container plants. Move your different veggie species to different spots each year, and you'll see less disease and grow more food.

BRING IN THE HARVEST Various cereals are harvested in different ways. Corn can be picked off the stalk by hand. Some other grains, such as amaranth, may be collected by tapping the seed head over a bowl to catch the falling seeds. Without modern farm machinery, wheat, rye, and barley are commonly cut with a hand-held sickle and tied into bundles for easy transport to a processing and threshing area. However you do your work, make sure you invite some helpers over—especially if there is a lot of work to be done. This is an ancient tradition that still makes a lot of sense in the modern world, and is a lot more fun than going it alone—especially if you can share some tasty beer from last year's bounty!

T/F

GEORGE WASHINGTON GREW WEED

FALSE It is true that the father of our country grew hemp plants, but the myth that he was a marijuana farmer is just that . . . a myth. Our nation's first president was indeed a successful farmer who grew a number of useful crops—including industrial hemp, which was (and to this day still is) a highly versatile plant that can be used to make rope and canvas, as well as clothing, twine, and other fabric products. The one thing you can't do with that kind of hemp is smoke it, as the plant doesn't have the psychoactive compounds found in pot. (I suppose you can, but if you do, you'll be sorely disappointed—it'll likely just give you a bad headache.)

GOOD TO KNOW

ROCK-A-BYE BABY The agricultural meaning of the word crib isn't far off from the familiar baby crib. Essentially, they are both cages. We put our babies in "cages" to keep them from crawling away. And we place our corn in these cages to keep the animals from crawling in—a much better plan than just piling up ears of picked corn inside the barn. The airy corn crib also helps to dry out the ears of corn. People have built their own corn cribs for centuries and you can easily build your own, too. Build a small shed frame on stilts or piers, about 1 yard (1 m) off the ground to keep it and its contents away from dampness. Instead of siding, line the frame with sturdy metal mesh. Use two layers of chicken wire or, even better yet, a layer of wire fencing and then a layer of chicken wire. Put a roof on the shed, add a sturdy door, and then fill it with dried ears of corn.

STORE GRAINS SAFELY The keys to preserving your hard-earned grains are insect control and dryness. After growing and harvesting crops, you should remove the seed hulls by threshing, and strip the corn husks. This interrupts the life cycle of many insect pests which would devour your grain while in storage. Then, you should store your grain in the driest place available. For our remote ancestors, this was in baskets or bags in the rafters of their homes, or in granaries or silos that were kept dry. Low moisture is the main factor for grain longevity and food safety, and this can be a major challenge in a wet or humid climate. For those living on the grid, another option defeats insect pests and spoilage, but requires a steady source of electrical power. Freezing the grain in buckets or bags will kill any grain pests like weevils, beetles, or moths. For the off-grid crowd, grain storage can be performed using those same buckets or bags, with the addition of oxygen absorbing packets and/or desiccant packs. This creates an inhospitable environment inside the container, thus preventing the takeover of a variety of grain-devouring insect pests.

DON'T TAKE THIS TRIP Some grass species naturally have purplish-black seeds, while some varieties of rye host a dark purple fungus which grows as a replica of rye seeds. These impostor "seeds" contain potent chemicals, including lysergic acid (the source for the drug LSD). Eating ergot-laced food can cause violent muscle spasms, vomiting, hallucinations, and many other symptoms, matching some strange tales of history—including possibly the Salem witchcraft trials. Ergot poisoning is a potential explanation for the Salem witch trials, because of the cold and wet growing conditions in rye fields that are the typical breeding ground for ergot, and 1691 was a cool, wet year in Salem, Massachusetts. By the summer of 1692, the grain had been used up and the season was drier, which may just explain the sudden end of the "Salem bewitchments." Ergot poisoning may have also been an element in other historical events such as the French Revolution and the alleged werewolf outbreaks of Medieval Europe.

ESSENTIAL SKILL

BE YOUR OWN THRESHING MACHINE Throughout history, corn has been instantly popular among those who encountered it. Sure, it's tasty and versatile, but it may also have had something to do with the fact that corn doesn't need to be threshed. Most grains grow surrounded by a tough-to-remove outer hull, which is then stripped off by a process called threshing. Without a factory-built threshing machine, threshing can be a serious challenge for the small-scale grower—but it's not entirely impossible. The first step is to choose grain varieties that can be threshed without modern machinery. Emmer wheat and spelt are notoriously hard to thresh. But these are some top picks for easily-threshed grains:

- Hull-less or "Faust" barley
- Hull-less oats (not entirely "hull" free, but close)
- Red fife and marquis wheat
- Rye and triticale

When you're ready to thresh, there are many homespun methods. You could lay a pile of seed heads on a tarp and beat them with a length of garden hose. Or, you could put the grain in a pillowcase and flail it with *nunchaku*—there's a theory that the iconic ninja weapons may have originally been used for threshing. Yet another reason to invite Chuck Norris to your compound.

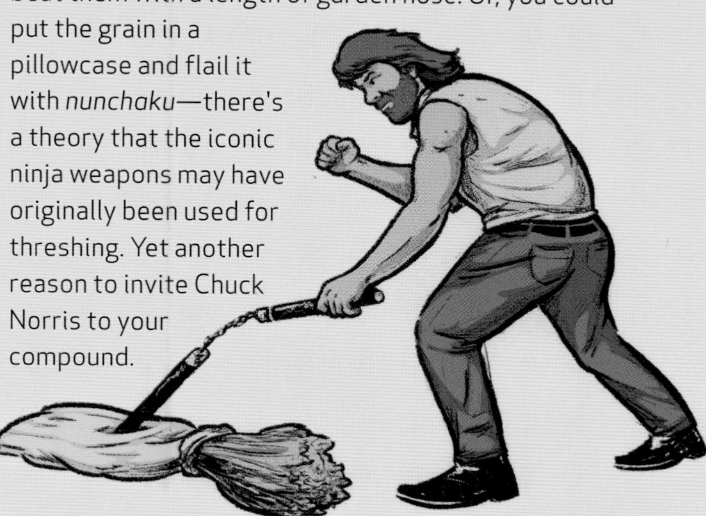

THRESHING BY HAND? DO IT ON A BREEZY DAY AND WORK OVER A TARP. WITH A LIGHT BREEZE, THE CHAFF NATURALLY BLOWS AWAY AND THE GRAINS ARE EASILY COLLECTED WHERE THEY FALL ON THE TARP.

BACKYARD CRITTERS

SMALL LIVESTOCK CAN HAVE A BIG IMPACT ON YOUR SURVIVAL—IF YOU KNOW HOW TO RAISE THEM AND SAFELY TURN THEM INTO FOOD. WHETHER CHICKENS, RABBITS, DUCKS, OR GEESE, THESE DIMINUTIVE DYNAMOS CAN ALL BREED QUICKLY AND PROVIDE MANY USES FOR YOUR FAMILY.

If you've never taken care of a farm before, then starting with small animals is a great way to begin your OTG homestead. Without a doubt, your responsibilities will increase. But many people also enjoy the routine of caring for their animals and they find it to be well worth the effort. Before you come home with a pair of rabbits in a cardboard box, remember what happened to that plastic bag of fish that you won at the carnival. They didn't make it—quite often because you just weren't properly prepared to care for them at the time. Be sure to take that lesson to heart, and do your research before making the commitment to animal husbandry. Decide which animals are the best fit for your life and your location. Learn how to care for them, what you can feed them, how to spot any problems, and what kind of home will make them comfortable. Once all the pieces are in place, then go buy your critters. And if you're lucky, you may find that caring for and raising small livestock is a stepping stone to a more purposeful life.

CAGE TO TABLE When we talk about raising small animals for meat, that generally means rabbits or chickens. In South America, however, guinea pigs have long been a staple on the menu, and some trend-spotters are asking whether the United States might be ready to start looking at an animal that's long been thought of as a cute kindergarten pet, and seeing it as a tasty entrée instead. The trend for authentic native cuisine means that some Peruvian and Uruguayan restaurants in the United States are serving *cuy*, which is traditionally grilled or fried. These furry rodents are also very efficient to farm—they don't take up much space at all compared to a cow, which requires 8 pounds (3.6 kg) of feed to make 1 pound (0.45 kg) of meat, for guinea pigs, the ratio is 4 to 1.

COMMON MISTAKE

BAD LUCK CLUCK More and more folks are raising backyard chickens, but there can be a devastating learning curve. Learn to diagnose and prevent the spread of diseases in your birds before you get them. You can prevent most with a clean coop that's warm at night, but there's still a risk for common ailments that can harm your flock.

Marek's Disease This common and contagious disease can be fatal in younger chickens. It is spread by lost feathers or dust, and may manifest as labored breathing, paralysis, and weight loss.

Fowl Pox A viral disease spread by mosquitoes, fowl pox can present as a "dry" form (with warty bumps on the bird's face or legs) or "wet" (creating lesions in the mouth and airways).

Infectious Bronchitis A highly contagious disease of the respiratory tract, this may cause difficulty breathing at night, and lower egg production.

DO FENCE THEM IN Whether we're talking about bunnies, chickens, ducks, or geese, it's a consistent fact that small critters have a tendency to wander, hop, or flap away—and they're also easy prey for all sorts of varmints. Protect your investment with proper fencing; if you do it right, this enclosure can also be part of your overall land management strategy.

Build a Chicken Tractor The term "tractor" has been loosely applied to all sorts of enclosures that allow animals to live within a portable pen, which can be frequently moved to a new spot for continual grass, weed, and bug consumption. This can be done for chickens, rabbits, and other small livestock, and it makes a big difference in their health and happiness. It also disperses their manure to fertilize the land, and can help prepare garden beds for planting. You'll still probably have to till the earth, since the chickens don't scratch that deep, but the hungry birds are relentless on weed seeds and seedlings. The tractor can be built from chicken wire over a lightweight wooden frame and it can even have an attached coop for egg laying and wheels for easy mobility.

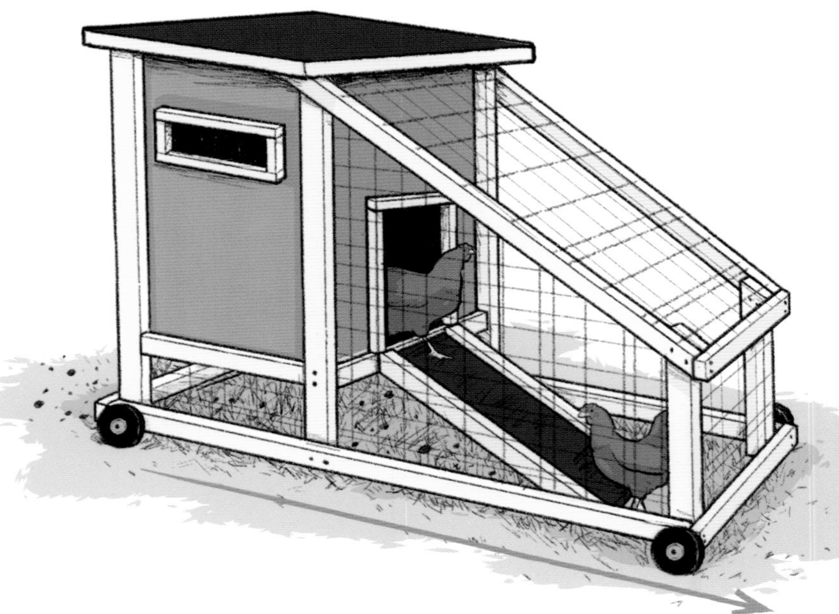

ESSENTIAL SKILL

PICK UP THE RIGHT CHICKS Things start going right when you do your homework in the selection of the right bird breeds for your needs. There are three main types of chickens that are commonly available to raise: hybrids, pure breeds, and bantams.

Hybrid Chickens Most commercial birds are hybrids, which are a cross between a number of different chicken breeds. These bird varieties are tough and less prone to disease, and are also great egg layers.

Pure Breeds Numerous heritage breeds will fall into this category. They can be very old breeds, raised for centuries. They are ideal for dependability in your future birds, if you choose to breed your own.

Bantam Chickens These are typically smaller birds, ideal for those who don't have a lot of free space.

For meat chickens, Brahmas, Jersey Giants, Langshams, and Cochins are popular breeds. For egg production, Leghorns and Australorp hens can lay up to 300 eggs per year per bird. Plymouth Rocks and Rhode Island Reds are also very popular layers, though not as productive.

Shock a Predator Few things are as heartbreaking as checking on your birds in the morning only to find them slaughtered by a nocturnal predator. Luckily, this scenario is largely avoidable if you have an electrified fence. One of the on-grid benefits is the wallop that a plug-in electric fence delivers. Canine predators yelp in pain and surprise, while other varmints hiss and howl. Whatever form the trespasser takes, even stray pets, they learn that the fence is painful and scary, and they want nothing to do with it (or the tasty chickens just beyond). Even if you're off the grid, you can still use a solar-powered fence. It doesn't quite pack the sting of a grid-tied model, but it still may save the birds.

GOOD TO KNOW

CHICKENS WON'T KILL YOU Don't worry, the chances of your flock doing you in with the bird flu are very unlikely. In fact, there's very close to a zero percent chance of that happening. But there are other zoonotic (communicable to people) diseases that humans can catch from livestock. The three main bacterial pathogens that should be on your radar are *E. coli*, *Salmonella*, and *Campylobacter*. In most cases, people have fallen ill after eating any eggs or meat that had been improperly cooked or handled, and thus ended up contaminated with those bacteria. However, people will only very rarely acquire these ailments while working with live, healthy chickens or eggs. Of course, birds do carry these pathogens regardless, but adherence to a good handwashing and sanitation regimen is usually sufficient to stop the spread of disease.

BARE MINIMUM

DIY RABBIT CHOW If you are looking for the easy way, this isn't it. But if you want to provide delicious and healthy meat for your family's dinner table—and with just the resources at hand—then read on. Using only natural or wild plants for rabbit food is great for the rabbits, and it will only cost you some time. The majority of a healthy rabbit diet is usually dry hay. It's high in protein, vitamins, and minerals, and it's great for a rabbit's digestive tract. The same cannot be said for those commercial food pellets, which may not even be available in an emergency. You can cut your own hay several times a year, when the green wild grasses reach maturity but the seeds haven't fallen from the plants yet. Cut down all the grass, dry it thoroughly, and feed it to your rabbits. You can also read up on wild edible plants, and feed your furry critters almost anything that is edible to humans.

SLAUGHTER A RABBIT There is always going to be at least a little bit of sadness when the time comes to for you to dispatch your livestock, but it's a necessary part of being a self-reliant omnivore. It does help if the work goes quickly. Once you get the hang of it, you should be able to process a small animal in mere minutes. Here's how to prepare a rabbit yourself.

STEP 1 Begin by swiftly piercing the rabbit's skull using a stout knife blade to dispatch it quickly. Then take the rabbit and a sharp filet knife to a clean cutting board, and continue by cutting off the head and all four feet.

STEP 2 Lay the animal carcass on its back, then set the knife edge above the anus. Tap the knife with the club again to cut off the anus and tail. (You could also cut a circle around the anus in order to isolate it, but this time consuming and can be fairly tricky when working on small game.

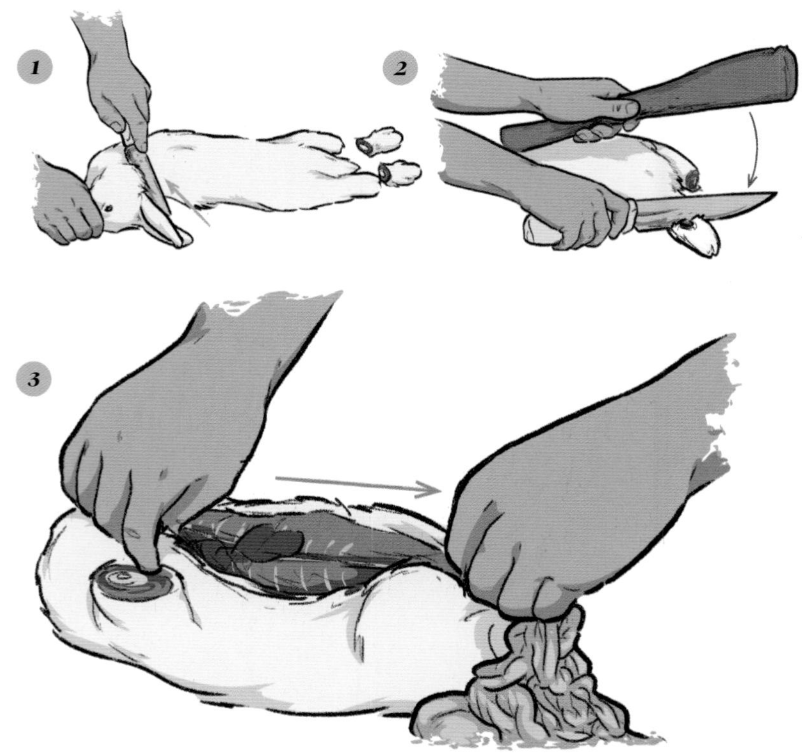

STEP 3 Make an incision in the belly skin and muscle, starting at the breastbone and cutting down to the anal cut. Slice shallowly, being careful to keep all stomach and intestines whole. Scoop out the guts from liver to colon.

STEP 4 Now that the abdominal guts are gone, you can insert the knife into the chest cavity, blade edge up, and slice through the center of the rib cage, all the way to the throat cut. Remove the heart and lungs (the only contents of the chest cavity).

STEP 5 Peel off the hide: Start at the hind section, which is thinner and easier to remove, working your thumb under the skin. Save the skin for tanning.

STEP 6 Pick off any remaining hairs, and give the carcass a rinse with clean water to remove blood. Refrigerate, freeze, can, or cook the whole animal (or its quarters).

ON THE GRID

YOUR BACKYARD FOOD COURT Even if you're not going to be fully off the grid, you can still raise your own small livestock within an urban environment. But first, be sure to check all of your local rules, laws, and ordinances on livestock and living space, to make sure that you're going to be on the right side of the law—and then recheck those regulations every few years because complaining neighbors tend to get these things changed periodically. Once that's done build your backyard critter palaces, rooftop coops, urban barnyards, and rabbit hutches as you see fit, so long as they're in a safe place for both the construction and your critters. I also like to put a red light bulb inside my chicken coop and keep it lit at night, to both help give the birds a sense of security and to keep them from pecking at any of their wounded fellows.

TRUE STORY

BEWARE OF GOOSE Not a dog person, but still seeking a domesticated animal to guard your off-grid homestead? Consider the sharp-eyed goose. These insanely territorial animals have outstanding vision, great hearing, and are unimpressed by food bribes (sorry, Fido). The first recorded instance of geese saving the day comes from ancient Rome. In 390 BCE, geese were kept in the temple of Juno as sacred animals. One night, those geese heard or saw an enemy force approaching the city. The honking gaggle of geese alerted city guards and likely saved the city from an impending Gaul sneak attack. In much more recent times, geese have been adopted as guard animals outside police stations in the Xinjiang province of China. They are also being used to guard United States military bases in West Germany, and at least one prison in Brazil.

LOOP THE LOOP Modern agriculture students may be quick to spout off terms like "zero waste" and "closed-loop farming," but at the end of the day, it's simply a return of the farming methods of their grandparents and great grandparents. They lived frugally and nothing went to waste, which is the definition of a closed-loop agricultural system. You can build your own system which generates no waste by taking a step backward in time and producing as much as you can from start-to-finish. This ecologically sound practice puts you in control, so you'll know exactly what you're eating and how it was produced.

Think Small How does one go about this process with small livestock? You've already gained some tricks from this section. Let a field of grass get tall, then cut it into hay for your rabbits. Use the rabbit droppings for worm beds. Use the worms to feed your fish or chickens, and the dirt they produce (castings) in your garden. It's the same kind of frugal living that people have done for ages, but with a more scientific understanding of the relationships between the land, the plants, the animals, and the people.

Bring In the Birds Can a closed-loop agricultural system involve different types of birds? You bet! Fowl such as geese and ducks are voracious bug eaters, but very gentle on garden vegetables. You can turn them loose in your garden beds to eat cabbage worms, cucumber beetles, and many other crop-ruining pests, with little fear of them pecking holes in your perfect produce. For a more intensive ground force, use chickens to clean up spoiled fruit lying around in an orchard. Chickens absolutely love juicy fruits, and will virtually purr with contentment as they make a feast of fallen fruit. And if you're looking to control insect pests and get some free protein for your chickens, all you have to do is lay out a bunch of old boards and lumber on the ground within the chicken pen. After just a few weeks, the boards' undersides will likely be crawling with a variety of insects—all of which the chickens will happily wolf down when you flip those boards over for them.

GOOD TO KNOW

THE CIRCLE OF LIFE I'd wager that most folks don't know that you can feed rabbit poop to many fish, with no harm to the fish or to you when you chow down on them. While the finicky cold-water trout may turn its scaly nose up at rabbit manure, plenty of warm-water and bottom-feeding fish ,such as catfish, tilapia, and carp, will gladly feast upon your rabbit's leavings. Some savvy homesteaders have actually built their mesh-bottomed rabbit hutches over their fish farms, so that the "bunny berries" drop right in automatically! But if all this has you a little squeamish, you can always employ a middleman: the humble worm. Some rabbit farmers keep worm farms under their rabbit hutches for the same automatic recycling system that fish farmers are using. The rabbit droppings fall into the worm beds and get eaten by the worms. The worm population grows, giving you plenty of worms to treat your fish or chickens, and worm castings to help grow veggies (or maybe even some hay for your rabbits).

BREEDING YOUR OWN RABBIT POPULATION IS EASY SINCE RABBITS BREED LIKE, WELL, RABBITS. ONE HEALTHY DOE FROM A LARGE-LITTER BREED COULD PRODUCE AS MANY AS 100 KITS PER YEAR FOR SEVERAL YEARS!

GET YOUR GOAT

WHERE WOULD WE BE WITH HAM, GOAT CHEESE, AND WOOL CLOTHING? HUNGRY AND COLD, FOR STARTERS. ONCE YOU'VE LEARNED TO TAKE CARE OF BUNNIES AND CHICKENS, IT MIGHT BE TIME TO UPGRADE TO SOMETHING LARGER: PIGS, GOATS, SHEEP, EVEN THE EXOTIC ALPACA.

Goats, sheep, alpaca, pigs, and a few other animals can be herded into the medium-sized animal category. These creatures can provide us with companionship, and so much more besides. Goats are often used for both meat and dairy production. Sheep can also give meat as well as wool. For top grade critter hair, the alpaca can produce amazing wool-like fiber. Any or all of these useful animals can have their hide turned into supple leather, and they can provide some valuable services around the home site as well. Sheep and goats can easily replace your noisy lawn mower for trimming grass; pigs and goats can become the living garbage disposals of your agricultural operation by eating up food waste and vegetable scraps; and all of them help fertilize the land as they go. The pig even will plow it up with its powerful ability to root through the soil. Together with all of your various small animals and your garden, you can have virtually everything that you'd need for a diverse (and delicious!) menu.

MIXING LONG LEGS AND SHORT By now, you've learned that you can grow different vegetables together for mutual benefit. What about letting medium-sized critters, like sheep, in the same pasture with big animals, like horses? If the individuals get along, they can graze together, and mixed species grazing is highly beneficial. The grazing patterns of different species increase the overall productivity of your pastures. Also, sheep and horses are typically infected by parasites from different places. Sheep eat the taller grasses that horses don't favor, and eat closer to horse manure (with little risk of contracting horse parasites). The horses eat the shorter grass exposed by the "mowing" of the sheep, and they will be safer as well. This system works for everybody!

GOOD TO KNOW

PICK A PIG Deciding to raise pigs means a wide world of options. There are more than a hundred recognized breeds, either fat or meat producers. Be sure yours are bred for meat; consider getting at least two. Pigs are smart, social animals, and they tend to be better off with friendly competition for their feed. Here are some popular meat breeds.

American Landrace Good mothers; high post-weaning survival rate.

American Yorkshire Typically good mothers; large litters and a large frame.

Berkshire Good sires and don't mind small spaces.

Chester White Good mothers.

Duroc Fast-growing and feed efficient.

Hampshire Lean and meaty.

Poland China Meaty pigs, good feeders with calm dispositions.

MEDIUM-SIZED FARM ANIMALS What makes pigs, sheep, and goats such good livestock for OTG living? There are many reasons why these barnyard buddies can fit into your self-sustaining lifestyle. Once you have them on board, you may wonder what took you so long.

Pigs These creatures have been accused of being the smartest domesticated animal. Their personalities are as varied as ours and their appetite knows no bounds. Always glad to scarf down virtually any food, whether plant or animal in origin, pigs are easy to feed and they make a meal out of food that other creatures won't eat. Got plenty of whey after making cheese? Feed it to the pigs. Have a heap of leftovers? Feed it to the pigs. Found some spoiled fruit? You get the idea. It should also be noted that the four best forms of meat come from this animal: pork, ham, sausage, and bacon.

Sheep These typically gentle and always woolly animals are a good fit for homesteads with wide open spaces, and plenty of grass to manage. If you like lamb and mutton, they can be your source; if you want to try your hand at fiber arts, they can provide wool. The enterprising homesteader may also try their hand at milking sheep, to make unique cheeses and dairy products. Do keep in mind, however, that certain sheep are bred for their milk production and their temperament for milking, so not every sheep may be a good candidate. That said, I was surprised to discover that sheep milking has been around

ESSENTIAL SKILL

MILK A GOAT So, you want to milk a goat? Well, roll up your sleeves and grab a clean bucket. Since goats can't kick you nearly as hard as an uncooperative cow, the goat is a great place to begin your OTG dairy farm. Even tall goats are low to the ground, so it's best to build a milking platform for your goat to stand on. This can include a ramp for the animal to walk up, a head gate to keep the goat in place, and a feed tray to keep them happy while they're being milked. Once the goat is in place and nibbling on some hay, clean their udder and commence with milking. Gently squeeze the top of the teat with your thumb and index finger, then close the rest of your hand moving down the teat. This pushes the milk down and out, to spray into your waiting bucket.

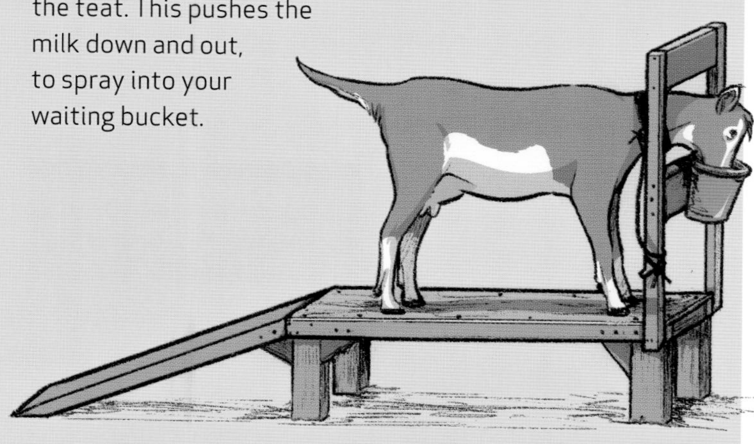

GOOD TO KNOW

SKIP THE LAWN MOWER We've all seen cartoons of a goat eating a tin can, and that's not far from the truth. Goats are relentless foragers, and they can eat almost any plant, even woody vines and shrubs, with enough time. This voracious nature, and their natural love of climbing, lets that herd of goats become a land-clearing machine. Rocky, brushy terrain can't defeat a hungry goat army. One mouthful at a time, even plants that are troublesome for humans (like poison ivy) go down the goat's throat to become nutrient-rich goat droppings. Before you burn a brushy area, or worse, dump poison on it, consider the goat as your partner in land reclamation. They're all too happy to help. If you don't want to purchase your own herd, there are even companies that rent out herds of goats for eco-friendly, sustainable land management.

for thousands of years and pre-dates cow milking. Today, Europe is the world's commercial center for the dairy sheep industry.

Goats What can we say about these capricious caprines? Tons of personality. The ability and desire to climb almost anything. A source of milk and cheese. Goats are many things to many people, and they might even become your favorite creature, once you understand that they cannot resist head-butting you when you aren't looking.

GOOD TO KNOW

WAX ON, WAX OFF If your hands are dry, scaly, rough, and unhappy, then go and shear some sheep. Working with raw wool can coat your hands in a waxy substance called lanolin, which is an excellent skin moisturizing agent found in sheep's wool. Lanolin has the ability to penetrate your skin's outer layer and nourish it from the inside. Also known by the name "wool fat," lanolin is the sheep's version of sebum—the stuff that gives us humans greasy hair and pimples. But the sheep have it much better: Their lanolin wicks out into their wool; a naturally waterproofed sweater growing all over their bodies means that sheep can stand out in the rain all day, warm and surprisingly dry! Once the sheep are sheared, you can extract the lanolin from the wool to make moisturizer or waterproof your boots—or leave it in and knit a lotion impregnated sweater!

YOUR WOOLLY FRIENDS So, you've decided to bring a few sheep or alpacas off the grid with you. You've made a good choice—your grass will stay shorter and better fertilized, your sweaters will be silky, and your taste for lamb chops will also be satisfied, if you decide that you will be gearing up for meat as well as wool production. Here are some of the commonly asked questions about caring for these quiet animals.

What Do They Eat? Sheep and alpaca will eat mostly grass, either fresh or dried in the form of hay. However, they should not have any access at all to certain plants, including acorns, buttercups, bracken fern, yew, or wilting cherry leaves, all of which are highly poisonous to both varieties of animals.

Can I Have Just One? Both alpaca and sheep are herd animals, and they should both be kept with at least one other member of their species. Males in particular, when kept alone, can develop some behavioral problems, so you should get two or three (or more) to give them a herd that they can call their own.

When Do You Shear Them? Most wool-bearing animals are sheared once a year (or even twice, if they have especially fast-growing wool). This is often done in the spring, and it helps to keep them from overheating in the warmer weather. With ewes (female sheep), shearing will often be performed about a month before lambing (birthing). This can keep them from being stressed near lambing time and it will also help the newborn lambs find their mother's diminutive teats.

Do They Need Shelter? Depending on the weather in your region, these animals may or may not need some cover from the elements in order to remain healthy and happy. Simple sheds may provide all they shelter they need, except in the coldest of climates. But you will see an increase in lamb survival rates if they are born in shelters, rather than open pasture.

COMMON MISTAKE

THE SPITTING IMAGE Llamas and alpacas (who are closely related) get a bad reputation for being cranky or dangerous. Reading about these critters, you may run across the freaky-sounding "berserk llama syndrome." So, are alpacas friendly farm animals or spitting, stomping jerks? The answer is "yes," and the reason may surprise you. Thing is, alpacas and llamas are naturally friendly animals. So much so, that people often treat the super-cute babies like household pets, cuddling them, wrestling around with them like a puppy, maybe even bottle-feeding them. As the alpaca grows up, he sees the human as his alpaca buddy, and will play like llamas play. Unfortunately, llama play involves kicking, biting, and, yes, spitting. That's cute when they're babies, less so once your alpaca weighs 200 pounds (91 kg)—llamas can go up to 300 pounds (136 kg). The solution? Treat them well, but remember that the babies are farm animals, not teddy bears.

ESSENTIAL SKILL

SHEAR PERFECTION
When it comes time to shear your woolly beasts, there's nothing wrong with calling in a pro. But if you want to embrace the rural life at your off-grid home, you can also learn to do it yourself. The best way to learn is from a skilled practitioner, though in an end-times situation with no help, you can teach yourself. Either way, start on young animals. Don't try to shear a huge and feisty old ewe for your first haircut customer. Start by shearing the belly, then the legs, and finally the back. If done correctly, the wool should remain in one matted piece, looking something like a thick rug. Shearing can be tiring, dirty, and smelly work—but if done successfully, your animals will be happier and more comfortable. And you'll have some wool to work with or sell. Wool can be cleaned and spun into yarn for fiber arts, or felted into solid items.

HAVE A COW, MAN

DO YOU WANT TO HAVE A BUCKET OF FRESH MILK A DAY WITH NO MILKMAN? OR MAYBE YOU'D LIKE TO STOCK A FREEZER FULL OF GRASS-FED STEAKS? LARGE ANIMALS HAVE LONG BEEN A FIXTURE AT HISTORIC FARMS, AND THEY CAN STILL BE A VIABLE OPTION EVEN IN MODERN TIMES.

Big rewards and big responsibilities are what you'll get when you up-size to big farm animals. Horses, donkeys, mules, cattle, camels, llamas, and more can turn your off-grid farm from a lively barnyard into a serious operation. Meat and milk, transportation and towing, pooping and plowing; all can be yours when you make the commitment to add large animals to your OTG plan. These big beasties can provide food, labor, and abundant fertilizer in exchange for their supper—usually just your excess grass. Be warned: big and cheap don't usually go hand in hand. With larger animals, expenses will climb, leaving novice farmers with an empty wallet. If you're not going to be on that mini-ranch full-time, you should line up some help. Dairy cattle need milking every 12 hours, year-round, so forget about that long vacation if you're doing all this by yourself. But don't let the negatives outweigh the positives. Large animals were necessary on our ancestor's farms. If you want to be truly self-sufficient, you're likely to need some of them as well.

ALL HAT AND SOME CATTLE Keeping a few cattle is not a decision taken lightly. The initial cost of livestock and fencing may be enough to dissuade many people altogether. But if you already have good fencing around a decent pasture, purchasing a few calves can be a wise investment. The average calf weights 75 to 90 pounds (34–41 kg) when born, and quickly puts on weight by drinking its mother's rich milk for about 200 days, until it reaches a weaning weight of 400 pounds (181 kg)or more. Their weight will more than double by eating grass and hay over the next two years, depending on sex, breed, and other factors. Barring any losses or major expenses (like vet bills), many come close to doubling their money in a few years by buying and selling their cattle.

GOOD TO KNOW

MEAT VERSUS MILK

To most, at first glance, your average cow will just look like, well, a cow. But once you start to pay attention to the details, the differences will begin to jump out at you. Of course, any cow could be eaten for its meat, and any lactating cow could be milked. But over the past few millennia, people have selectively bred their livestock to produce specific traits from certain breeds. Beef cattle have been bred to be, well, beefier. Dairy cattle, meanwhile, have been bred to have massive udders and a long lactation period after calving. Take one look at the bony hindquarters of a dairy cow and your hope for steaks will quickly shrivel. Having a look at the small milk bag on a beef cow will be equally disappointing. Good luck milking her, too—these ladies usually will not have a good disposition for that particular task.

WITH A GREAT HERD COMES GREAT RESPONSIBILITY

The benefits of a herd of milk- and meat-producing cattle are fairly obvious. Who doesn't like the idea of potential cheeseburgers on the hoof, right there on the back forty? But as we keep harping on, this is a big commitment. So, know what you're getting into, plan accordingly, and then you can stock up on ketchup and relish.

Make Room Large livestock farming requires land for them to graze and move about. If they're confined to feedlots as in the conventional cattle industry, disease rates and calf mortality rises. Adequate pasture means these problems are far less common. Depending on your climate, the grass species, and the length of your growing season, you'll need about 2 acres (0.8 hectare) of land for each animal. In arid climates, they need much more room; in tropical locations, they may only need a fraction of that space.

A Different Breed There are more than 800 recognized cattle breeds worldwide. Depending on their lineage, some perform better in different climates. A few breeds do it all, as meat, milk, and draft (or "draught") animals. These beasts of burden pull carts, plow fields, and carry loads for their owners. Crossbreeding them can create nearly limitless possibilities. Keep one for your own slaughter, and you'll have a lot of beef to feed your family.

Meat on the Hoof No freezer? Store your food "on the hoof." If you can handle the slaughter of a large animal and wait until winter to do it, the beef can be aged by hanging in a cold barn until you're ready to prepare it for longer storage.

HORSES & MULES Figuring out the right animal for the job can be tricky, until you get some experience with these animals. Getting a mule team to pull a wagon or an ox to pull a plow is something of an art form, and these activities require training for both the people and the beasts.

Mounts For riding, nothing beats a horse, although most large animals can be ridden. You can also ride donkeys,

GOOD TO KNOW

HORSE SAFETY Things can take an unhappy turn when you have a problem with a 1,000 pound (454 kg) animal with a mind of its own. Observe these rules when working around horses and mules, and you and your animals will stay safe.

- Talk to the animal as you approach from the side. Don't sneak up on them. Their blind spots are directly in front of them and behind them.
- To take control, attach a lead rope to their halter, and don't get the rope coiled around your fingers, hand or arm. Lead the animal with a physical pull combined with verbal commands. It doesn't hurt to praise their successes, either.
- Stand to their side of the animal when grooming and brushing it, rather than in front of them or behind them. This helps to keep you out of the path of kicking and biting.

mules, and camels, if they are trained. Put the appropriate tack and saddle on your mount and ride off into the sunset.

Pack Animals Mules and donkeys, as well as horses, llamas, reindeer, and camels, have been used as pack animals. Some have been carefully bred for load-bearing. Just be sure you're using the right panniers or load-bearing equipment to avoid hurting your animals.

Harness Animals Oxen, cattle, dogs, goats, alpaca, elephants, and all the beasts above can be used as harness animals to pull various loads. From dogs drawing a sled across the tundra to elephants pulling entire trees out of the jungle, the right sized beast with the right training can perform all sorts of tasks. For OTG living, packing and riding chores could fall to horses and mules. Slow, yet strong, oxen can pull plows and carts with their mighty frames. Even your large dog could carry a load on a hike. Make sure to take care of them, and they'll take care of you.

COMMON MISTAKE

DON'T GO OVER BUDGET It's a bad sign if you can barely afford to purchase a cow. It typically means you're not in the financial position to handle the hidden costs of being a herdsman. Here's an idea of what to expect.

Vet Bills The average farm visit from a large animal vet could cost hundreds of dollars. Even if you have some veterinary skills yourself, animal medicines aren't free.

Fencing Even if you've got adequate fences already, they won't last forever. Barbed wire, boards, nails, and mesh fencing will all cost money.

Hay Unless you're in the tropics, keeping cattle or other large animals over winter usually requires a lot of hay. A single cow may eat 25 pounds (11.4 kg) of hay per day in winter, more if the conditions are unusually cold. If the cow has been successfully bred, she'll also need more feed as the fetus develops.

FISH AND BUGS

MOST PEOPLE WON'T SAY NO TO A TASTY SERVING OF FISH—BUT HOW ABOUT A HANDFUL OF CRUNCHY CRICKETS? FISH AND INSECTS MAY NOT BE THE CUTEST THINGS, BUT THEY ARE A FORCE TO BE RECKONED WITH WHEN CONVERTING FEED AND WASTE INTO FOOD FOR HUMANS.

When Spanish explorers first colonized the deep southeastern coast of North America, these colonists suffered some serious growing pains while attempting to adjust to their new homes and the available resources. Cut off from their normal European trade routes, supplies, and familiar food sources, they were forced to adopt new foods to their diet instead. In the 1600s, the local fish were considered nasty creatures to eat, and the locally abundant oysters were unimaginable as a menu item. But through hunger and necessity, these foods were eaten and the colonists eventually learned to like them—even oysters, which at the time, were considered "boogers" inside a rock. Spanish colonists, sailors, and soldiers learned to live off new resources—ones that they could collect with their own two hands. Isn't that just the same kind of adaptability you'd need to be a modern day, off-the-grid homesteader? Wouldn't you need the creativity to come up with new food sources as well as the flexibility to make them work?

EAT YOUR BUGS It's hard to say how long humans have practiced entomophagy (the eating of insects). Eating of witchetty grubs in Australia dates back to ancestral times for the native Aborigine. There are also references to eating insects in the Bible and other ancient writings. Today, human entomophagy is widespread throughout southeast Asia. Roadside vendors sell fried or roasted grubs, beetles, scorpions, spiders, and other treats to hungry local customers and intrepid tourists. Even in the United States, adventurous eaters use products such as cricket flour as a high-protein, high-mineral food supplement. Edible insects convert organic matter to edible body mass far faster than other animals. They may be the next big thing in the future of food.

ON THE GRID

FARM SOME FISH IN YOUR BACK YARD A plastic kiddie pool can make for a great micro fish farm for your urban or off-grid homestead, plus it's fairly easy for you to set up. Fill the pool with water. If it's chlorinated, then just let it sit for about a week to evaporate from the water before you finish the setup and add in your fish. Put in the pool's filter, minus any disinfecting elements such as chlorine tablets or salt. Then set up your filter's discharge hose to spray water up in the air a short distance to help aerate the pool. Purchase some catfish, tilapia, or other hardy species from your local agricultural supplier. Then just add them to the pool, feed them daily, and watch them grow until they're ready to catch. If you happen to be living in an area that stays above freezing during the winter months, you can even run this operation year-round.

SMALL-SCALE FISH FARMING Many species of fish can be grown for food in small tanks or containers, so long as the water is clean and aerated and you're supplying them with enough food. Here are some of the most popular species for fish farming.

Tilapia These fast growing and tasty fish are best suited to warm climate aquaculture systems. In their warm water comfort zone, around 80 °F (26.7 °C), they can convert over three quarters of the feed weight they are given into body mass—and that means more meat for you later on!

Catfish For temperate or cool water, the hardy catfish is a great choice. These tough creatures can eat almost anything and grow to enormous sizes.

Perch Various species of perch can be another good fish for warm or temperate waters. The jade perch will need warm water to live in, but it will pay you back with the highest levels of omega-three oils of any fish species in the world. The silver perch can handle cooler water and, though it is slower growing, it can eat vegetable scraps.

Trout If there is a fast moving mountain stream on your property, and you can legally divert part of it, then trout farming could be for you. These cold-water fish demand clean, cold, and very aerated water. They're the least hardy of any fish on this list, but their taste is excellent and they will grow well on commercial fish food.

Carp Tough and long lived, carp won't grow very fast—but they are veggie eaters and can even subsist on things such as kitchen scraps and lawn clippings.

PROTECT YOUR PISCES You're not the only one interested in your farm: Fish-catching birds, such as kingfishers and herons, would love to eat your fishy friends when they are vulnerable little fish fry and marauding raccoons will be happy to take your fish at any size. An easy fix to prevent most predation is to install bird netting over your entire

TRUE STORY

YOU FED YOUR FISH WHAT? Fish are a very interesting creature to farm. A few years ago, our family had an above ground fish farm made out of a repurposed metal tank. Inside the water-filled enclosure, we had dozens and dozens of catfish. We aerated the water with a small pump that squirted water up in to air to splash back down into the tank. We fed them store-bought fish food when it was available and pet food when the fish food wasn't in stock. Of course, the kids threw in worms and bugs when they found them near the tank, but it turns out that these scavenging fish can eat many different things. Chopped vegetables, insects, dog food, other fish, and even rabbit droppings are fed to catfish, carp, and tilapia in aquaculture systems around the world. While it's best to use fish feed and foods that the animals would naturally eat, their diet can be very diverse in a pinch.

fish farm. This lightweight and affordable mesh material will still allow you to feed your fish (just throw it over the mesh and it will fall through the gaps) and it allows light, air, and bugs to get to your fish. This may discourage the raccoons somewhat, but they can chew through the mesh if strongly motivated enough by hunger. For them, you could install a strand of electric fence wire around your fish farm's perimeter, close to the ground. When the critters touch this wire with their little wet nose or tender paws, they'll get a jolt that reminds them who's in charge (that's you!). For particularly stubborn cases, use fish as bait in a trap and remove that predator permanently.

A WORM A DAY Worms are a great protein supplement for your fish (and chickens). Worm castings (waste) can also make an excellent soil amendment in gardening. You can even eat them yourself by frying them until crisp and sprinkling them with salt.

NOT INTO BUG EATING? BUMMER! U.S. NO. 1 GRADE FOODS CAN HAVE A SURPRISING AMOUNT OF INSECTS, INCLUDING 30 FRUIT FLY EGGS PER 100 GRAMS OF KETCHUP, OR UP TO 10 PERCENT OF COFFEE BEANS WITH LARVAE. ENJOY!

GOOD TO KNOW

A BUG'S LIFE Insect farms can be somewhat hardy, as the bugs can handle cold snaps, food shortages, or other issues they normally face in the wild. But your controlled bug farm ecosystem still has to keep your creepy crawly critters living in a habitable range to help keep all of your bugs happy and healthy.

Guard Against Heat The hot summer sun can cook your bugs, especially if the habitat is dark colored and in a sunny spot. Keep your bug bins in the shade, and you'll keep them alive.

Avoid Drowning Excess fluid collecting in the bottom of certain insect habitats can lead to bug drowning. Drain off the fluid periodically. Use it as a soil drench to water and fertilize your vegetables.

Don't Dry Out All bugs need moisture to live. Find out the optimal level of humidity and liquid water your bugs need in order for them to thrive.

JIMINY CRICKET! Bugs aren't just handy snacks for your chickens or fish, many can be eaten by people. Crickets, for example, can offer things that more conventional food sources do not. 3.5 ounces (100 g) of crickets contains a goodly 121 calories. Less than half of those calories come from unsaturated fats, which could reduce your risk of heart disease. Your cricket dinner plate also contains one-half ounce (about 13 g) of protein, 76 milligrams of iron, calcium, and several B-vitamins. These crunchy little chirpers also turn 100 pounds (45 kg) of feed into 40 pounds (18 kg) of edible "meat". Cattle, by contrast, can only turn that much feed into 10 pounds (4.5 kg) of meat.

Farm Some Crickets Put on your overalls: You're about to become a bug farmer! Start with roughly three dozen adult crickets. Catch them in the yard or buy them from a pet shop. Set up a well-ventilated, escape-proof container for them. A plastic or glass aquarium with a tight wire screen top is a great choice. Give your crunchy friends some structure to climb on, with places to hide. Paper egg cartons work great, and they can even nibble on the paper if they get peckish. Keep their habitat out of direct sunlight, but warm. It should ideally be kept between 75 and 85 °F (23.9–29.4 °C). Add a very shallow water dish with a rock or something in the middle to prevent drownings. Feed them vegetable scraps and fruit, or store bought cricket food. Once they are at home, add a breeding dish. This is a container of moist soil. The crickets will naturally lay their eggs by burying them in the dirt. Keep the dirt slightly moist for 2–3 weeks. Then place it in a second habitat to hatch, or use all of the adult crickets, thus vacating your only habitat. Just keep those adults away from the hatchlings, as the grown ones will eat their young.

WHAT'S THE BUZZ? Humans have craved and collected honey for thousands of years. The proof is in an ancient cave painting in Spain, which depicts people collecting wild honey from the native bees. This remarkable piece of ancestral art dates back around 8,000 years. And in all this time, our love of that sweet food hasn't changed a bit. At 60 calories per tablespoon (about 300 calories per 100 grams), it's also a very valuable food source. Whether you are a beekeeper or a wild honey collector, it pays to know the bees that are working hard for you.

In addition to honey making, bees are also very helpful around the homestead as natural pollinators. Fruit, nut, and vegetable yields can be increased with their beneficial pollination services. The hive can be moved near orchards at blossom time or even into a vegetable garden to give the bees easy access. Bee stings have also been used to treat arthritis, multiple sclerosis, chronic pain, and more.

You might even find a wild hive, if you are observant. Honey bees are not native to the New World, but they have been here since British settlers brought them in 1622. They eventually spread from coast to coast in North America, and wild colonies are now common. These wild populations favor hollow trees for hive sites, but they may set up in any cavity. One year, we had a hive in the space between the floors of our house.

Honey's Many Uses We all know how sweet honey is, but this sticky stuff isn't just a one-trick pony. Honey has been used for centuries as a natural wound covering, particularly for burns. Manuka honey from New Zealand is regarded as the world's most potent medicinal honey, and it is used now for Staph and MRSA infections. Then there's mead (possibly the world's oldest alcoholic beverage), a wine made from honey, clean water, and yeast suitable for making white wine or champagne. Let it ferment for about two months, then pour the wine off the sediment. Bottle it, and let it age for a few months more.

GOOD TO KNOW

THE BIOPOD MAGGOT FARM Don't confuse this with a worm farm. It may look similar, but this one carefully engineered to raise fly larvae (aka maggots). Yes, maggot farming can be stinky, and you could throw a dead raccoon into any plastic bin and grow maggots. This revolutionary bug barn, however, is designed to let the larvae harvest themselves. Just fill the interior cavity with a starter medium such as used coffee grounds. Then toss in some old meat, a road-killed animal, chicken guts, or whatever, as long as it's something that maggots will naturally eat. Keep the unit level and in the shade. After a few days, flies will lay eggs inside the unit and the maggots will begin to crawl up two proprietary ramps, dropping into an external canister for harvesting. Then serve the canister's contents as a protein-packed snack for your chickens or fish.

SURVIVE THERE

So far, you've learned about setting up an independent off-grid home and building a resilient (and delicious) food supply chain. In a perfect world, the material we've covered would be enough to live off the grid indefinitely, but bad luck can strike at any time, and we all make mistakes. It's time to take your self-reliance skills to the next level.

Now, we'll focus on the long-term living skills of an independent lifestyle, such as food processing, preparation, and preservation. We will also delve into the skills that you will need to protect and sustain yourself and your family in the event of an emergency, such as wilderness survival, emergency medicine, creating a secret food cache, fortifying your home, repairing and modifying your own vehicles, collecting wild game as a backup food supply, building a still, and of course, how to bug out in a crisis. Whether you're off the grid because you want to be, or because you had no choice, these are the skills you'll need to survive.

THE LONG HAUL

IF YOUR IDEA OF THE GOOD LIFE INCLUDES BACON, BEER, AND PICKLES, READ ON! THESE HERITAGE FOODS TASTE AMAZING AND THEY KEEP WELL TOO. FOOD STORAGE AND PREPARATION ARE THE NATURAL (AND DELICIOUS) END GAME FOR THE FOOD YOU WORKED HARD TO RAISE.

You've taken the plunge and are living at your home site. You're growing some crops and raising a few animals, too. It's not all drudgery and watery gruel for dinner when you're self-reliant. Life can still be filled with comfort and good food, even if you're outside of the limits of pizza delivery and well off the grid. The fresh and wholesome foods you have produced can be turned into delicious meals, made all the more savory because you know exactly what went into the food and how it was grown. It doesn't even have to be gourmet to be great. Fried eggs from your own hens and a slab of fresh homemade bread, still hot from the oven, are excellent for breakfast, lunch, or dinner. Because it's so fresh, this humble fare can be far more flavorful than the average person can imagine. Bread and beer, bacon and cider, pickles and cheese—all these await you in the next few pages. These foods are nourish the body and please the palate, and many of them will last for weeks or months—that is, if you don't devour it all well before then.

UP IN SMOKE You might not know that tobacco can be grown anywhere in the United States, and lots of other places worldwide. Even if you don't smoke, you can still grow it, cure it, and use it as a trade good. Tobacco will grow in the same types of soil and conditions as a tomato plant. All you really need is protection from pests, and roughly 100 frost-free nights after planting your tobacco seedlings. Once the plants have reached full size, they can be cut and hung upside down to dry and "cure" to improve their smell and taste. Your tobacco yield will depend upon the specific growing conditions and the variety that you grow, but generally each tobacco plant will produce about 5 ounces (142 g) of dry cured tobacco. This means that just a few plants can turn into a carton of cigarettes.

ON THE GRID

CHOOSE YOUR BATTLES
If you're starting out with seed saving, keep in mind that all seeds don't store equally. Some plants will produce seeds with a very high germination rate (nearly all of the seeds sprout under the right germination conditions), while others may not sprout as well. Start out by focusing on easy ones, and skipping the difficult seeds. Carrots, peppers, parsnips, okra, parsley, celery, Swiss chard, and New Zealand spinach regularly have low rates of germination and they may not be worth the bother of trying to save them. But if you do decide to save these seeds, save extra amounts of them. This will make up for the ones that don't sprout. If you really want to make it easy on yourself, save the seeds of plants that have a high germination rate. Cucumber, squash relatives, lettuce, beans, peas, corn, and melons are all forgiving seed to save.

BE A SEED STEWARD The ultimate way to be sustainable in your OTG garden is to save your own vegetable seeds from one year to the next so that your supply is secure. This is best done when you are growing single varieties of each vegetable, to avoid any unpredictable results from cross-pollination. Allow the veggies to mature completely, remove the seeds, and dry them for storage. An easy rule of thumb in seed storage is to add the temperature of the storage area in Fahrenheit to the humidity percentage. As an example, 60 °F (15.6 °C) added to 30 percent humidity will give you 90 points. The total of these two numbers should always be below 100 points. Lean toward the drier side in storage and your seeds will sleep happily for years. These steps should get you well on your way to being a seed saving savant.

Keep Them Dry Seeds will go bad if they become damp. Use a watertight container and some desiccant packs to soak up the stray moisture in the seeds and packaging. These packs can be repurposed silica gel packs that are used in shoe packaging, vitamin bottles, and other retail applications.

Keep Them Cool Someplace cool is an ideal place to store your seeds for the long haul. Many folks use their refrigerator for this task. Just be careful when you take the seeds out of this cold storage, as they have a tendency to sweat a little.

Keep Them in the Dark Some seeds are light sensitive, and will not last as long if they are exposed to bright light. Most storage methods for "dry and cool" will also keep them dark, but just to make sure, consider a container that will eliminate light as well as moisture.

GOOD TO KNOW

DON'T THROW THAT OUT Next time you're eating an orange or about to toss an apple core, think again. Why not save those seeds from your food, plant them, and grow your own vegetables and even trees. This could be merely for fun, to satisfy your curiosity, or as a cool project with kids. Or it could be for food production, even if you live in an apartment or other small space. Start off by picking winners. Fruits and vegetables that are fully ripe will usually have fully formed seeds inside. Avoid the hybrids. Play favorites by choosing things that say open-pollinated or heirloom in the description. You never know what you'll get when the hybridized DNA falls apart in the next generation of that plant. Finally, be patient. Most seeds respond well to a long and gentle drying process, and they sprout better after being fully dried. If you try to plant them too early, they may not sprout at all.

STRIVE FOR VERY STABLE TEMPERATURE AND HUMIDITY WHERE YOUR SEEDS ARE STORED. THIS WILL HELP YOUR SEED STOCK KEEP A HIGHER GERMINATION RATE FOR A MUCH LONGER PERIOD OF TIME.

GOOD TO KNOW

STAY FOOD SAFE
Trichinosis has always been a concern when butchering swine, handling uncooked pork and eating underdone porcine products. But barnyard pigs aren't the only creatures that carry the nasty *Trichinella* parasite. Horses, feral hogs, bears, foxes, wolves, skunks, and raccoons can all carry this species-jumping pathogen. To protect yourself and others from this sneaky roundworm, wear disposable gloves when butchering, and wash very thoroughly when finished. Protect yourself in the kitchen by cooking meat to safe temperatures (at least 145 °F/63 °C internal temperature with a three-minute rest before serving). You can also minimize the chance of *Trichinella* infection in your own OTG swine herd by not allowing your pigs to eat raw meat scraps (particularly pork, raccoon, or bear meat).

HIGH ON THE HOG Why not go "whole hog"—using everything but the squeal? When it comes to processing your own pigflesh, all you need is a bone saw and a sharp filet knife to unlock this porcine puzzle. Even if you don't eat pork, don't skip over this section. These cuts can also be made on virtually every other four-legged mammal.

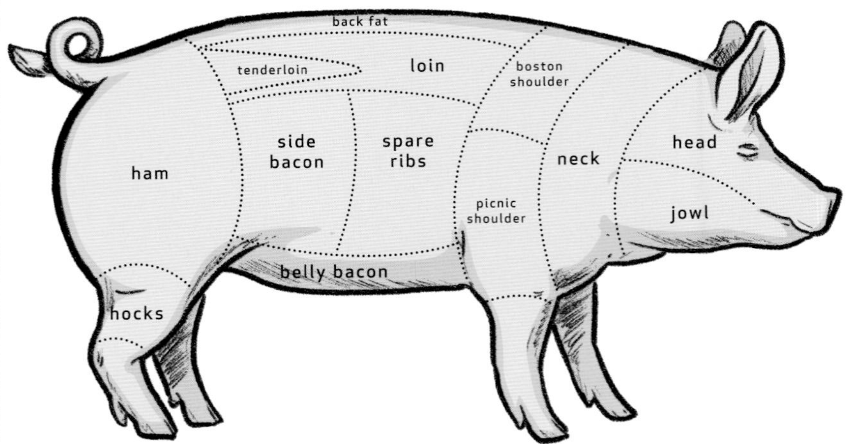

Top Shoulder Also called the pork butt (or Boston butt) though it's not the pig's butt—it contains part of the neck, shoulder blade and upper arm. A tougher cut, it's good for stews and braising, and excellent for slow cooked barbecue. It's also handy for ground pork or sausages.

Picnic Shoulder This is the lower front shoulder, and even tougher than the top. It could be tender if slow cooked for hours, but it's more commonly turned into sausage.

Pork Loin Modern hogs are now bred for very long loins and even extra ribs. The entire loin is very tender, making great chops, roasts, and cutlets. The actual tenderloin itself comes from the rear of the loin and baby back ribs come from the upper rib cage area of the loin. On top of the loin is a section of fatty tissue called fatback, which is great for making lard and salt pork or as an added ingredient to sausage.

RECIPE FOR SUCCESS

MAKIN' BACON Anyone can make homemade bacon—and it's easier than you think. Here's how you do it.

HOMEMADE BACON

Supplies:

3 pounds (1.4 kg) of thick, skinless pork belly

½ cup (120 ml) white sugar

1 tablespoon (15 ml) maple syrup

2 tablespoons (30 ml) coarse salt

1 teaspoon (5 ml) curing salt

1 teaspoon (5 ml) freshly ground black pepper

2-gallon (7.5-l) freezer storage bag

Directions:

Rinse the pork belly and pat it dry. Trim it into a rectangular shape (for easy slicing later).

Thoroughly mix the wet and dry ingredients until well blended. Place the meat and mix into the freezer bag, and massage all the contents around until you have coated the pork evenly.

Place the bag in the fridge, and massage the pork daily, for the next 7 days.

After a week, check the meat for soft spots; if there are any, add another sprinkle of salt and wait a few more days. When fully cured, it will be firm to the touch everywhere.

Once cured, rinse and dry the meat, and smoke it for its signature smoked flavor. Make sure it reaches 150 °F (40.6 °C) for safety. Slice it into strips, and your bacon is complete.

Pork Belly This is where bacon comes from. That's all you need to know about this part.

Ham The rear quarters of the pig are the hams. These can be parceled out as roasts, cut into steaks, or roasted whole until they fall from the bone. The ham hock, a staple of cuisine in the southern United States, comes from the joint at the bottom end of the ham. It is used for flavoring in beans, cooked greens, and other southern fare.

Jowls The neck, cheeks, and the rest of the head can end up in the stew pot or sausage grinder.

T/F

SAUSAGE CASINGS ARE INTESTINES

TRUE Many people are shocked when they find that "natural casings" for sausages are intestines. An adult pig has 15 to 20 yards (meters) of small intestines, with various diameters and strengths based on the size and breed of animal. And you can easily process your own. Remove the needed section from the gutted animal, along with fat, connective tissue, and flush internal contents (I squeeze an open end of the intestine onto running garden hose). Turn them inside out and soak in water overnight. The next day, strip the mucosa and muscle layers by hand. Use immediately or store in cold heavily salted water for a few days.

BARE MINIMUM

BAKE A HOE CAKE

The stories vary on the origin of this classic American flatbread, but some people do believe that this simple colonial cornmeal cake was actually cooked on the blade of a garden hoe, suspended over a small fire (although there is also a historical skillet known as a "hoe"). Whichever story is true, the basic recipe hasn't changed in centuries. Grease your frying pan, griddle, or wiped-off hoe blade with a bit of butter or pork fat, or fry a few strips of bacon and leave the grease. While the fat and metal get hot, add small amounts of water to finely ground cornmeal. The addition of some wheat flour or an egg to the mix will improve it, but the classic recipe is nothing but cornmeal and water. Pat out a small cake of dry dough. Fry lightly and flip periodically, until it has cooked to a golden brown on both sides.

BAKE FLAT BREADS Bread is an ancient food, dating back to the earliest days of agriculture, when it was likely a version of a cooked paste of ground cereal grains. Humans may not live by bread alone, but they're a lot happier with it.

Loaf Bread If you have an oven of any kind, you can bake your own loaves of bread and enjoy them while they are still hot. You could use a combination woodstove/oven unit, a solar oven, or build a brick oven outside. Get a bread recipe book and start working through it until you find your favorite recipes.

Flat Breads Around the world, people with limited resources have created delicious and sustaining flatbreads as a dietary staple. No bread machine required. Pitas, tortillas, naan, and Scottish oatcake hail from different shores, but share a common lineage that shows just how complex and varied world food traditions can be.

Sourdough Like sourdough bread? You can make your own starter with 3 cups (720 ml) warm water, 1.5 tablespoons (4.5 g) active dry yeast, a teaspoon (4 g) of sugar, and 3 cups (420 g) all-purpose flour. Combine the water, yeast, and sugar first, making sure the yeast starts to foam. Add the flour and stir in lots of air. Let it sit in a warm, dark place for 12 hours. Use the starter one cup (240 ml) at a time, replacing it with one cup (240 ml) of water and one cup (140 g) of flour to maintain the original starter batch.

RECIPE FOR SUCCESS

PITA BREAD Originally made by bakers residing in lands from the Mediterranean to the Middle East, pita is now known virtually worldwide. Here's a simple recipe that goes with just about any spread or dip (including the goat cheese we'll be learning to make next).

PITA BREAD

Supplies:

2 teaspoons (6 g) active dry yeast

½ teaspoon (2 g) sugar

1 cup (240 ml) lukewarm water

¼ cup (35 g) whole-wheat flour

¼ cup (35 g) all-purpose flour + 2 cups (280 g) unbleached, all-purposed flour

1 teaspoon (6 g) kosher salt

2 tablespoons (30 ml) olive oil

Directions:

Blend the yeast and sugar in the lukewarm water.

Add the whole-wheat flour and ¼ cup (35 g) of the all-purpose flour and stir. Place the mix in a warm spot for 15 minutes.

Add the kosher salt, olive oil, and the rest of the all-purpose flour. Stir and then knead the ingredients to form the dough.

Dust with additional flour if sticky and knead for two more minutes. Let it rest 10 minutes, then knead another 2 minutes.

Let the dough sit for 1 hour at room temperature. Near the end of the hour, preheat your oven to 475 °F (245 °C) and place a heavy baking sheet on the lowest rack of the oven.

Punch down your dough, then cut it into 8 or 10 equal dough balls. Let them rest 10 minutes.

Roll a dough ball flat with a rolling pin and place on the baking sheet. Bake it for about 2 minutes, flip it, and bake it for about one more minute. Repeat with your remaining dough and serve while warm. Watch carefully, they can burn quickly at this temperature.

RECIPE FOR SUCCESS

MAKE SOME HARDTACK This food has been around since the time of Egyptian sailors, but it is better known from the American frontier. Hardtack lasts for years if it's kept dry and away from pests. It's dehydrated, so it's light and easy to transport. It's also very dense, and packs a lot of nutrition in a small package. To soften it, our forebears soaked it in water, coffee, or rum.

HARDTACK

Supplies:

5 cups (600 g) flour

2 cups (0.5 L) water

3 teaspoons (15 g) salt

Directions:

Mix the flour, water, and salt, making sure the mixture is fairly dry. Roll it out to about 1/2-inch (1-cm) thickness, and shape into a rectangle. Cut the rectangle into 3x3-inch (8x8-cm) squares, and poke holes in both sides. Place on an ungreased cookie sheet, and bake for 30 minutes per side at 375 ° F (190 ° C).

ESSENTIAL SKILL

MAKE GOAT CHEESE

If you get your own milk from the source, why not try making cheese? This easy soft recipe doesn't need rennet, and the results are delectable.

STEP 1 Heat milk in a saucepan to 180 °F (82 °C) over 10 to 15 minutes.

STEP 2 Remove from heat and add ¼ cup (30 ml) of fresh lemon juice. Let it curdle for 1 minute.

STEP 3 Line a colander with several sheets of cheesecloth. Place the colander in a large bowl. Ladle the milk into the cheesecloth.

STEP 4 Tie the corners of the cheesecloth around a wooden spoon, and set it over a very deep bowl. Let it drain for 60 to 90 minutes until you have a smooth, ricotta-like mixture.

STEP 5 Put the cheese in a bowl and add coarse salt and herbs. You can eat it now or store it for a few days in the refrigerator.

SAVE IT FOR LATER In the days before refrigeration, people had to get creative when it came to storing food for the winter or for long journeys. Today, even with all our modern conveniences, these tips and tricks for how to stock a pantry are still useful—and delicious!

Pickling A salty brine or an acidic bath can turn most veggies, hard boiled eggs, and even some fish and meats into savory, sour pickles. Both salt and acidic environments act to limit the growth of bacteria and keep your food from spoiling. Pickles can be made by submerging the food in a vinegar and salt solution, or fermentation can turn vegetables into pickles. Cabbage is one of the most popular fermented vegetables in the world, turning into kraut and kimchee. Fermenting can smell pretty rank a few days into the process, but just wait, and it will soon smell like inviting kraut. Cabbage naturally has the organisms on it to ferment, and all you have to do is smash it down into a glazed crock or other fermenting vessel, and sprinkle on sea salt, press it down with a weight, and let ferment.

Drying Dehydrator units are a great way to preserve many foods, while cutting down the food's weight and volume, but they can be expensive. A less costly option is to make your own dehydrator by using something that you probably already have: window screens. Pop the plastic screens off of your windows, set them up on a few cinder blocks to get air flow underneath, and dehydrate many types of food in dry, sunny weather. Just avoid galvanized wire screens, as these can leach into your food, creating off flavors and potentially introducing toxins into the food. Slice fruits and bulky

ESSENTIAL SKILL

SMOKING FISH Being off-grid doesn't mean living like a savage—you can still have lox for your bagels! If you've caught or grown fish, you can turn them into flavorful smoked fish, without much modern equipment. There are two traditional ways to smoke fish: hot and cold. These can be done with the same apparatus; the big difference is the heat.

Hot Smoking This technique involves a closed box to hold in the smoke and the heat from your smoke producing materials. The fish is cooked by this heat, and permeated with a smoky flavor. Fish prepared in this manner can last up to a week at room temperature.

Cold Smoking Done at cooler temperatures, for a longer period time, the goal in this method is long term fish storage. This requires more of a drying process than a cooking process. It should not get hot enough in the smoker to actually cook the fish.

vegetables into thin pieces. Apply a little fruit preservative powder (available at most grocery stores) or dip them in lemon juice to ward off oxidation and browning.

Salting Encrusting your meats, fish, and other foods in salt is a great way to limit bacterial decomposition. The traditional salted hams of my home state of Virginia have been a global favorite for centuries. Salting usually starts out with a brine soak that lasts for about a week, which then progresses to a drying process with the food items buried in salt, sugar, and perhaps spices.

T/F

BOTULISM RUINS FOOD

FALSE The bacterium *Clostridium botulinum* creates a toxin that can cause tiredness, speech and vision issues, followed by weakness in the limbs, paralysis, and even death. The spores that cause it are found in improperly canned foods (fish is a major culprit), but are also common in water and soil. Honey is another source, so honey is not recommended for babies under 1 year old. Their immune system cannot defend against it properly. We may be rightfully wary to eat old or expired canned goods, but there is a way to guard against this deadly toxin. The botulinum toxin can be naturally destroyed by heating the food to at least 185 °F (85 °C) for about 5 minutes or longer.

RECIPE FOR SUCCESS

DANDELION ROOT COFFEE Dedicated to the glorious coffee bean? Try growing the real thing in a greenhouse—or you can just make dandelion root coffee. Once you're satisfied about the plant's identity, dig up the roots of 10 to 20 plants and get ready to make a healthy, caffeine-free coffee alternative.

Step 1 Preheat your oven to 350 °F (175 °C). Wash the dirt off your roots and cut them into small bits.

Step 2 Spread the roots on a cookie sheet and bake until chocolate brown, about 30 to 40 minutes.

Step 3 Pour boiling water into a coffee mug and add a spoonful of roots for each mug of water. Cover and let the brew steep for 10 minutes. Sweeten to taste and enjoy your drink.

Store roasted roots for a month or two in a breathable container like a paper bag, or freeze for longer-term storage.

BREW YOUR OWN Home brewing is much easier than you think! In the simplest of terms, brewing happens when you add yeast to a sugar-water solution. The yeast is going to eat the sugar, producing carbon dioxide and alcohol. This is the process of fermentation, which will take about a month for home brew. During this time, a special cap will let the CO_2 bubble out, but keep oxygen, unwanted debris, and microorganisms from entering the brewing jug. Pretty simple, right? Welcome to the smallest microbrewery around: your own home!

Collect Your Supplies You'll need a 1-gallon (4-l) glass jug; a package of beer or wine yeast (in a pinch, use the stuff that makes bread rise–*Saccharomyces cerevisiae*. The same microbe for bread also creates doughy tasting alcohol); a source of sugar, such as honey, malt, table sugar, or molasses; clean water; and a wine lock cap for the jug. One other item of note is a sanitizer–a quick fix is cheap vodka. The only part that may need to be improvised is the wine lock (if you don't pick one up where you buy your yeast).

Be Sweet To brew beer that tastes like beer, you'll need malt. This can be found as a canned product with hops already added or as a powdered extract. For old-school brewing, sprout some barley, then toast and grind it. Simmer the ground grain in water for an hour, then filter out the malt-rich water, and finally, boil with the hops for another hour. If you're making wine, you can use a mix of fruit and table sugar. For mead, all you need is honey and water (plus wine yeast).

Get Carbonated To make your beer bubble or your sparkling wine fizz, you will need to carbonate it after fermentation. This can be done by adding more sugar to the brew and sealing it in a pressure-safe vessel. The dormant yeast will wake up to produce a little more CO_2, carbonating the beverage. Add an ounce (28 g) of table sugar or corn sugar to each gallon (4 l) of brew and seal it in bottles. Clean soda bottles and self-capping ones will work fine. Let it sit for one week, then chill and enjoy.

STEP BY STEP

PRESS SOME CIDER It's not hard to make your own hard cider from apples (or other fruits). You'll just need to buy or borrow a cider press, or get creative and make one.

STEP 1 Squeeze the chopped and mashed fruit in the press to extract the sugar-rich juice, then feed the solids to your livestock (they will love it). Pour your juice into a large enamel or stainless pot.

STEP 2 Boil the juice for 30 minutes to kill any stray organisms (wild yeast and bacteria). Let it cool to room temperature.

STEP 3 Add a packet of yeast to the cool juice and stir with a sanitized spoon.

STEP 4 Pour the juice into a large sanitized glass jug. Add a water-filled wine lock on top, the same as you would to make beer.

STEP 5 Watch it bubble for 45 days, then pour the cider off (leave the sediment). Bottle it or enjoy immediately!

GOOD TO KNOW

AGE YOUR WINE, NOT YOUR BEER It's been said that waiting is the hardest part of home brewing. I agree. I'm always eager to try a new batch of wine, but wine is not a beverage to rush. In general, you'll want to age your homemade wine at least three months before you start tasting it. Even then, it may still have a "green" flavor, but this will typically mellow and disappear over time. Once your wine has aged a year or two, it should be very smooth and a pleasure to drink. But oddly enough, we can't apply this same aging technique to our regular proof beers. The average beer is around 5 percent alcohol by volume and filled with lots of grain residue. When this beer ages, it develops a "skunked" flavor. The only beers that can last a few years without losing their good taste are heavily hopped, high-proof beers over 9 percent alcohol by total volume.

COMMON MISTAKE

PACK IT RIGHT Just as critical as the "what" part of your food cache plan, is the "how" part. Your cache container should be able to withstand the natural environment it is located in, and protect against the enemies of storage, like moisture, rodents, insects, freezing, heat and theft. Avoid any places where it is likely to receive water damage or be assaulted by rodents or other animals. Skip the spots that will get too hot in the summer. Additionally, you really shouldn't hide all your goodies where thieves could easily find them. In the event of a basic burglary, all the way up to a full scale looting and pillaging spree, then your cache should defy discovery and be able to withstand it all. Finally, don't hide your cache so well that you can't find it again. That would add insult to injury if you really needed your food cache and couldn't find it.

MAKE A FOOD CACHE Have you ever thought about making a stash of food supplies at a remote site, a bug-out-location, or your off-grid homestead? It makes a great back-up plan to add to your food security. Whether you're trying to keep your supplies safe from critters or provisioning a remote outpost of your land, you don't have to bury your treasure to have it count as a cache. You could have your container stored virtually anywhere on site, so long as it is accessible in an emergency and hidden from view. You could even bury your cache outdoors. Just make sure that you can find it again later. Let one or two responsible family members know of the cache, just in case you don't make it.

Waterproof containers are the best choices for damp conditions, along with home-made vaults made out of PVC sewer pipe with caps glued in the ends. And for scenarios that aren't so damp, metal boxes are often a good choice, as they are impregnable to the gnawing teeth of rodents. Just remember that space is at a premium in a cache, especially a small one. Picking the right food is also a dicey selection process, as you are trying to balance calorie density, shelf life and package size. Mountain House's line of Pro-Pak meals are the most space-saving options for freeze dried foods, and they are touted to last 25 years (in ideal storage conditions). Carefully packaged white rice, jars of honey, and many other grocery store items can fit the bill for nutrition and longevity also.

One final point to consider with your food cache is the conditions under which you'd be using it. If times are tough enough that you'd be relying on your own food supply, you would want that food assortment to be easy to prepare, without any strong odors, and able to provide complete nutrition for yourself and your family. You'd also want the food to be safe if your home is plundered. Consider dividing your food supply by storing it in many different locations. This way, you may still have something to eat after a burglary. Don't be shy about mislabeling your food bins, either. Looters may pass right by your food bin labeled "X-mas Keepsakes" underneath a stack of real holiday decorations in the back of the basement.

ON THE GRID

URBAN FOOD CACHE Do you want to hide some food, supplies, and other stuff, but have only limited room to do so? Think about the empty spaces in your walls. Interior walls (between rooms) which are covered in drywall or paneling usually don't have much insulation inside, if any at all. These hollow spots can store quite a bit of food. Open up the wall, load in your stuff, and do your best repair job. Tell only those you trust the most about its location, such as your family or close friends.

DON'T STORE LIQUIDS AND DRY GOODS TOGETHER IN THE SAME CACHE CONTAINER, UNLESS YOU LIKE MAKING MOLD FARMS. WHEN THE WET STUFF LEAKS INTO THE DRY (AND INVARIABLY IT WILL), IT WILL ALL BE RUINED.

HUNT & FISH

WITH THE CAST OF A FISHING LINE, OR THE RELEASE OF AN ARROW, OUR FOREBEARS TOOK THE WILD GAME THAT FED THEMSELVES AND THEIR FAMILIES. TODAY, WE CAN STILL FOLLOW IN THEIR UNSHOD FOOTPRINTS, HARVESTING GAME ANIMALS IN BOTH GOOD TIMES AND BAD.

By hook, arrow, bullet, or trap, we can still take many of the same animals our ancestors once hunted for food, fur, feathers, and the many other ingenious uses they discovered, uses as diverse as the people who continue these arts. These days, procuring your own wild game can mean many different things. For some, hunting, fishing, and trapping are a means to a backup food supply. For others, they are a thrilling pastime. For the few who live way off the grid, wild game is a major supplement to their family's food supply—a necessity, in fact. Wild game is the original locally-sourced food, and it comes in a wondrous variety. You won't worry about palate fatigue when you're eating different game every day and preparing it fresh without any preservatives or commercial processing. On a wild game diet, you're eating as nature intended. Yes, I'm talking to you, paleo enthusiasts! You're following in the footsteps of your forebears. And the patient and perseverant outdoorsperson will eventually be rewarded with meat.

YOU DON'T NEED MUCH Contrary to the "buy it all" motif in the sales circular from your local sporting goods store, you don't need lots of equipment to hunt, fish, or trap. A basic rifle, some snares, or a fishing pole will do—if you have the skill to use them. Of course, you should always obey the regulations of your local fish and game authority, which usually include the purchase and carry of a license for the activities you'll be engaging in. But after those expenses, everything else is just whipped cream and sprinkles. Sure, the extra gear is nice, handy, and cool. Really, though, all you will need is the instrument of your game animal's demise and the experience to use it. And if everyone around you is dressed like Mad Max, you probably don't even need the license anymore.

ESSENTIAL SKILL

HAND FISHING By far the simplest method of fishing is hand fishing, and it's about as primitive as you can get. You actually grab the fish (typically catfish and other large slow species) from its watery lair with your hands. To get started, use your feet to feel for structures that could harbor a fish, and then reach your hand into them. The fish will often move forward and bite your hand. Fight your natural urge to pull your hand away. Leave it in the fish's mouth and pull it toward you. Wrap your free arm around the fish, being careful to avoid contact with the barbs on the fish's fins. You should never try this solo; go with others so that they can help you if you become injured or entangled in debris. Common injuries when practicing this form of angling include cuts, scrapes, and scratches, which can be avoided by wearing gloves.

SURVIVAL FISHING What if all of your fantastic food plans go sideways? Or, more likely, what if you're caught off-guard while away from your home base? That's when survival training kicks in. You'll need quick and easy methods of catching fish if you're angling for food in a survival situation. You probably won't have much gear to work with either. These emergency fishing techniques don't require much tackle, but they do demand that you put in some practice, before you have to rely upon them.

Hand Line The basic survival fishing kit (hooks, line, and split-shot weights) and a fat juicy worm or grub are all you need for hand lining. Tie your hook to the line, squeeze on the weights, impale the bait, and then toss the line into the water by hand. Hold onto a coil of the line when you're sure there are only little fish present. Tie the end of the line to a stick and wind the line around it to create a handle when you're not sure how big the fish might be. Tie a floating stick into the line for a bobber to do top-water or mid-water fishing. Skip the float for bottom fishing.

Cane Pole It doesn't have to be cane or bamboo, but any flexible pole or sapling can make a nice fishing pole to help you reach further out into the water, and keep your looming figure from scaring away any fish. Tie the rig as you would for hand line, and tie the free end of your line to the slender end of the pole. Fish as you would with rod and reel, except for the reeling-in part.

Nets You may also need a net to help you land the fish that you've caught with your hook and line. Find a flexible stick with long forks, wind the forks around each other to make a hoop, and tie a piece of fabric over it for a quick survival dip net.

Bait For successful fish traps and fishing with hook and line, your best bet is to select irresistible bait. Since most fish species are carnivores, it's hard to go wrong with worms, grubs, crickets, and other natural

TRUE STORY

NATIVE FISH POISON Around the globe and across the centuries, native peoples have used various plant compounds to stun fish in fresh and salt water for an easy catch. Seeds, bark, fruits, and roots have been crushed and dumped into waterways to paralyze fish, which will usually float to the surface due to their buoyant swim bladders. Today, these practices are illegal in most areas, but something to remember for dire emergencies. In the Eastern United States, many Native peoples once used crushed green nut hulls and bark of black walnuts (*Juglans nigra*) which contain juglone. This compound affects fish respiration, bringing them to the surface in an attempt to breathe. The seeds of another common plant, mullein (*Verbascum thapsus*), can be crushed to release rotenone in the water, which affects the nervous system of fish. This "fish doping" was typically done in very slow moving rivers, with massive amounts of plant material.

bug bait. Flip over a rock or tear into a rotten log to find these spineless creatures and use them accordingly. You can even cast out a net to catch small fish—an irresistible bait for the bigger local fish.

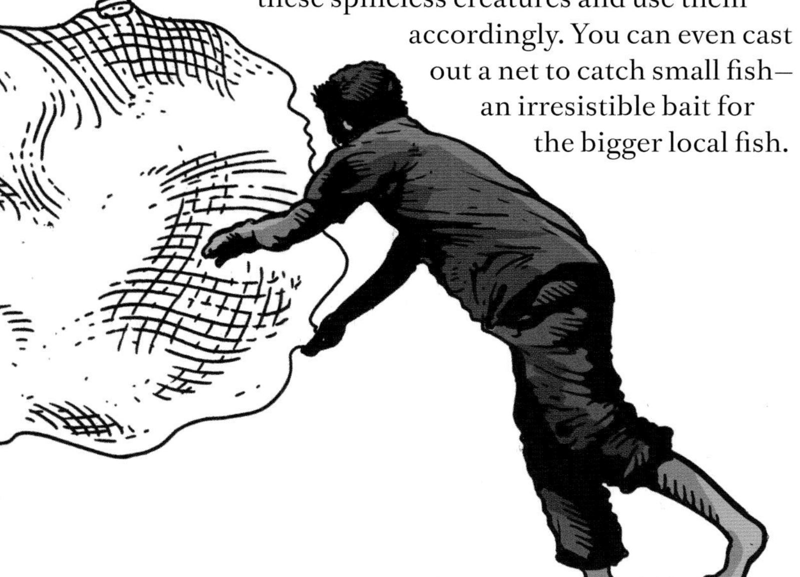

BARE MINIMUM

BASIC FISHING TACKLE You might think that you would need a huge box of tackle for all your survival fishing needs, but in truth, you really only require just a few items. A combination of large and small fishing hooks is, of course, a great place to start. You are likely be hungry in a survival scenario, and you will want to hook whatever varieties of fish are out there, whether large or small, so a set of different size hooks are important. A dozen little split-shot weights can make a big difference in your survival fishing game too, so you should choose a set of weights that can be crimped onto the line by hand and removed easily the same way as well. Last, but not least, a sturdy bundle of monofilament line should be part of your survival fishing kit. 40 yards (37 m) of 8- to 10-pound (3.6- to 4.5-kg) test should work well for most kits.

GOOD TO KNOW

TYPES OF TRAPS The real beauty of trapping is that it can generate food, and you don't even have to be there for it to work. It's like getting other people to hunt for you. There are many different types of traps that work in both urban areas and wild places.

Snares These strangling traps can be primitive snares made of string, or wire taken from strong braided-steel cable.

Foot Hold These feature clamping jaws that hold an animal by the foot, should they step on the trigger.

Body Grip Like oversized rat traps, minus the board, they use one or two heavy springs that move the trap bars together, killing the animal quickly.

Live Catch Ideal for farm, urban, or suburban settings, live catch traps lets you safely release any animals you don't want to kill, such as your mouse-murdering barn cats.

SET A SNARE A specific kind of trap, snares are defined by the fact that they restrain or strangle game animals. Thousands of different trap configurations are used worldwide, but often the simplest are the best. Find out about your local trapping regulations, and test the traps that are legal in your area. At the most basic, snares can be classified as fixed or active. Here's the difference.

Fixed Snares The key feature here is rope, cord, or wire that is connected to an immobile object, like a tree or a stake in the ground. Typically unbaited, fixed snares restrain an animal until you come around to dispatch it.

Active Snares Active snares have moving parts in addition to a constricting snare-noose and provide your greatest selection of traps that utilize baits or rely on habitual animal movement to set them off. The classic example is a spring pole snare that lifts small game by a flexible tree branch or sapling tree.

ESSENTIAL SKILL

USE COVER SCENTS Smell is usually one of the strongest senses an animal possesses, and the various rich smells of plants are a normal part of a terrestrial animal's daily life. If they smell strongly to us, imagine how intense these odors are to the animals, and if you use these local, nontoxic plants on your skin and your traps, it'll just smell like everyday life for the animals. There are plenty of options out there to use as cover scents: Pine needles, onions, garlic, and yarrow leaves can all be crushed in order to release their oils, resins, and other odorous compounds. You can rub the stems and leaves of mint plants to use their mentholated oils. Even plants such as wintercress and wild mustard leaves can be crushed to release a short-lived, but very strong pungent scent.

AVOID INDISCRIMINATE BAITING You may be able to smear some cheese or peanut butter on a mousetrap at home and have good results, but putting the same salty and oily treats on a trap in the woods may not be such a good idea. To have any predicable luck with trapping, you'll have to use the right bait for the right critters. The careless or uninformed use of a bait can draw in the wrong creatures to be caught–or cause the right animals to avoid the trap altogether. Pick a species to trap, and select baits that match their normal and natural diet. You're never going to catch a rabbit using a chunk of meat for bait, and you're never going to catch a bobcat with a wild strawberry stuck on the trigger. When you're not offering them anything that is part of their diet, they're just not going to go after it. Instead, use fresh meat and viscera for bringing in the carnivores. Use old meat, stinky fish, or carrion to tempt the taste buds of scavengers. Stick to the plant kingdom for baits that would attract herbivores. Give them something they'd like, but can't easily get, and you'll see more success.

COMMON MISTAKE

DON'T TOUCH THAT TRAP Fixed snares are the safest to set and handle, as there's almost no way you can hurt yourself with just the noose. Active snares, on the other hand, can cause serious harm to an unlucky, careless or clumsy trapper. If you've bent a sapling or tree branch and attached it to a trigger and noose, be very careful. Once a trigger is set, never touch the noose part of the snare with your hands again. If you're holding the snare noose or have your fingers near it and the trigger should go off unexpectedly, the noose can tighten around your fingers or hand, ripping the skin and soft tissue right off. This injury is called degloving, and it is intensely painful and dangerous. This injury usually requires major surgery, such as skin grafts. If you must move a noose once a trigger is set, use sticks—not your bare hands!

SNARES AND THINGS

Snares are tireless companion hunters, whether you are working to acquire game for meat, fat, or fur: once they're set, they will do all the work for you when a target animal crosses their path. With the proper know-how and a little bit of time and effort, you can craft any or all of these snares, and plenty more aside from the ones seen here—this is just a small selection of the many snare varieties that humans have been using for trapping animals for millennia. All that you need to bring to the task is a sharp knife for carving wood, along with some lengths of cordage or braided cable. Nature provides the rest of the materials for you.

DROWNING SNARE This simple trap can acquire food for you while putting the critter out of its misery faster than many other traps. It's easiest to set when you have a steep-banked waterway frequented by creatures of habit.

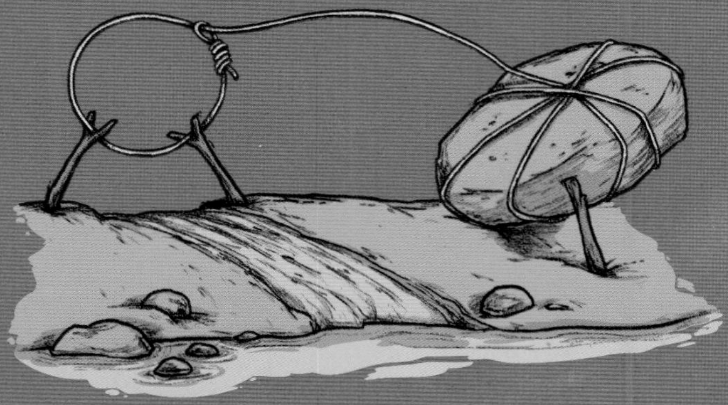

TREADLE SNARE This "spring pole and noose" trap is set off by an animal bumping the treadle stick, stepping on it, knocking it down, or by knocking it out of its way while running down its trail.

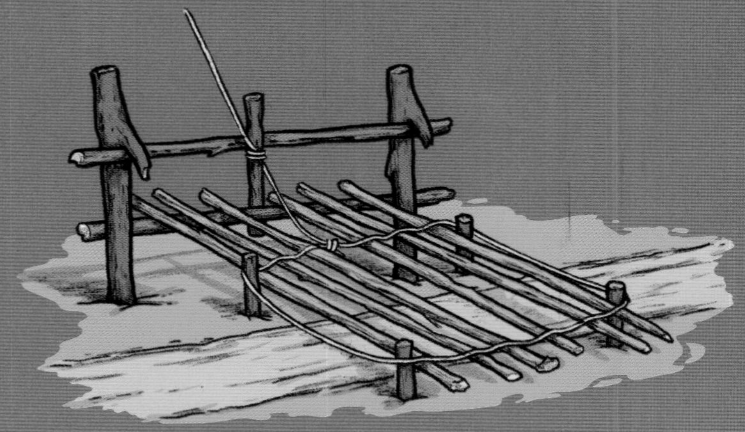

OJIBWA BIRD SNARE You can use this versatile trap year-round and in all conditions. If your cord noose keeps blowing off the perch, you can wipe a little sticky pine pitch on the contact points.

FIGURE-4 SNARE This low-to-the-ground snare combines a sensitive leverage trigger (one often used in deadfall traps as well) with the powerful lunch-launching capability commonly encountered in a spring-pole snare.

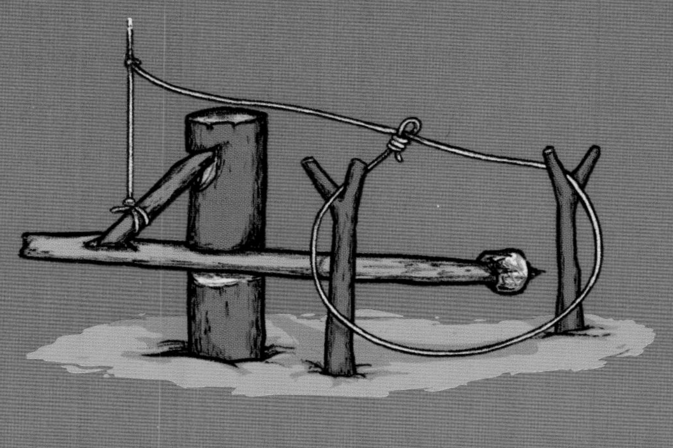

GOOD TO KNOW

TRAPPING SUPPLIES
You can build your own trapping kit with just a few basic supplies in a large backpack, and a firearm to dispatch wounded game. Pick and choose from this list to suit your needs.

- Braided cable snares
- Foothold traps
- Body grip traps
- Trap setting tongs
- .22 handgun
- .22 ammunition
- Knife
- Cordage
- Several stakes
- A large trowel
- A small hand saw
- A tarp to kneel on
- De-scenting material
- Work gloves
- First aid kit
- Headlamp
- Delectable and species-appropriate baits

OTHER THAN MEAT AND FUR, YOU CAN USE VARIOUS PARTS OF WILD GAME FOR OIL, GLUE, BONE TOOLS, LEATHER, AND CORDAGE. COLORFUL BIRD FEATHERS AND ODD ANIMAL HAIRS CAN BE TIED INTO FLY FISHING LURES TO CATCH YOU EVEN MORE FOOD.

IT'S A TRAP! Once you've mastered the basic snare, it's time to expand your repertoire to other traditional ways of snagging dinner with little more than a stick, some string, and a rock in some cases.

Drop a Deadfall If a trap uses a weight to crush your prey, then it's a deadfall. The triggers on these sorts of traps can be a little tricky to fabricate, but they are very versatile. Most deadfall triggers can be used to set up a crate or box (instead of a rock or log) to go from lethal trap to a live-catch box trap. Although deadfalls tend to squash your target animal into a pancake, they do have a real bonus. Many deadfall triggers can be field built with only a knife, and some can be put together using just your bare hands. Since the rocks and logs that you'll be using for weights are already out there in the wilderness or the backyard, you don't need much to build these traps.

Hold Tight Body gripping traps (also known as conibear traps) are some of the most devastating traps that you will ever have the opportunity to set. These can be set and placed in a remarkable variety of ways: horizontally, vertically, on land, or underwater. There are many sizes available, from small single spring traps to huge double spring traps that can be downright frightening to look at, let alone set. Small body grip traps start out with 4-inch (11-cm) jaw spreads, and they are well suited to catching animals such as weasels, muskrats, minks, martens, fishers, and rats. Medium and large body grips can tackle larger animals such as opossum, raccoons, skunks, foxes, bobcats, groundhogs, otters, and smaller coyotes. These stronger traps pose a greater risk to trappers, as the larger springs store more energy when set. The biggest models can measure up to 22 inches (56cm) wide. You know those are dangerous when you need to use a special tool in order to set them. A pair of conibear setting tongs is a real finger- and hand-saver (just ask any seven-fingered trapper about that). These tongs are like a set of large pliers, and they are used to grip the trap springs and compress them. I won't dare set larger versions of this trap without a pair of these in my hands.

TRUE STORY

BUILD A BOX During the Great Depression, one of my dad's childhood chores was to check on the family's box traps. In those days, if any meat could be found on the dinner table, it was rabbit or squirrel—courtesy of those traps. Jump forward 70 years, and a homemade box trap is still an option for meat on the table during challenging times. You can even build one yourself with a few tools, a little scrap lumber and a few odd bits of stick and string.

Step 1 Gather lumber and tools. You'll need boards, a few small nails and screws, a few feet of string, a piece of wire mesh, two pencil-sized sticks, a hammer, a drill, and a saw.

Step 2 Build a box shaped like a tunnel, with both ends open. Nail or screw four small wood strips at one end of the tunnel to act as guides to allow the door to side down securely. Nail the mesh at the other end of the tunnel.

Step 3 Drill a hole near the mesh end of the box for the trigger. Whittle a notch on the trigger peg, and tie your string to the other end of it. Attach the string's free end to the top of your wooden trap's door. Set your string to the top of the longer stick.

Step 4 Now comes the tricky part: adjusting everything. The trigger stick may need to be re-carved to be more or less sensitive. Bait with appropriate food or scent baits, and check twice daily (before they chew their way out).

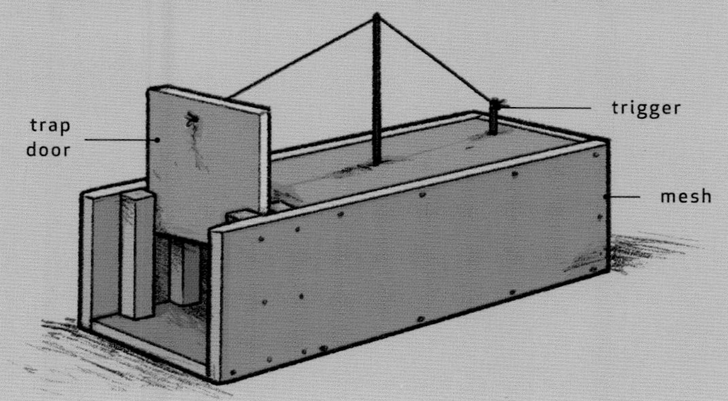

GOOD TO KNOW

IT'S A NUMBERS GAME
Traps are a great way to help get game meat for your table while you're busy doing something else. But you shouldn't expect each and every trap to catch an animal every time you set them. Even professional trappers typically only have about a 10 percent success rate on their trap lines (a circuit of traps that are checked and maintained daily). And these game animals aren't always dead, which is why trappers should carry a .22 caliber handgun along with ample ammunition to dispatch live trapped animals. But it's not at all uncommon, either, to find only a foot in your trap. The animal may have chewed off its numb foot to escape, or a predator may have come to take advantage of the trapped quarry. For these reasons and many more, you should set at least a dozen traps (or, if possible, several dozen) to maximize your chance of catching something to eat.

BARE MINIMUM

CALL A GOBBLER
Turkeys are smart birds; they're also very curious creatures. Any kind of sound which may seem like a stray hen could catch the interest of an amorous Tom turkey. You don't have to buy the latest high-tech call to make these sounds on your next turkey hunt. You can use the same apparatus that natives used to bag these birds for centuries. Get a thin piece of slate, and find a large clam or mussel shell (or shell from a small box turtle) about the same size as your slate. Next, cut a piece of cedar wood into the size and shape of a fat pencil—point and all. Hold the shell and slate in one hand, to create a sound chamber. Scrape your cedar stick against the slate with your other hand. With a little bit of practice, you'll get yelps, purrs, and all kinds of sounds from this call. With some practice, you'll get the bird too.

GO BIG WITH SMALL GAME You don't need to shoot a deer, a moose, or an elk to come up with some meat for the stew pot. Many hunting cultures have gotten along just fine with game animals. And if you're not convinced, let me tell you that rabbits and squirrels taste very good. I would rather have them on my plate than any other meat, wild or farmed. These serving-size creatures may be all you ever need.

Rabbit This animal has fed countless hunters in history. Its lean meat is tender and flavorful. A 3-ounce (85-g) serving of cooked rabbit has 147 calories, 28 grams of protein, 3 grams of fat, and 23 percent of your daily allowance of iron.

Squirrel The grey squirrel is my favorite on this list, and the most chicken flavored. 3 ounces (28 g) of squirrel has 147 calories, 26 grams of protein, 4 grams of fat, 32 percent of your daily iron, and 14 percent of your daily riboflavin.

Opossum These small, shy creatures are one of the most overlooked wild game meats. When eating a natural wild diet, the meat can taste like pork. However, the opossum often gets a bad reputation for flavor by living on garbage and taking on a poor flavor when living close to civilization. A 3-ounce (85-g) serving of opossum includes 188 calories, 26 grams of protein, 9 grams of fat, 22 percent of your daily iron and 18 percent of your daily riboflavin.

Raccoon These bandit-masked creatures can be found pretty much everywhere, and they can eat just about anything. Their adaptable diet always keeps them in food, and probably has a role to play in their high levels of nutrients. 3 ounces (85 grams) of raccoon meat contains 217 calories, 25 grams of protein, 12 grams of fat, 34 percent of your daily allowance of iron, 26 percent of riboflavin, 33 percent of thiamin, and 118 percent of B-12.

COOL TOOL

OLD-SCHOOL SLINGS

Ever wonder how you might go hunting if you don't have a firearm? Or how to get by when everyone's out of ammo in the End Times? The basic sling is a deadly weapon that's existed since prehistoric times, and compared to a bow, it's easy to make, though there's a steep learning curve in learning to aim it. And the ammunition is stones—a completely free and plentiful source of projectiles! Cut a piece of leather or stiff cloth into an oval shape that's palm-width and as long as your entire hand. Next, tie a 1-yard (1-m) piece of cordage to each end of the oval. Then tie a loop in one free end of one cord, and a big knot in the end of the other cord. Slip the loop over your thumb, hold the knot in the same hand, and load a rock into the pouch. Whirl the sling over your head to build up power, then release the knotted cord to fire!

DIY CROSSBOW

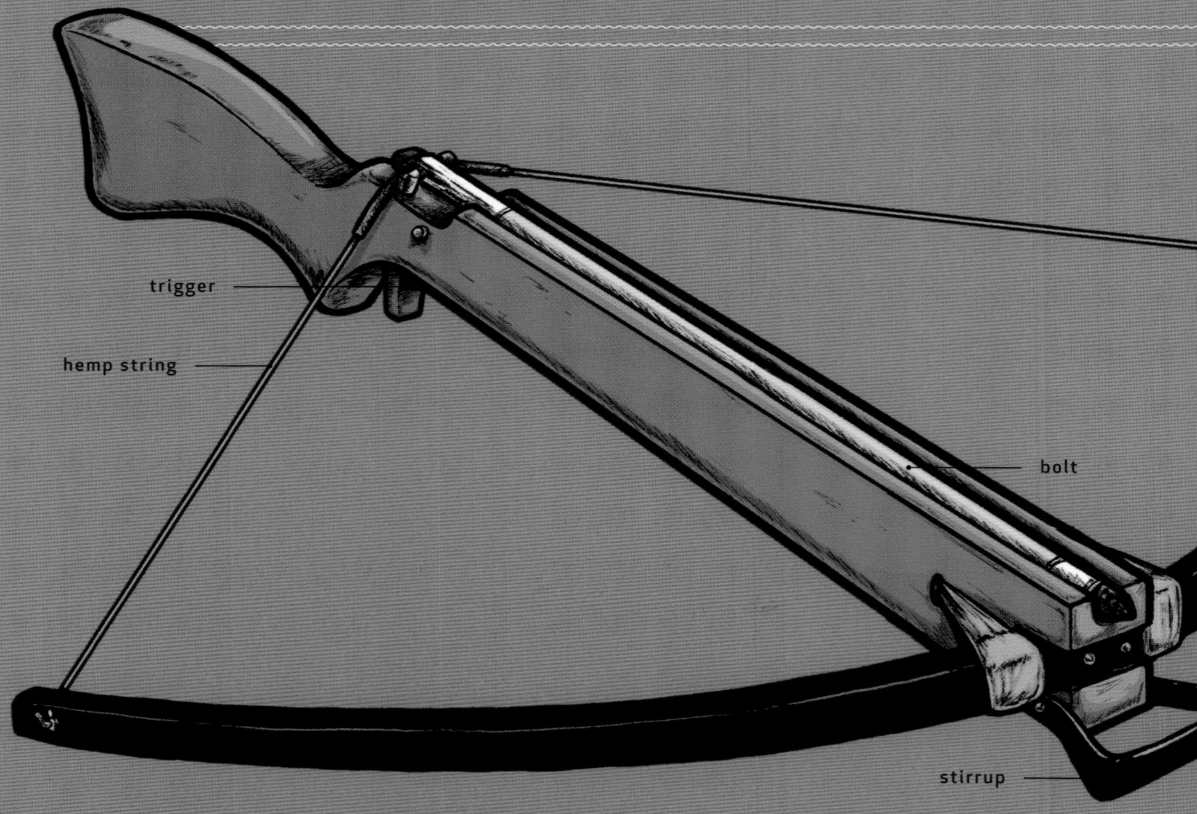

Crossbows are remarkable devices whose origin dates back at least 2,500 years. You shouldn't let their antiquity fool you into thinking that these time-honored weapons are ineffective, however. In medieval times, they were not just for hunting but warfare, capable of punching through leather, chainmail, and even plate armor. They've even had their skull-penetrating power demonstrated by dispatching zombies on postapocalyptic TV shows and movies with a single shot to the head. That power means that these hunting tools can take down animals just as well as other archery tackle—and plenty of hunters out there use them to this day. While store-bought varieties are available, you can even build one yourself.

STEP 1 Build the stock, which provides a handle to hold the weapon, mass for stable shooting, and the frame to hold the crossbow components together. The top of the stock is grooved to guide the bolt, cut out to hold the crossbow string, and drilled out to receive the trigger mechanism.

STEP 2 Shape the prod, the bow-like component of the crossbow. Select a dry piece of wood from a good bow-making species such as yew. Taper the prod as you would a normal bow, so the limbs bend equally.

STEP 3 Add a string. Historical crossbow strings were made from hemp. Today, we can use Dacron and twist up a 20-strand bow string for the prod.

STEP 4 Add a stirrup and trigger. Pin or screw on a foot stirrup made from bent strap iron to assist with cocking. Next, install the trigger pin that pushes up through the stock.

STEP 5 Build some bolts. Fashion these like short arrows, with no notch and two feathers. The length of the bolts should match the length of the drawn crossbow prod, plus an inch or two (2.5–5 cm) of overhang on the end of the weapon.

STEP 6 Test your weapon. Once the crossbow is complete, there's only one thing left to do: launch some bolts!

GOOD TO KNOW

BRING ON THE POUNDS The energy stored in a crossbow is measured the same way as a bow's strength, in pounds of pull at the maximum draw length. Just because they are short doesn't mean that crossbows are wimpy. They can be just as powerful as a longbow, or more so with the right prod. Use flexible hardwoods like locust or hickory for a powerful traditional prod, or try fiberglass or leaf-spring metal for an upgraded prod from modern materials.

COMMON MISTAKE

SHOOT SAFELY Treat a crossbow like a firearm. Unload and unstring it if not in use. Store it and the bolts in a dry place away from kids. Don't point it at anything you don't mean to shoot. Beware of what's past a target, or that may cross the line of fire (kids or pets). Make sure all parts are in working order before you begin shooting.

COOL TOOL

BREAK-DOWN RIFLE
A portable, collapsible rifle, such as the Henry U.S. Survival AR-7, can be easily assembled and broken down, and it has upheld a reputation for ease of use, accuracy and reliability for decades. Today, bush pilots (and U.S. air force pilots) still carry the AR-7; it has also become a staple for backpackers, survivalists, and off-grid homesteaders who may need to hunt small game but don't want to carry a heavy firearm. The AR-7 is available as an ultralight semi-auto model which only weighs 3.5 pounds (1.6 kg). With all components stored in the stock, the weapon is just a little longer than 16.5" (42 cm). You can even store extra ammunition in it too. Once the tough ABS plastic stock is sealed, the rifle actually floats in water! If you need an affordable and dependable survival rifle, consider this one!

HUNT FOR FOOD You can absolutely hunt for meat rather than raising it. In game rich areas, colonial hunters went on "long hunts" which lasted at least a year. During that time, they survived on game meat, with just a few staples such as corn. Today, a big freezer or a lot of canning jars are important if you plan on scoring a large game animal. You could have hundreds of pounds (kilograms) of meat to deal with in short period before it spoils. And as you eat through your meat stockpile, you'll need a little something extra. It's been said that there are three things you need to eat a whole moose, elk, or other sizeable creature: the gun to shoot it, the knife to butcher it, and a whole lot of different spices so you can stand to eat it all. One of humanity's secret survival traits is palate fatigue. We tire of eating the same thing and crave diet diversity to avoid malnutrition. If you're stuck eating a whole moose over a long winter, you'd better have a lot of different spices, or eating will become drudgery.

(Field) Dress Quickly As soon as your big game is down, it's time to remove the internal organs. It's important to open up the animal quickly so that the meat can begin cooling. You should also remove the stomach and bowels to prevent the meat from becoming tainted. But just because we want to vacate the animal's body cavity quickly doesn't mean the contents are trash. The heart, lungs, liver, and kidneys are all safe, nutritious organ meats. When every calorie counts, even the stomach and intestines can be cleaned, cooked thoroughly, and eaten. Save the guts as you field dress your game, and use the quick-spoiling meats as your next meal.

Hang 'Em High Once the game has been field dressed, it should be hung to drain and cool in a shady place, well off the ground out of the reach of scavengers (but not in your camp in bear country). Leave the hide on it, and the limbs intact, to make it last longer. Carcasses with the hide and limbs still attached may safely hang for a few days in warmer weather (ideally wrapped in cloth) or they may hang for weeks in cold weather. In sub-freezing conditions, it's even possible to leave the hanging carcass frozen for months, until you're ready to butcher.

Save Your Skin Once it's time to remove the hide, you'll want to work carefully if you intend to use it for leather. Cut the hide down the belly, from one end to the other. Cut from this center line down each limb, and cut around each "ankle". Then put your knife away. People who skin with knives end up with sliced up hides. Even if you use a knife and don't cut all the way through the hide, it's still covered with shallow slashes called score marks, which ruin the appearance of the leather and weaken it. Once all your cuts are made, begin peeling the hide off the carcass starting at the rump and working your way toward the neck. If you need help separating the hide from the underlying tissue, you can use a wooden spoon or something similar to "chisel" the hide off the animal. Once removed, the hide should open up into a large semi-rectangular shape. This can be flopped over a log, flesh side up, and scraped to remove remaining meat and fat. For long term storage before tanning, you can sprinkle a little salt on the flesh side of the hide while it is still moist. For short-term storage, don't waste the salt. Either way, dry the hide in the shade until stiff and store it away from pests until you are ready to tan the hide into leather.

Make Some Jerky Do you have more meat than you can easily handle? This may be a happy problem, but it's still ultimately a problem. In warmer temperatures, without a freezer or the equipment to pressure can the meat, you may have no other choice but to make jerky. It's an easy process and one that's best done in dry weather with plenty of sunshine. Cut all visible fat off the meat (throw the fat in your stew pot with some meat and veggies for lunch). Slice the de-fatted meat into thin strips and apply a little salt while it's still damp. Hang the strips to dry in the sun. Ideally, maintain a tiny, smoky fire near the meat, so that the smoke drifts across the meat to discourage flies, but the heat doesn't cook it. Jerky *must* be raw in order to be safely preserved. You can tell that the jerky is done when it is brittle. This may take only a few hours or all day. When finished, the jerky should be stored in a paper bag or cloth sack to prevent sweating and molding.

ON THE GRID

URBAN HUNTING The suburbs and nearby urban areas can be home to lots of wild game. A deer that devours your garden can be a source of wild game meat in a crisis. So can the squirrels raiding your bird feeders, or a raccoon going through your trash. But don't assume that these critters are easy to hunt. Animals use their sharp senses to remain undetected in suburbs. To increase your chances of a successful hunt, spend some time observing your quarry. Look for trails, tracks, scat, and other signs to give you an idea of their movements. Watch where they travel at dawn and dusk, for a better chance of getting them in your sights. And be careful when hunting near homes or businesses. Use a tree stand or high vantage point and never shoot toward areas where people could be. Trees, brush, and fences are not a safe backstop for bullets or arrows.

LEVEL UP

COULD MAKING YOUR OWN SOAP, LIQUOR, OR DOOMSDAY RIDE BE THE KEY TO YOUR SURVIVAL? YOU NEVER KNOW WHAT MAY SAVE YOUR FAMILY SOMEDAY. LIVING OFF THE GRID MAY REQUIRE YOU TO BECOME YOUR OWN ROPE MAKER, DISTILLER, OR MECHANIC. YOU MIGHT EVEN ENJOY IT.

Basic short-term survival is simple enough and quite easy for most people to wrap their heads around. In a nutshell, you need enough shelter, water, food, and protection to stave off death until your situation resolves itself or your circumstances improve. That's basically all you need. But when it comes to long-term survival and the self-sustaining lifestyle, the list of things you need to know becomes a lot longer and a lot less intuitive. We would need to be handy with a wide range of tools, good with ropes and knots, and it wouldn't hurt if we knew how to work on a car. Some of the following things in this section may not seem like survival issues, such as soap. If we pay no attention to hygiene, however, illness and disease are inevitable outcomes. It could be that something as obscure and "un-survival-like" as soap making could be your salvation. In this next section, we're moving way past the foundation of self-reliant living. It's time to learn the skills that will take your homestead or survival camp to the next level.

DON'T GO OFF-GRID WITHOUT ONE
The trusty pocketknife! Few tools are as necessary or versatile on a day-to-day basis. Whether you favor a fixed blade or folding knife, straight edge or serrations, there are a few must-haves for your faithful knife. First, it needs to be easy to sharpen. Even if your knife is sharp right out of the box, it's no good if you can't hone it to a razor edge again. Find a knife that's easy to sharpen with a basic whetstone. Next, consider the grip. The material doesn't matter. It just has to offer a solid, comfortable grip, wet or dry. As for the eternal "fixed or folding" debate, fixed-blade knives can generally take more abuse and are better in the field. Folders are more discrete, and a better fit for every day carry (EDC). But why not have several of each?

ESSENTIAL SKILL

GET SHARP Putting a keen edge on a knife or tool is nearly as important as having knives and tools in the first place. Follow these steps, and soon you'll be a sharpening wiz .

STEP 1 Survey the edge angle. Look for nicks, which take extra work to remove. Pay attention to the angle you will sharpen.

STEP 2 Remove major damage. Use a coarse stone or file on nicks, keeping the proper edge angle (most knives have a bevel of 20–23 degrees). If there are no nicks, run a coarse stone down each side of the edge twice.

STEP 3 Sharpen with stones. Grind the edge using tiny circles, making the same number of strokes on each side—medium, then fine.

STEP 4 Remove burrs and polish. Strop the blade on a leather belt several times, drawing the spine of the knife forward and dragging the sharp edge against your strop.

STOCK YOUR TOOLSHED Pappy's toolshed wasn't just where he hid his moonshine from grandma. It was the storehouse of all the necessary tools and supplies that were needed around the farm. We can take a page from our collective family history, and set up our own tool repository, to be ready for any chores that arise.

Saws A chain saw can cut wood very quickly; hand saws are slower but make finer cuts.

Wrenches End wrenches, monkey wrenches, and crescent wrenches are critical for mechanical work and repairs, as well as plumbing.

Vice This holds items so they can be repaired or modified.

Hammers A variety of hammers and mallets are needed for carpentry and mechanical work.

Screwdrivers Vital for repairs and carpentry.

Rakes Metal rakes and fan rakes are very handy around the farm.

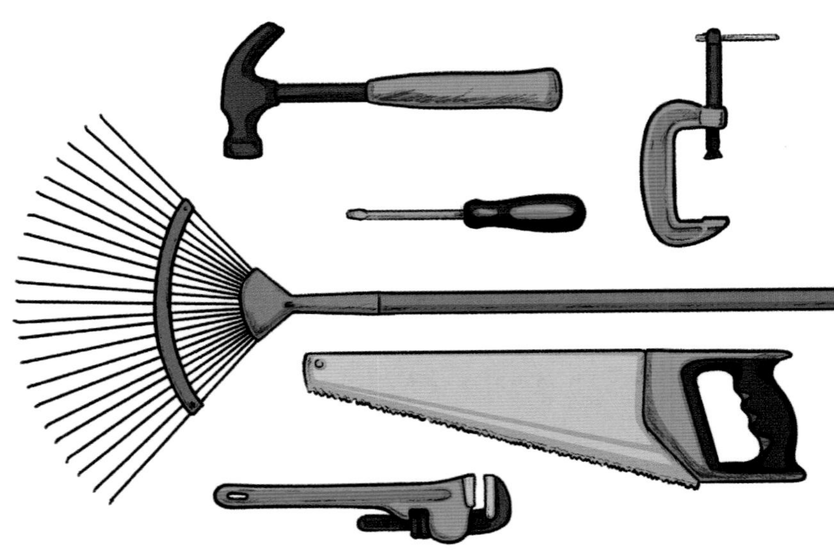

Shovels Round shovels are for digging, square shovels are for shoveling sand or grain, or for shoveling up material on hard surfaces.

Axes Felling axes bring down trees and cut off their limbs. Splitting mauls split firewood. Hatchets are good for making kindling and camp craft.

Machetes and Brush Axes These clear brush and heavy vegetation.

Pitchforks These move hay, straw, debris, and animal bedding around.

Power Tools If you have a place to plug them in, power tools will save you a lot of work.

Files Some files can sharpen your edged tools and help to repair metal items, while others are strictly for carpentry.

Logging Tools Log tongs and cant hooks will help you roll and pull logs to wherever you need them to be.

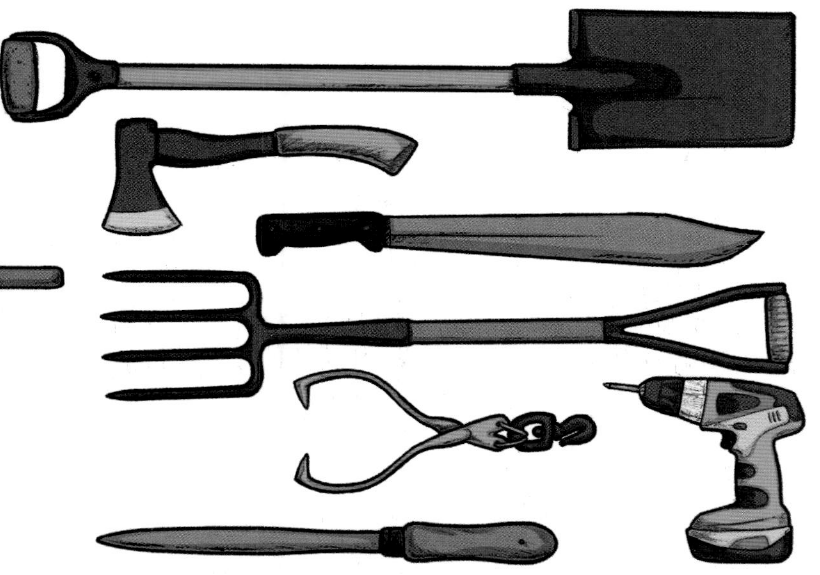

GOOD TO KNOW

HANG AN AXE HEAD If you use axes, you break axe handles. Sometimes the only way to replace a handle properly is by "hanging a head".

STEP 1 Clean the hole in the axe head, filing off any rough edges.

STEP 2 Sand the end of the new handle to a very snug fit in the axe head.

STEP 3 Hand fit the axe head on the handle, so it barely sticks on there.

STEP 4 Hold the end of the new handle, with the barely-stuck-on axe head dangling near the ground, but not touching anything.

STEP 5 Tap the free end of the axe handle with a hammer. Because of the mass, the axe head tends to hang in mid-air as the wooden axe handle drives into it, and the head creeps up the handle with each blow. Hammer the handle until it emerges from the other side of the axe head. Drive in a wedge to lock the handle in place.

COOL TOOL

PARACORD Also known as "550 cord", this versatile braided line was first used in parachutes in World War II (hence the name). Paratroopers found that the cord was incredibly useful for everything from pitching tents to repairing gear. Astronauts even used this resourceful rope to mend the Hubble telescope. Survivalists have learned to keep some in their emergency equipment; anyone is lucky to have this stuff handy if we get into a bind. You can use it as a replacement for boot laces, or weave it into bracelets and belts to ensure it's right there when you need it. Aside from a 550-pound (227-kg) breaking strength, each length of cord is made of a hollow sheath with several inner strands. This cord can be stripped to make 8 or more pieces of cordage, used for a wide range of tasks. It's like a floppy nylon multi-tool with endless uses.

GET ALL WOUND UP Back in the day, yarn, twine, string, and rope were all made by hand on the farm. These days, we've become so used to buying these essential items at the local hardware or home-and-garden store that the art of twisting them up has been lost to many modern folks. If you're truly going off the grid, the day will come when you need to tie up some bean plants, rope a steer, or something else like that, and all those store-bought supplies will be gone. Here's what to do to make sure you never run out of rope, line, or twine.

Grow a Field of Rope In modern times, plastic is one of the most common materials for rope and cord, but both flax and hemp have been grown for fiber all around the globe for millennia. If your land will support it (and if it's legal in your area), you could grow a crop of the stuff for fiber production. Plenty of early American colonists grew flax for their fibrous stalks along with their oily edible seeds. Once the flax had gone to seed, the dry stalks would then be cut down and broken to separate the fibers from the woody material. The raw fiber would then be pulled through large wire combs to clean it, and finally spun into thread for sewing, twisted into rope, or woven into linen cloth. Hemp can be similarly processed.

Make Your Own Two-Ply String You can get started on your own string by collecting the strongest fibers that you can find. This may be flax or hemp that you have grown, or fibrous inner bark from trees such as basswood, mulberry, cedar, and poplar. Wild plants, including jute, dogbane, stinging nettle, and milkweed, can also be made into cord. Grab a small length of fiber and begin twisting it. Continue twisting until it kinks (A). Hold the kink, and keep twisting each bundle of fiber (B). If you twisted clockwise to begin the cord, then keep twisting the fiber bundles clockwise, while also allowing them to encircle each other counter-clockwise (C). It is the opposing force that makes the line strong. As you work, take time to meticulously splice in new fibers in order to continue twisting to make a long length of cordage.

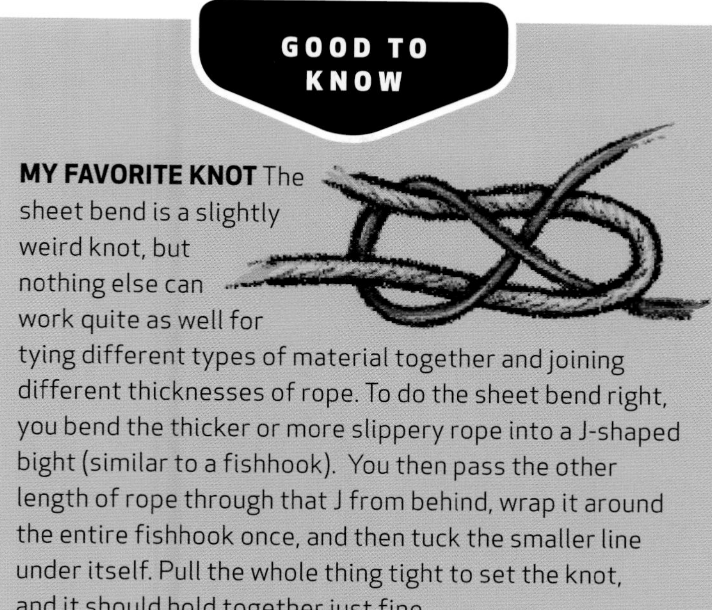

GOOD TO KNOW

MY FAVORITE KNOT The sheet bend is a slightly weird knot, but nothing else can work quite as well for tying different types of material together and joining different thicknesses of rope. To do the sheet bend right, you bend the thicker or more slippery rope into a J-shaped bight (similar to a fishhook). You then pass the other length of rope through that J from behind, wrap it around the entire fishhook once, and then tuck the smaller line under itself. Pull the whole thing tight to set the knot, and it should hold together just fine.

ALL THE ROPE IN THE WORLD WON'T HELP YOU IF YOU DON'T KNOW HOW TO TIE KNOTS. LEARN A FEW COMMON KNOTS, SUCH AS THE SQUARE KNOT, SHEET BEND, BOWLINE, AND PRUSIK, AND YOU'LL BE ABLE TO HANDLE MOST JOBS THAT ARISE.

ESSENTIAL SKILL

RENDERING FAT Fat is a little tricky to keep on hand unless it's rendered, which removes water and impurities that can make it rancid. Rendering means cooking the fatty tissue for a long time at low temperatures, and filtering the fat before storage. Cut animal fat into 1-inch (2.5-cm) cubes, removing all visible meat and non-fatty tissue. Drop these chunks into a pot with water about 4 inches (10 cm) deep. Bring the mixture to a simmer, keeping it below 150 °F (65.5 °C) for a few hours. When no more fat is melting, pour it through a cheesecloth-lined strainer. After pouring your grease into another container, you can also simmer it a little longer (30 minutes) and filter it again. The final product is then poured into small jars or cans, and kept in the coolest, darkest place available. It should last weeks in warm weather, or months in cold weather.

FUN WITH FATS Many products around the home rely on fats or, more precisely, on lipids, which is the scientific term for the molecules that make up substances such as fat, wax, and lanolin. If you learn to harvest and process these handy—if slightly greasy—products, then your home will be shiny, waterproof, and well-lit, among other things.

The First Rule of Soap Club Yes, the soap-related scenes in the movie *Fight Club* are true. Lye will burn the crap out of your hand, and soap can be made out of liposuction leftovers (or any other sort of plant or animal fat). And it turns out that people have actually been using soap for a very long time indeed. The most basic form of soap comes from non-toxic plants that contain some form of saponin, a group of soap-like compounds. The proper crushed plant part will lather up in water and get you clean. Yucca root (*Yucca filamentosa*) crushed in water has been a Native American beauty secret for centuries. When used a shampoo, it gently cleans hair, leaving it silky and soft. But it's often the case that these soap-bearing plants aren't available when you need them. This still leaves you with another option—making your own soap from fat and lye (see our recipe on the opposite page).

Let There Be Light Dipping your own wax candles is really very easy and the only things that you need to make your own are cotton string and paraffin or, better yet, beeswax! If you have your own beehives, you'll naturally have plenty of leftover wax from your honey collection. Beeswax candles will burn several times longer than paraffin candles of the same size. Start by melting the wax down to a liquid inside a deep container, and then lowering a cotton string into it. Dip the string once and pull it out to

RECIPE FOR SUCCESS

MAKE YOUR OWN SOAP
This process revolves around a reaction called saponification—the chemical change from oil and lye into functional soap. Here's how to mix up your own batch of old-timey soap.

DIY SOAP

Supplies:

A Pyrex glass measuring cup

Wooden spoon

A pot

3 cups (700 ml) purified water

9¼ ounces (270 g) lye

4½ cups (955 g) of olive oil—the cheap stuff works best

2 cups (390 grams) coconut oil

2 cups (515 g) grapeseed oil

Directions:

Be careful! Lye is very caustic to the skin and eyes, with some nasty fumes. Use gloves and goggles, and work outside when making lye soap. Start by adding the lye to the water in the glass container. It will get very hot, so use Pyrex (which is shatter resistant). Let the lye mixture cool to 110 °F (43.3 °C), while you warm the oils to the same temperature in your pot. Slowly pour the lye into the pot of warm oil and stir with the wooden spoon until the texture changes, looking like a gritty milkshake. Pour the soap into molds to harden, and let it age one month before use.

cool and harden. Dip it quickly again to add another layer and thicken the wax skin without melting off the previous wax layer. Keep repeating this quick-dipping and long-cooling process until you have created the desired length and diameter of candle. If you decide to use a long string bent over double, you can even make two candles at once—and you'll have that cool pair of candles on a string like the ones that they used to sell in general stores.

ON THE GRID

SIMPLE OIL LAMP If you've heard that you could insert a plant fiber string into a dish of fat, light it with an open flame, and watch it burn like a candle, you heard right. Fat lamps can burn as brightly as a wax candle, and serve as a great terminal use for grease that may have gone rancid. You can use liquid or solid fat, and it can be animal, vegetable or mineral. Old bacon grease, a chunk of fresh animal fat, expired shortening, leftover frying oil—any of these materials can work in a fat lamp. Just put your fat in a heat-safe container (such as a canning jar or ceramic bowl), stick a wick into it, and light it up. Grease lamps are handy if you lose power in your on-the-grid home, and very useful out in the boonies. Just treat it like a candle—keep it out of the wind and away from flammable objects—and your lamp will light up the darkness.

GOOD TO KNOW

THE PURE PRODUCT Do you ever wonder where essential oils come from? Producers use a still to make these medicinal and healthful oils. Note: once you use a still for this, you won't want to use it for anything else—unless the next hipster trend is rosemary moonshine!

Add fresh plant matter and water to cover it to your still. It's best if it's packed tight. Add the still head and connect your condensation coil. Turn on your heat source followed by the cooling water as the coil starts to warm. Once liquid begins trickling out, adjust the cooling flow to keep the distillate lukewarm. When you've distilled 80 percent of the liquid in the still, turn off the heat. Let your distillate sit for several hours, so the oil can separate. Nearly all oils are lighter than water and float. Skim the oil off when the water is cleared, and bottle it in labeled dark glass containers.

MAKE MOONSHINE AND MORE Stills aren't just used for moonshine, although they can definitely brew that stuff along with plenty of other uses: They can also be used to purify water, distill essential oils, and even make fuel! You can build your own small still by using a pressure canner and a length of small-diameter copper tubing. The best part of this small operation (aside from getting safe water) is that the pressure canner stays intact. This allows you to shift gears from water distillation to food preservation very easily (assuming that you are not distilling water to remove radiation from it). If you're good at metal work and soldering, you could also make a full-sized still for more generous batches of your distillate.

First, build or improvise your "kettle". This is the big pot (typically copper) that holds your undistilled material, and it's where the heat will go. It could be heated by wood fire, propane burners, or even solar power if you are particularly creative. Atop the kettle, you'll have your still head. This is tightly fitted so that no vapor can escape and it is tapered to connect the kettle to the condensation coil. If the still isn't portable, all of the metal joints can be soldered to make them airtight. Otherwise, you could caulk them with flour and water paste. From the still head, the worm spirals down into a container of cold water, condensing the vapor to a liquid. Whatever you are distilling is collected at the end of the line.

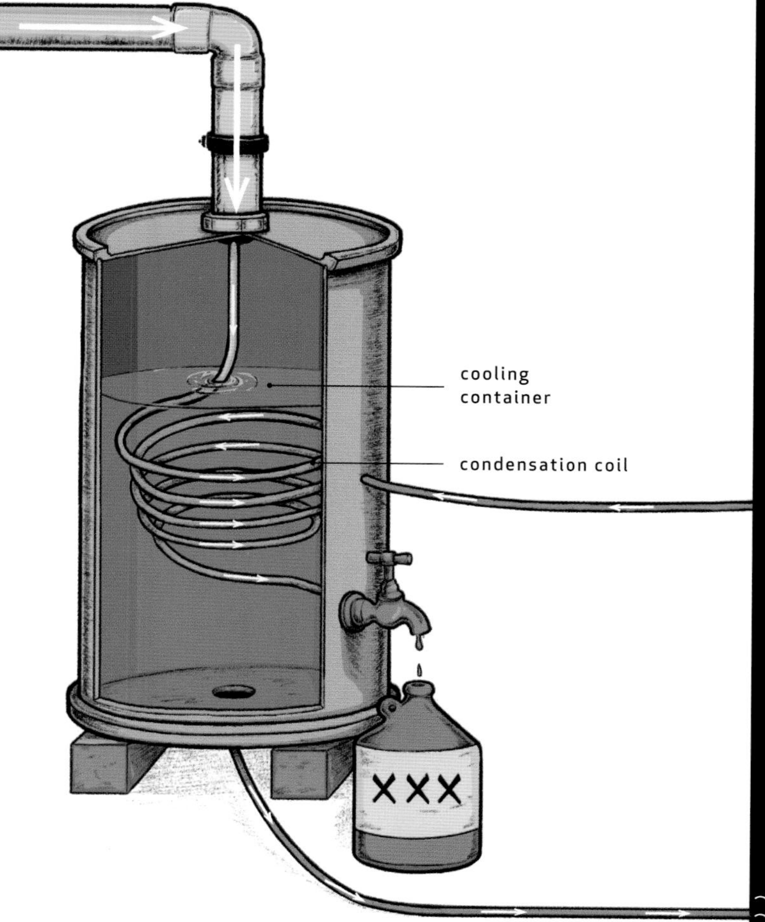

T/F

GUNPOWER WAS USED TO TEST ALCOHOL

TRUE Modern distillers have an easier (and safer) time measuring the proof of their alcohol these days. A small glass float called a hydrometer is dropped into a tall cylinder of alcohol, and it settles at different depths for higher- or lower-proof hooch. Since alcohol is less dense than water, higher proof drinks allow the float to sink deeper. But when this system wasn't working for the British Navy, sailors would blend alcohol and gunpowder. If the alcohol was strong enough, the gunpowder would ignite; the higher the alcohol percentage, the bigger the flash! This was their "proof" that the liquor was good, and why we use that word for alcohol.

THE BARE MINIMUM

OFF-ROAD OPTIONS
What's the perfect way to travel around your OTG property? A quad, dirtbike, dune buggy, horse, or your own feet? Any or all of them could work for you and the terrain you call home. For sustainability, your feet and a horse are good as they don't need fuel. To go quickly through rough terrain or narrow trails, the dirtbike is nimble and fast. If you need passenger room or cargo capacity, you can add a sidecar to the bike. A quad can carry two or more people and a generous amount of supplies, especially with a wagon in tow. And a 4x4 or other off-road ride can carry people or supplies in comfort and ease. In the end, the mode of transport that makes sense is one you know how to operate safely and that can handle your biggest tasks and chores. You'll have to answer that question yourself.

CHOOSE YOUR WHEELS We're not here to plug any specific major vehicle manufacturer. Selecting the ideal off-grid auto is a matter of personal preference and your should take into account the environment you'll be driving it through, as well as many other factors. You'll probably also have to consider the price tag. Indeed, you'll need to do your research. But this list is, at least, a place to begin.

Toyota Land Cruiser 70 There have been many different incarnations of this hardy truck since it rolled off the line in 1984. This off-road workhorse has been used by 4x4 enthusiasts, military forces, and safari providers, just to name a few. This "bush taxi" is built tough per Toyota's concept of a 25-year service life. This means more expensive and durable components all around, even the windshield is thicker than other Toyotas!

Land Rover Defender This modern version of the tried and true Land Rover blends luxury, performance, dependability, and a big fat sticker price to go with it—but it's one of the toughest SUVs ever made. Don't expect this vehicle to go quietly into the night.

Jeep Wrangler The Jeep first rumbled across the broken landscape during 1942 in the middle of World War II. It tirelessly transported GI's to the world's battlefields, and survived many different manufacturers buying and selling the brand. Although many models of Jeep have come and gone, the original Jeep (renamed the Wrangler in 1987) is still an off-road icon. It's tough and affordable, and there are many aftermarket parts available.

Mercedes-Benz G-class Easily the most expensive vehicle on our list, the G-class is the off-grid luxury vehicle for those who spare no expense. You could buy about four Jeeps for the price of a single G-class, but its track record, power, and off-road engineering have kept this line of vehicles in demand for over 30 years.

FUEL STORAGE The gas-powered equipment at your off-grid oasis is always going to need fuel. No matter how much liquid fuel you're planning to stockpile, certain considerations remain the same. You're dealing with a combustible, poisonous material, so use all due caution.

Containers Liquid fuel should be stored in airtight containers that do not vent. You should be able to walk into the area where your fuel is stored and smell nothing. Only store your fuel in approved plastic or metal containers, and check them frequently.

Location Don't store fuel in your basement or even in your garage. The ideal spot is a storage shed on your property located at least 30 feet (9 m) from your home (safer in the event of a house fire). If you want to stockpile fuel in bulk, you can even purchase aboveground storage drums.

Temperature You should keep your fuel somewhere that's clean, dark, and as cold as possible. Direct light and higher temperatures can degrade fuel quickly and, in a worst-case scenario, pose a fire risk as well.

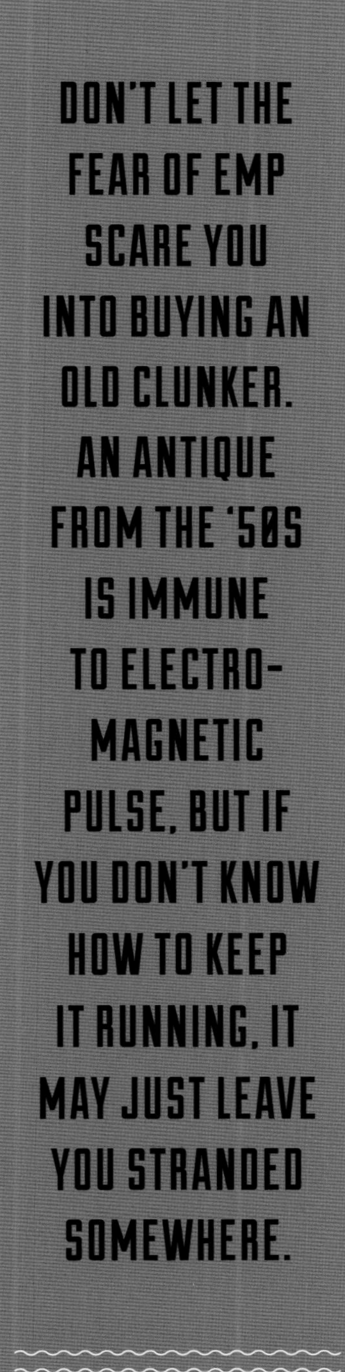

THE BARE MINIMUM

SHOP 101A If you flunked shop clas, it's possible to fix ailing vehicles, but you need the right tools. Here's what you'll need in case you can't make it to a professional.

Tools Get wrenches along with a metric and standard socket set. A good car jack and stands are also important. Don't forget things such as hammers, pliers, cutting tools, and screwdrivers.

Parts Oil filters, spare fan belts, and headlight bulbs are all cheap and easy to store. (You're going to need them at some point.) Make certain that you have exactly the right parts you'll need, and any specialty tools needed to replace them (can you hand me that oil filter wrench?).

Fluids Stock up on motor oil, antifreeze, and washer fluid, at a minimum. You can also keep some brake fluid and power steering fluid to top those off if they are running low.

SET UP AN OFF-GRID GARAGE A humble shed or outbuilding can become a glorious off-grid garage if it's properly stocked up with all of the right tools, supplies, and equipment. You don't need a full hydraulic lift and a 1,000-piece socket set (though it'd be cool, right?). You can turn your basic garage into a DIY auto shop with a lot less, and there's a good reason to do it. Being able to work on your vehicles is a key skill for the true OTG type.

Start with the Basics Your shop will need some electrical power and lots of lighting, since it's usually pretty dark under the hood. A set of strong overhead lights and numerous drop lights will let you see what you're doing. And don't forget about safety: your shop needs at least one large fire extinguisher, a smoke alarm with a carbon monoxide detector, and a great first aid kit.

Add the Tools A battery charger and a set of jumper cables are handy when your vehicle's battery needs a boost. All the bare minimum tools and supplies will be needed too. Add a large air compressor and some pneumatic tools, such as an impact wrench, and your shop will look, act, and sound like the real deal.

Get Jacked A simple jack and stand set can get your vehicle up off the ground and allow you to work underneath it in relative safety, but the sky is the limit (that is, if your budget is generous). I have a friend with a professional grade full lift in his backyard garage, and I know of another crafty fellow with a solar-powered, full-size lift in his own OTG auto shop.

Store Things Securely Your tools, parts, and supplies all have value. It's important to keep them in good order, and keep them secure from thievery. Locking tool boxes and security measures around your garage are a must in remote areas. These would be increasingly important during

GOOD TO KNOW

ADD SOME FLAIR Aftermarket options for vehicle accessories can be nearly limitless. Brush bars, spotlights, and winches are common and useful accessories. But what about the weirder stuff? The things you might not have known about could make all the difference if you're in a roadside emergency.

Larger Gas Tank Fill up less often with a bigger tank. Many makes and models of vehicles can support a bigger gas tank, up to twice the size of the original. Yes, your fuel purchases will be pricy, but now you can drive twice as far.

Onboard Air Compressor The ability to pump air makes it possible to repair flat tires and run pneumatic tools. Electrically powered by the engine, small air compressors are lightweight, yet very powerful. Imagine using an air wrench to pull off a tire and an air chuck to inflate it in the middle of nowhere!

Electrical Power Vehicle engines are not meant to be electrical generators, but they can act as such in order to run small appliances while the engine is running. Electrical inverters with outlets can be plugged into the vehicle, while hardwired versions can be mounted and wired to the vehicle's electrical system.

FLAT TIRE IN THE MIDDLE OF NOWHERE? YOU CAN FIX IT WITH A CHEAP TIRE PLUG KIT AND A SMALL AIR COMPRESSOR THAT PLUGS INTO A CIGARETTE LIGHTER. JUST PUT GLUE ON A RUBBER STRIP FROM THE KIT, INSERT IT INTO THE HOLE, AND REFILL THE AIR.

tougher times as well. There's no point in buying all of this equipment, to just leaving it lying around for thieves.

Work on Your Welding Since certain car and truck parts would be hard to replace in a catastrophe, learning how to weld properly and adding a small welder to your garage would make a lot of sense. Auto body and chassis repairs, exhaust work and other mendings (both minor and major) will become a whole lot easier with a welding machine in your off-grid garage and some welding experience in your OTG "toolbox".

THE ULTIMATE RIDE

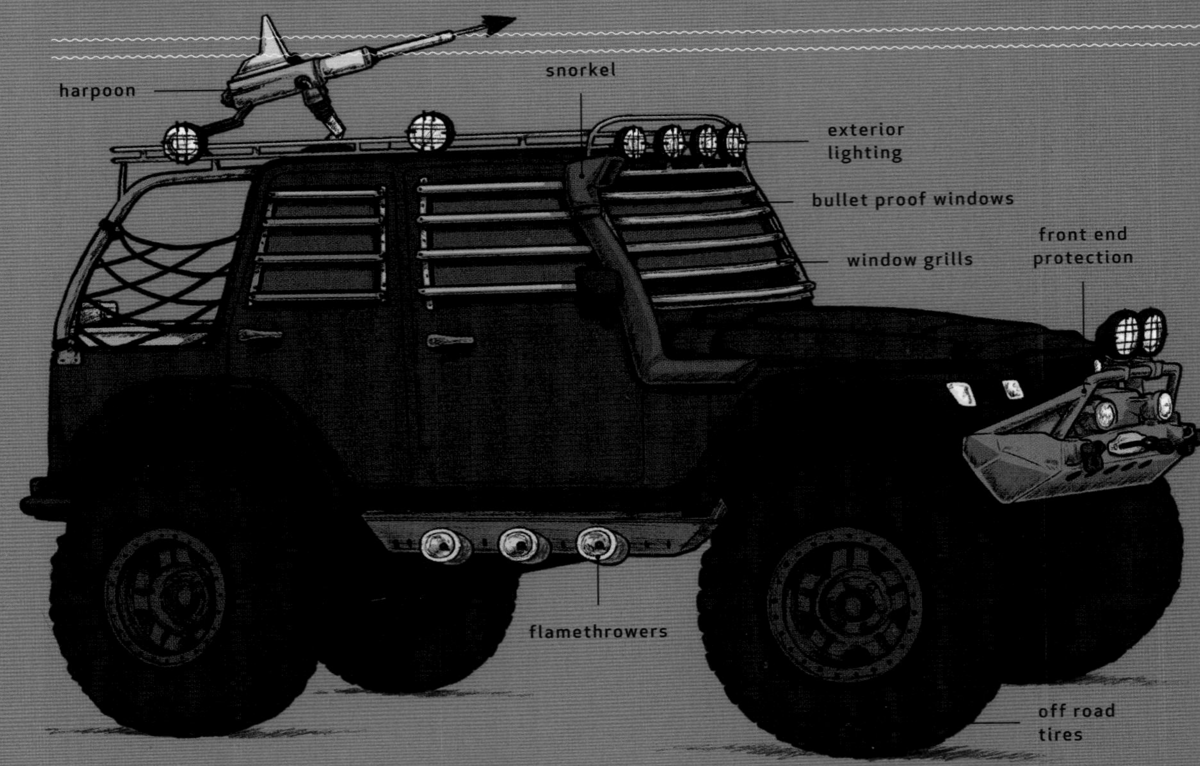

If you're looking for a doomsday-worthy battle bus, consider something like the Land Rover Defender with a few Mad Max approved upgrades. Defensibility, room for the kids, and tons of attitude? Check, check, and check!

Front End Protection The terms can get a little confusing. Push bars, brush bars, and bull bars are all different forms of front end protection. Push bars are small, and just for pushing against other autos. Brush bars protect headlights, grill, and radiator. Bull bars are low and heavy guards to push down brush (or cattle). Whichever suits your needs best, add it to that Franken-wagon.

Off Road Tires Big, knobby tires should be on your list if you build a vehicle like this.

Bulletproof Windows Hey, people may not be so nice in the future. Keep what's yours by avoiding bullet holes in your windows (and your body).

Exterior Lighting Science has proven that it gets dark at the end of each day. Brighten things with side and rear lighting.

Flamethrowers No joke—a new product that's on the market in South Africa is an underbody mounted flamethrower that shoots from under the driver and passenger sides to foil carjackings and mob attacks.

Window Grills Bulletproof glass isn't always enough.

Snorkel To lose bad guys by driving through a swamp or river, you need a snorkel for air intake during water crossings deep enough to flood your engine.

Caltrops A dispenser in the rear of the vehicle can dump these on the roadway, flattening tires and halting your pursuer.

Harpoon You never know.

Locked Cargo Area You could strap tools, cans of gas, and jugs of water to the exterior, but it's easy for people to steal them. Keep your supplies secure with a locking storage area.

Onboard Distillery It might be nice to make brandy for the driver and ethanol for the engine.

Armor Plating The sheet metal on vehicles doesn't normally stop small arms fire, despite all the action flicks you've seen that suggest otherwise, but bullet-proof paneling can be a life saver in real life.

GOOD TO KNOW

PACK FOR PASSENGERS

Your doom wagon design still needs to account for passengers. Add these items to your ride.

- Several gallons of water (and disinfection kit)
- Long-lasting foods
- Blankets
- Flashlights or headlamps
- Sanitation supplies
- Fire starting materials
- First aid kit and manual
- Signaling equipment
- Mobile phone charger
- Clothing and rain gear
- Morale items

COOL TOOL

ADD A TANK TO A TANK

To refill the air quickly on big tires, consider adding an air tank to your ride to top off low tires and refill flats. Get a long enough hose to reach all tires, and be sure it's big enough to refill at least two tires (if it's a smaller sized tank).

SAFE AS HOUSES

WITH ISOLATION COMES TRANQUILITY—AND VULNERABILITY. WITHOUT OTHER PEOPLE AROUND, AND FAR FROM LAW ENFORCEMENT, YOU'LL NEED TO BE YOUR OWN SECURITY FORCE. THE OUTLYING HOMESTEAD CAN BE A PRIME TARGET, UNLESS YOU MAKE IT YOUR STRONGHOLD.

According to crime statistics, the average professional burglar only needs about one minute to break into your home and ten minutes to sweep through the house picking up valuables. While a lot of these scary incursions happen at night, the majority of burglaries actually happen in broad daylight. Some smart criminals dress as workers or delivery people and walk right into unlocked homes. And what about the home invasions that aren't motivated by burglary? Assault, kidnapping, or murder might be the goal of a home invader. Does this mean that we should live in perpetual fear and paranoia? Do we have to board up the windows and hide inside the house? No, but it does mean that we need to be aware of the ever-present nature of crime. The good news: You don't have to live in a hermetically sealed bunker with a time-lock door to be safe. Common sense security measures can give you both the safety you need and the freedom you want—even in a remote area. With some of these security measures in place, intruders beware!

YOU'RE IN CHARGE No one else will be as concerned and invested in your security as you. As the head of (your) home protection, you can learn a lot with an objective look at your security through the eyes of a bad guy. Walk around your home with a note pad. Pretend that you're a burglar and write down every way you could get into the house at the ground level and with some climbing. Note anything you see that would deter you. Be brutally honest. This exercise could give you the clues to prevent a home invasion and save lives. Make notes about all defensive and protective items. This can range from prickly bushes, to alarm systems, to your big, loud dog. Finally, determine how you can make each of the entry points of your home unappealing or unusable to a criminal.

DURING CIVIL UNREST, IF THE PERCENTAGE OF THE POPULATION RIOTING AND LOOTING EVEN GETS CLOSE TO THE PERCENTAGE INVOLVED IN LAW ENFORCEMENT, DON'T EXPECT HELP TO COME WHEN YOU CALL. YOU MAY BE ON YOUR OWN, SO HOME DEFENSE IS CRUCIAL.

BUNKER UP AT HOME You may have a great basement in your place that you can turn into a small bunker, or you could have a storm cellar that could pass for your secret underground lair. Either way, your mini-bunker door should be your last line of defense, not your first. Think of your defenses as being like an onion—a series of layers, with each one completely covering the next. If your property has layers of defensive obstacles to keep out rogues, then the innermost ring is the bunker. To do this, you will need to install defenses in and around your homestead that an intruder would have to tackle to get to the bunker. Fences and locked gates could be your outer layer. A couple of dogs inside those fences could be the next layer. Great locks on the doors and windows of your home are next after that. More advanced tricks could include the concealment of the bunker door and other acts of camouflage. Just remember to reinforce the walls as well, if you decide you are going with the basement bunker idea. That steel-bolted security door won't do you any good if the homicidal maniacs can smash their way through the drywall next to it.

PREFAB BUNKER If money is no object, and you're looking for a hellaciously good storm shelter (or a zombie apocalypse hideout) with plenty of great features, there are plenty of companies out there that can deliver a prebuilt bunker and drop it into a hole at your chosen off-the-grid location. This turnkey approach to below-ground shelters is much different than the brick-by-brick construction of old-fashioned storm cellars. And this new breed of doomsday bunkers can come fully loaded. Blast doors, escape hatches, air filtration, sewage systems, low voltage power, various bells and whistles for comfort while you take shelter from the elements—you name it, they'll add it to the bill. The latest architecture and building materials are going into these prepper paradises, and all of the age-old issues such as ground water leaks, stale ventilation, and cracking walls are nearly solved with the latest and greatest designs. If you live in America's "tornado alley," one of these could make a lot of sense (and raise your property value). But this isn't for everybody.

COOL TOOL

WHEN YOU GOTTA GO If you've opted for outside sources of water and power, and they go out while you're in the bunker or sheltering in place, you're going to need to do some emergency hacks until they come back on or you get a more self-sufficient set-up going. If you don't have an outhouse, you'll need a sanitary way to easily manage human waste. Here's a safe short-term solution.

MAKE A TOILET

Supplies:

- Thick plastic trash bags
- A small bag of kitty litter
- Toilet paper
- Duct tape
- A permanent marker
- Disposable gloves
- Hand sanitizer
- A 5-gallon (20-liter) painter's bucket

Directions:

As an extra-comfort option, you can buy a special toilet seat from disaster supply stores that's designed to fit on the bucket.

Place all of the supplies inside the bucket except one of the plastic bags. Seal the bucket and place it into the plastic bag to keep moisture out and keep it in storage.

When you need to use the bucket, double-bag the inside and sprinkle kitty litter generously after each use. When the bucket is about half full, seal the inner bag with a knot, then tie the outer bag with another knot, then finally seal the knot with duct tape and write "Human Waste" on the duct tape with the marker. Place bags someplace out of the way, preferably out of direct sunlight. Check local regulations on how to properly dispose of waste after services are restored or you get your proper OTG systems in place.

GOOD TO KNOW

GO TO YOUR ROOM
A safe room (also known as a panic room) is a major investment in your home defense strategy. For most people, it may not be warranted; in some situations, it has even left people trapped. However, for those who live in remote areas (where it would take some time for police to arrive), for high crime areas, or those who are concerned about civil unrest, a safe room could be a lifesaving asset. These rooms are often fortified basement or second floor rooms, with reinforced door jambs and a heavy exterior door. They often have a landline, a spare mobile phone, weapons, and supplies similar to those in a home disaster kit. And don't forget to stock one of the most vital things to keep in a safe room: a trauma first-aid kit. This can help to keep you alive until assistance arrives, if you've been wounded in a home invasion.

ON THE GRID

GO WITH A PRO The police aren't able to be everywhere at once, and dead-bolt locks aren't nearly as impenetrable as you might expect, so you should consider going with a professional alarm system while the grid is still up. Here are some of the features that might make this a good fit for you.

- Monitoring for every possible entry point (in high-end systems)
- Infrared motion and glass-breakage sensors (on mid-level systems)
- Pressure mats
- Interactive services from the company providing security monitoring
- Panic buttons
- Smoke and carbon monoxide detectors
- Systems that can be wirelessly linked to the monitoring service
- Flood and heat-loss detection

HARDEN YOUR HOME If your home is your castle, shouldn't you be able to defend it like one? One trick that anyone can do with existing elements is to merely keep their doors and windows locked. This basic defense will eliminate a lot of home invasions before they start. Exterior security doors and beefy deadbolts are a great way to discourage break-ins too. Yes, these can be pricey, but they should add value to the dwelling as well as a little more peace of mind to your night's sleep. Cheap hollow-core interior doors could be replaced with stronger solid doors. Sliding-glass doors are extremely vulnerable; be sure they have a locking steel pin to keep them from being forced open or go low-tech with a length of dowel or a piece of 2x4, cut to the exact needed size, that you can place in the door's tracks to keep it from being forced open by intruders.

Protect your parking Your house's garage door is going to be a particular point of weakness in your security, since most of them have rather flimsy construction. If you have a security system, be sure it covers the garage door (you'd be surprised how many people forget this step). If you have an automatic garage-door opener, you can reprogram it to have a different code than the factory setting. Contact the manufacturer for details—it's usually very simple and adds an extra layer of security. If you're going out of town (or want to be extra secure overnight, or when home alone), you should consider installing a slide-bar latch or a padlock to keep the door from being manually rolled up. You can also cut a piece of wood to fit snugly into the door's track and clamp it in place, preventing it from rolling up. Disable the opener beforehand, so that if you forget and try to open it, you won't damage the door.

RELEASE THE HOUNDS (OR SNAKES) While it's generally illegal to create "man traps," you could still legally employ some unorthodox tactics. How about releasing your snake collection in the hallways of your home? Or tying a set of tripwires on the stairs? If any home invaders think that they're up against a crazy person who has rigged their home with traps, that could very well send them running.

GOOD TO KNOW

DEFEND WITH STONE Besides being beautiful, stone walls have a lot of benefits for the home owner (or castle owner). They can last for years, withstand fire and insects, and are relatively maintenance-free. And did I mention they will stop small arms fire? Here's how you can use stone to make your home into a stronghold.

Real Stone Walls Actual load-bearing stone walls are a thing of beauty. They can last for centuries, and withstand most of the weapons that would be available in a time of crisis. The windows and doors are the only vulnerable points in a stone wall, unless your attackers have a cannon or a bulldozer.

Stone Façade Thin pieces of real stone and artificial stone are commonly used today as an exterior home siding alternative. These do add defensibility, though they are nowhere near as tough as actual stone walls. But it is an achievable DIY project and it will render your home more fire-resistant.

Gravel Walls Your walls will have to be engineered (or re-engineered) to hold this kind of weight, but the standard 3.5-inch (9-cm) void in modern walls can be filled with a half-inch (1.25 cm) of gravel to prevent small arms penetration. This technique has been proven to stop rounds up to .308, and it may even go higher.

COMMON MISTAKE

DON'T GET BACKED INTO A CORNER No matter how invulnerable you think your home, bunker, or safe room may be, you will always need to have an escape route ready. It's been said that bunkers are just tombs with lots of room and safe rooms are the places where the chalk outlines are drawn. This could very well be true, if your home should ever be invaded by very determined people with plenty of time on their hands. No matter how tough, virtually any defenses in your home can be breached with enough time and by people who are using the right tools. So, make sure your Alamo doesn't end up like the real Alamo—a battle synonymous with last stands. There needs to be a window egress, a secret tunnel, back door, or other way for you to get out of a barricade situation. Otherwise, you will be cornered and at the mercy of your foes.

USE THE LANDSCAPE FOR YOUR DEFENSE. ROCKY AND STEEP TERRAIN, SWIFT RIVERS, AND TALL CLIFFS POSE HAZARDS TO YOU, SHOULD YOU BUILD YOUR HOME NEARBY—BUT THEY ALSO PROVIDE A NATURAL "WALL" ON YOUR PROPERTY'S PERIMETER.

PERIMETER DEFENSE During social unrest and mayhem, you probably won't have the time or resources that you would need to build a set of barbed-wire-topped walls, high powered searchlights, or manned guard towers. However, there are still some things you can do almost anywhere to create a more defensible position.

STEP 1 Decide what you are willing to defend. Basically, here is where you are marking out the boundaries of the area that you intend to protect. Consider the roles that any existing walls, waterways, buildings, and fences can play in your defense.

STEP 2 Establish a controlled entry/exit point for the homestead, or even the neighborhood. This may mean blocking off a street with derelict vehicles (if things are really that bad). If vehicles are operational, several could be parked to create a "gate" to keep out other vehicles.

STEP 3 Enhance existing defensive structures. This can be anything from locking fence gates to boarding up windows and doors around the perimeter. Look at your perimeter from the outside, try to figure out ways in, and do your best to seal them off.

STEP 4 Set up a fallback position. This would be a place of refuge if you had to retreat within your perimeter, like the strongest and most defensible home within the neighborhood. Keep it well supplied with water and food, in case you have to spend a few days waiting out rioters.

SET OUT SOME WARNING SIGNS If you can dissuade trespassers, looters, burglars, and other ne'er-do-wells at your property's perimeter, then you won't have to deal with them yourself later on! An imposing fence, threatening signage, bright exterior lights, and packs of roaming dogs should do the trick.

GOOD TO KNOW

BURGLAR PROOFING In a crisis, crime rates can go up sharply. Defending your home also puts you in harm's way, but with a few upgrades your home could defend itself.

Animal A big dog with a loud bark is a wonderful addition to the family. It's a wise move that will scare off most intruders. If you're dead set against it, at least set a big dog bowl full of water and a huge chew bone on the back porch. It may make the burglars think twice.

Vegetable Thorn bushes or cacti under windows will keep people from crawling through, or at least not silently.

Mineral Gravel around your house as a mulch substitute discourages insects—and prowlers. Pea gravel can't be used to break your windows like larger stones. Under your windows and around the back door, it makes noise that the aforementioned dog can pick up.

GOOD TO KNOW

OPEN CARRY VERSUS CONCEALED In the United States, "open carry" refers to carrying your firearm in a visible holster (or on your vehicle dashboard) in plain view of the public. This is very different from concealed carry, in which the firearm is hidden. Most American states allow concealed carry with special permit, and there are reasons to consider this. An open carry weapon tends to upset some people; a hidden weapon doesn't make waves. A concealed weapon also may give an element of surprise, which could help in a tough situation. Open carry weapons can also draw the wrong kind of attention. The practice of open carry has been on the rise in recent years, but it's smarter to play your cards close to the chest. I suggest getting the permit for concealed carry in public and saving open carry for your off-grid property.

PROTECTIVE GEAR This is a very broad category, covering everything from safety glasses to a full-body hazmat suit. Depending on the calamity you're facing, you may need some very specialized gear to protect you from a wide range of dangerous elements.

In a Pandemic Masks, gloves and goggles can protect you from a great many germs in the event of a pandemic. Basic N95 masks filter out 95 percent of the particulates that a person would normally breathe in. The goggles can protect you from cough droplets and the gloves can shield you from touching contaminated items.

In Heavy Smoke Smoke hoods are a very important product that allow you to both see and breathe in the dangerous fumes and smoke of a fire. The average home owner may not need something like this in a house fire, since they would be relatively close to an exit in a small home. But for those who live in big houses (or big buildings), the hood can give you as much as 20 minutes of air filtration, which would be lifesaving during a lengthy escape scenario. This item is also important for those with impaired mobility.

In a Fire Smoke alarms and fire extinguishers save lives. Battery-operated smoke and carbon monoxide alarms should be near heating sources, in the kitchen, outside bedrooms, and on each level of your home. Fire extinguishers should be in the kitchen, but not right next to the cooktop in case the area is engulfed in flames. Extinguishers are also great in garages, sheds, and workshop areas.

When Bullets Fly Body armor is both expensive and heavy. The more pricy and weighty, the bigger the bullets it will stop. Although there are plenty of places on your body that body armor doesn't cover, it's still covering a lot of vital territory. Do you really need this? I can't read the future, and neither can you. If it helps you sleep better to have a bullet-proof vest within reach, right next to the handgun and tactical flashlight, go for it!

COOL TOOL

NBC GEAR A suit that protects you from nuclear, biological, and chemical warfare (shortened to NBC) may seem like a pretty extreme piece of survival gear—and it is. Having a full hazmat suit at the ready just in case sounds good, but isn't practical for all kinds of reasons—the main one being that high-quality hazmat suits are very costly and, in any situation where you and your family might actually need them, there will be so many other serious issues that the suits themselves aren't likely to save you (they also require support and maintenance that won't likely be available to you). That said, in a number of disaster scenarios, you may want to be protected from airborne or environmental pathogens or contaminants. A low-cost solution is to buy Tyvek safety suits at a home-improvement store and add them to your home survival kit. These suits are very inexpensive; they're basically disposable protection for housepainters and construction workers. They certainly won't protect you from radiation or a chemical attack, but they will offer a layer of protection against a range of other toxins. For another layer, search online for "chemical protection suits," which can offer a higher level of protection against various radioactive particles and at least some chemically dangerous or toxic substances.

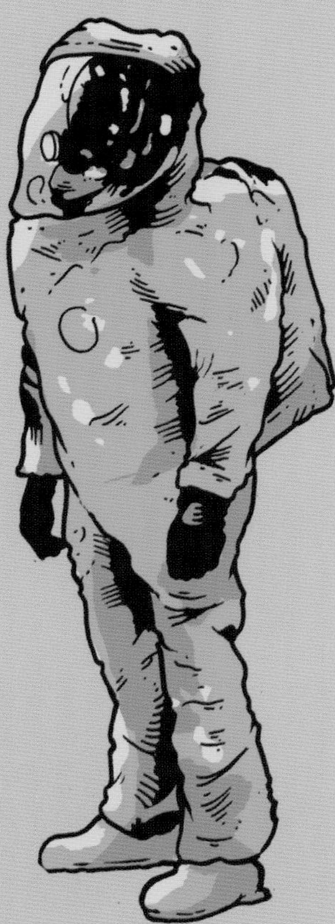

COMMON MISTAKE

ACCEPT NO SUBSTITUTE The internet is full of tips and tricks for defeating tear gas, but RCAs (riot control agents) aren't so easily foiled by any improvised protection. You can't actually rely on juice soaked rags or bandanas for protection from these irritants. Plenty of myths abound that certain fabrics soaked in mixtures of various fluids can become an effective filter or neutralizer for tear gas, but in actuality they won't work at all. Don't fall for any of these so-called urban survival hacks.

- Soaking a cloth in vinegar
- Wearing a wet bandana
- Soaking a medical mask in citrus juice
- Rubbing a wet bandana with crushed charcoal
- Making your own gas mask from a two-liter bottle and wet rags
- Holding your breath

BE YOUR OWN DOCTOR

DIGNITY IS FOR THE DEAD. EMERGENCY MEDICINE IN A REMOTE SETTING IS ROUGH, DIRTY, FRIGHTENING, AND EMBARRASSING. THERE'S NO TIME TO BE PRISSY, SQUEAMISH, OR MODEST WHEN SOMEONE'S LIFEBLOOD IS POOLING ON THE GROUND. GRAB YOUR MEDICAL KIT AND GET TO WORK.

It may seem like emergency medical care is too complicated for most to even try and that first aid for major injuries can only be performed by trained paramedics and ER doctors. The truth is in fact quite the opposite: Anyone can save a life. With just a basic understanding of anatomy, airways, breathing, and circulation, even a child can stop major bleeding and maintain a victim's airway until experienced help arrives. All you need is a bit of training and some first aid supplies (or the creativity to improvise them). First aid is the most likely "survival" skill that anyone will ever need and it's even more likely to be in demand at an off-grid location. Heavy work, sharp tools, and a remote location are the recipe for disaster if you don't add medical skills into the mix. We could have written a whole book on off-grid medicine, but that won't serve you as well as hands-on training. Ultimately, you should take a class in wilderness first aid or disaster medicine (or even basic life support training like that received by EMTs) . . . and then pray you never need to use it.

LOOK FOR THE X When you learn the ABCs of first aid, there's usually an "X" before the "A." The A stands for airway, which you need to check quickly. Then comes B for breathing, then C for circulation. But before the A, you'll check for X. This stands for "exsanguinating hemorrhage"—massive blood loss. Deep cuts, gunshot wounds, and other forms of trauma can mean severe blood loss that's lethal in a minute or two if unchecked. The average adult has about five liters of blood in their body. If they lose one or two, they are at risk for numerous issues, but likely to survive. Losing more than that is usually life-threatening. Since the human heart pumps several liters per minute, if an artery is opened, death can come fast if we don't stop the bleeding quickly.

NEED TO KNOW

USE EMT SCISSORS For those who aren't familiar with EMT scissors (also called trauma shears), these are very strong scissors which have blunt rounded tips so that they won't hurt an already injured victim. They're also strong enough to cut through seat belts, leather belts, and even a penny (although this will dull them considerably). As I mentioned earlier, there's no place for any modesty in emergency medicine. You may need to cut clothing off of someone in order to reach their wound and treat it properly. During an emotionally charged and stressful emergency situation, the last thing you need to do is try to cut anything with a sharp pocket knife or pointed scissors. In your haste, you are very likely to cause further injury. Use these shears instead, which are both sharp and strong—and protective of an already injured person.

WRAP IT ALL UP From a small nick or scratch on your hand after a brush with a thorn bush, to a nasty cut on your arm or leg after an accident with a tool or knife, bodily injuries are a risk of any labors or misadventures you might engage in. A first-aid kit should definitely include plenty of ways of patching up any injuries you or someone else might receive, whether you're off the grid or on it. Since you won't be able to fix that gash on your leg by just sticking a Band-Aid on it, this means having a wide range of both dressings (the term for items usually applied directly to injuries) and bandages (which are either placed on wounds directly as dressings or are used to help hold dressings in place). Have a look at the list below for a suggested list of both types, and how many of each of them you should add to your first-aid kit.

8x10-inch (20x25-cm) trauma pad (use sterile dressing to apply pressure and stop bleeding on a large area)

4-inch (10-cm) Israeli bandage (a wraparound bandage that can be tightened to add pressure and stop bleeding)

4 rolls of gauze (for bleeding control, wound dressing, and many other tasks)

6 4x4-inch (10x10-cm) non-stick gauze pads (to dress wounds, especially burns)

Triangle bandage (useful as an arm sling, a dressing, an improvised tourniquet, and more)

Eye pad (for dressing eye wounds or any other small wounds)

2 Ace bandages (get the kind with Velcro ends, for pressure dressings and to bind orthopedic injuries)

40 assorted flexible fabric bandages (for all those minor boo-boos)

GOOD TO KNOW

COMPLETE THE KIT Plenty of medical supplies can be improvised by a creative first aid provider, but it's far better to have everything you need at your fingertips.

Space blanket Wrap around patient to help fend off shock or as part of hypothermia treatment.

5 pairs of nitrile non-latex gloves Protects the caregiver from pathogens. Use nitrile or plastic gloves, since many folks have an allergy to latex.

Tweezers To pull out splinters, thorns and other foreign material from wounds. They're also handy for tick removal.

Trauma shears They can cut away clothing and even belts to give you access to wounds.

QuikClot ACS A treated sponge which causes rapid clotting to stop serious bleeding.

1 tube each of antibiotic ointment, anti-itch cream, and burn gel For small injuries or minor burns, and tending to mosquito bites or poison ivy.

Prescription medications If you need these to live—like heart medicine and asthma inhalers—make sure at least a month's worth of each is stashed in your kit)

Tourniquet To constrict the blood flow on a limb to stop severe bleeding.

2 ammonia inhalant swabs To revive a patient who has fainted.

8 oz. (240 ml) bottle sterile saline eyewash To remove foreign particles and chemicals from the eye, or to irrigate wounds.

20 antiseptic wipes To disinfect wounds and wipe bloody hands clean.

Roll of 1-inch (2.5-cm) medical tape (to keep all your nice dressings in place)

Ibuprofen or other NSAIDS

First-aid book My favorite is *The Survival Medicine Handbook* by Dr. Joseph Alton and his wife, Amy.

COMMON MISTAKE

GET SOME TRAINING Just because you've bought a fully-stocked medical backpack with enough supplies to start a field hospital doesn't mean that you can automatically start saving people with it. Medical gear, particularly advanced medical gear, requires the knowledge to be able to use it properly and in a timely manner. Your first time using a tourniquet (or worse, your first time even reading the instructions) should never be while your friend is bleeding out right before your eyes. Seconds count to first responders and blood on the ground cannot be put back in the body. Practice first aid skills, familiarize yourself with the supplies, and know where they are in your kit in order to be an effective first-aid provider. Otherwise, you're fooling yourself about the help you can render, and you're wasting your money on the gear.

GOT A BLEEDING WOUND WHERE YOU CAN'T USE A TOURNIQUET? TRY WOUND PACKING. MAKE A GOLF-BALL-SIZED WAD OF GAUZE AND INSERT IT INTO THE WOUND. ADD AS MUCH MORE GAUZE AS YOU CAN PACK, THEN APPLY A PRESSURE DRESSING.

CONTROL BLEEDING An exsanguinating hemorrhage can kill in mere minutes. But by quickly responding with the proper bleeding control techniques, it's possible to save a life. Study up on these three methods, go out and buy a tourniquet, practice with it (not using full pressure), and make sure you have the medical supplies to handle this life-or-death injury.

Direct Pressure Sometimes, your first instinct is the right move. If you see a heavily bleeding wound on yourself or someone else, use a large dressing (or a bare hand, if need be), and apply heavy pressure to the wound. It's best if there is a dressing over the wound, especially one that can be constricted. It's also helpful to elevate the wound, if it happens to be on a limb.

Tourniquet When direct pressure isn't working or you're dealing with a wound that is literally squirting blood, it's time for a tourniquet. Apply the tourniquet as high on the limb as possible, and crank down hard enough to stop the blood flow and eliminate the pulse on that limb, no matter how much the victim screams (tourniquet use will be very painful). Write down the time you applied the tourniquet and rush them to modern medical care. Never remove a tourniquet in the field, unless you are days away from medical care. In that rare situation, and only if you think you have controlled the bleeding, release the tourniquet after one hour, and very slowly—one turn per minute over a five-minute period. Never release it after two hours, as toxins may have built up in a limb without blood flow and releasing them by restarting circulation can be fatal.

Pressure Points This technique is used as a supplement to direct pressure and wound packing. First, learn where the femoral arteries and brachial arteries run (the inside of the groin and the center of the upper arm) and then learn how much pressure to apply. This is more like crimpling off a garden hose than performing medicine, but it can help to stop the blood flow when used in combination with pressure dressings.

AVOID FOLK REMEDIES Plenty of well-meaning folks believe in family recipes. Sometimes, these odd cures and home remedies make it into mainstream practice, but it doesn't make them right. Here are a few to avoid.

Butter on Burns This old farm remedy can actually increase the risk of infection in burns by creating a more bacteria-friendly environment. Use dry, non-stick, sterile dressings, and moisten them with sterile water or saline to facilitate removal when changing them.

Hydrogen Peroxide on Cuts Yes, this stuff does foam up on contact with wounds, making us think it is doing a good job. But peroxide, alcohol, and bleach on open wounds kills healthy cells too, which actually slows down healing. Instead, simply use warm water and mild soap, iodine, or a saline rinse, to cleanse small wounds.

Cut and Suck a Snakebite When dealing with pit vipers like rattlesnakes, copperheads, and cottonmouths, don't cut and suck. This removes less than a thousandth of the venom. Ice, compression bandages, and tourniquets won't work, either. Less than 1 percent of bites from these snakes are fatal, and 30 percent of bites don't even contain venom. Just get to the doctor ASAP. If you can't, bandage the wound lightly and let your immune system try to fight it off.

COOL TOOL

TRIANGLE BANDAGE
Some of you might scoff at my choice of triangle bandage as a super cool item over so many other remarkable new medical gizmos. Here's the thing: A triangle bandage—also known as a cravat—is one of the most versatile items in my medical kits (yes, I have several). Not only is it a great sling for arm injuries, but it can perform dozens of other medical and survival tasks. That's right, a big, stupid triangle of muslin cotton cloth is one of my most functional and adaptable items. I can tie it on a limb and add a stout stick, making it into an improvised tourniquet. I can cut it into strips for use over sterile dressings to bandage wounds. I can filter the chunks out of my drinking water so that other disinfection methods will be more effective. And its terminal use can be in fire starting, since it's made from flammable material.

TRUE STORY

TREAT KIDNEY STONES WITH BEER A dear friend of mine shared a backwoods remedy with me that has been used in his family for several years: drink a case of beer to get rid of kidney stones. While most (if not all) urologists would say that it's not a good idea to drink vast amounts of beer to help pass a stone, you can't argue with the fact that you would really have to pee and you may not be feeling as much pain after chugging down a bunch of frosty cold beers. Of course, modern medical assessments and treatments for kidney stones are your best bet in any situation. You could also simply use an ounce of prevention rather than a keg of "cure". If you or your family are prone to kidney stones, limit or eliminate the foods and beverages that cause kidney stones, and you won't have to worry about finding an off-the-grid cure later on.

GROW YOUR OWN MEDICINAL PLANTS Many wild and cultivated plants have medicinal benefits that would make a great addition to our OTG gardens and properties. Many of these plant medicines were once well known, but today have fallen into obscurity (since it's so easy and effective to just pop a pill). But many of our modern medicines trace their history back to where they were first discovered in wild plants, and these plants can still come to our aid, often with little or no side effects. A very basic herbal medicine garden could consist of yarrow, comfrey, lemon balm, echinacea, mint, and lavender. And should a few burdock, plantain, chickweeds, or dandelions pop up, then just let them grow too.

Make a Poultice A poultice is about as old school and simple as it gets: you just apply the plant parts directly to the problem area. This is used primarily on external problems, but it could be held in the mouth for gum or tooth problems—if the poultice material is nontoxic. To make a poultice, crush (or even chew!) the plant material into a pulp or paste and apply it directly to the affected area. Keep it in place using a bandage, piece of fabric, or similar item. Replace with new material once or twice daily, until you no longer need it. Great wound poultices include plantain leaf, comfrey root or leaf, and yarrow leaf.

Brew a Tea Tea is another medicinal classic. For most teas, fresh or dried plant material is soaked in water to create an infusion. Use about 1 tablespoon (15 ml) of plant material per 8-ounce cup (240 ml) of water and let the tea sit covered for 10 to 15 minutes. Mint is great for nausea and yarrow can induce sweating to help break a fever.

Sooth with Salve Salve is a thick, oily medicinal vehicle. Typical salve is a combination of plant-infused oil, with beeswax melted into it for a thickener. Chickweed salve is very soothing for itching. Comfrey and yarrow in salve form are excellent on wounds. Be sure to store any and all salves in a dark cool place, which will help extend their shelf life and maintain their potency.

RECIPE FOR SUCCESS

TINCTURE A simple and effective way to preserve the medicinal quality of a plant is to make a tincture from it. Here's the basic recipe.

STEP 1 Get the dried herbs for the tincture. Purchase the highest proof vodka or neutral grain spirits that your area supplies, to act as the solvent and preservative of this tincture. Moonshine is acceptable, too.

STEP 2 Cut, crush, chop, or otherwise break up the dried plant material, and pack it tightly into the jar. Pour enough alcohol over the plant material to cover it slightly, and put the lid on it.

STEP 3 Let the jar sit for six weeks in a cool, dark place such as a cabinet. Shake the jar once every day. Avoid sunlight on your jar, as the UV light can have a negative effect on tincture making.

STEP 4 Strain out the plant material with a cloth, and bottle your tincture in dark glass.

FORAGE FOR YOUR FIRST AID KIT You can take a page from the apothecary shops of our ancestors and put together your own first aid kit by using a range of herbal medicines. Alcohol-based tinctures are naturally disinfecting and, coupled with a plant that has known healing properties (such as comfrey or plantain), they are great for cuts, scrapes, and scratches. You can make ointments that will soothe and treat burns. Dried plants can be included to make healing teas or infusions when added to hot water. Plenty of these all-natural medicines can be made into poultices as well. Round out your kit with a few salves for itchy spots and burns, and you're ready to administer some frontier medicine.

T/F

DRUG STORES USED TO CARRY ONLY DRIED PLANTS

TRUE Today's chain pharmacy stores are truly a modern marvel, offering medicines, supplies, food, drinks, personal items, and many more things. But it's important to remember that it wasn't so very long ago when these stores simply didn't exist, and you'd have to go to your local apothecary shop to pick up medicinal plants to treat your ailments. In fact, many of our modern medicines trace their history back to the time where they were first discovered in wild plants. Even the word *drug* itself is still anchored in the past, as it comes from the old Dutch word *droog*, which means dried plant.

MEDICINAL PLANTS

People have been collecting and cultivating all of these helpful plants for centuries or millennia. In modern times, the cultivation and use of these healing plants may represent a much healthier alternative for the homesteader crowd, as well as a sustainable resupply plan for preppers and bug-out enthusiasts. While all these home remedies should not take the place of any professional medical care, it's still nice to have a sense that you are not helpless, should you end up having to fend for yourself.

Blackberry Yes, the berries are delicious, but did you know that the blackberry leaves are helpful for diarrhea? Make an infusion (like a tea) by pouring near-boiling water over the leaves and let steep 5 to 10 minutes. The usual amount to use is about 2.5 ounces (75g) of fresh leaf, or 1 ounce (30g) of dried herb to one cup (240 ml) of hot water. The infusion must be taken same day.

Lemon Balm This makes an outstanding topical agent for cold sores. Crush the fresh leaves and bind them over the sores—or use a cream with a high concentration of lemon balm.

Lavender Used since ancient times for bug bites, burns, and skin disorders. To relieve itching, rashes, and swelling, apply crushed fresh leaves to the affected area. You can also make an infused oil for skin problems. Fill a jar with dried leaves and cover them with olive oil. Allow this to soak for 6 to 8 weeks, then decant. It's not recommended for pregnant or nursing women, or small children.

Comfrey Cooked, mashed roots are a topical treatment for arthritis, bruises, burns, and sprains. (Avoid ingestion, as consuming this herb can potentially damage the liver if taken in large enough quantities.) Simmer the fresh peeled or dried root, about 3.5 ounces (100 grams), in 1 pint (500 ml) of water for 10 to 15 minutes, then mash into a paste and apply to the injury.

Yarrow Crushed leaves and flowers can be placed on cuts and scratches to stop bleeding and reduce the chance of infection.

Burdock The roots and leaves make an excellent liver tonic and help to purify the body and blood. Make a tincture of the dried root in alcohol and consume 10-20 drops daily. You could also eat

blackberry lemon balm lavender comfrey yarrow burdock plantain

the fresh leaves and roots (after boiling in water and discarding the water to remove bitterness).

Plantain While not quite strong enough to tackle snake bites, plantain can still help neutralize the venom of bees, wasps, scorpions, or other pain-inducing creatures. Just keep the paste of plantain leaf on the wound and replace as it dries out. Relief should be swift.

Echinacea If consumed at the first sign of cold symptoms, this can reduce the effects and duration of the common cold in adults.

Elderberry This may shorten the common cold, and have anti-inflammatory, antiviral, and anticancer properties. Just consume jam or wine made from elderberries. The raw berries are mildly toxic and they may have drug interactions with diuretics (water pills), diabetes medications, chemotherapy, laxatives, theophylline (TheoDur), or immune suppressants.

Jewelweed This stuff is a great cure for poison ivy, poison oak, or poison sumac. Crush the juicy, purplish-colored stalk into a paste, and briskly scrub it all over the affected skin. After two minutes of contact, wash off the mush with clean water. If you found and used jewelweed within 45 minutes of exposure to ivy, oak, or sumac, you should have little to no reaction.

Birch Birch bark, particularly the bark of the Sweet Birch, can be an effective analgesic. The bark is scraped from the tree's twigs before being brewed into a tea. Add ¼–½ teaspoon (1–2 grams) of bark to about 7 ounces (200 ml) of water and then boil for ten minutes. This tea can be taken up to five times per day.

echinacea elderberry jewelweed birch

GOOD TO KNOW

DON'T DIE FROM DIARRHEA Our bowels can stage a revolt for a wide variety of different reasons. A viral infection, tainted food, bad water, or unsanitary living conditions can each cause a dangerous case of diarrhea and, during an emergency situation, you will likely have enough problems without worrying about colon control and dehydration. Luckily, relief is close at hand in the world of traditional medicine, you can brew an anti-diarrhea tea. Woody canes in the genus *Rubus* (such as blackberries) produce thorny leaves that are often used as an herbal tea. This tea also contains at least one compound that can help to dry up diarrhea. Make a strong tea from the dried leaves, and drink one cup (240 ml) every couple of hours, until you notice a positive change. If this isn't strong enough, then you can also use blackberry roots for a tea, sipping it in comparable amounts to the leaf tea.

BUG OUT!

THE WORST HAS HAPPENED. YOUR ONLY CHOICE IS TO FLEE. BUT DO YOU HAVE WHAT YOU'D NEED TO SURVIVE? THE BUG OUT SCENARIO IS A LAST DITCH PLAN FOR SURVIVAL. IT MEANS LEAVING EVERYTHING YOU'VE WORKED TO ACHIEVE. BUT IT ALSO MEANS ESCAPING WITH YOUR LIFE.

So far, we've talked about going off the grid with a lot of thought and planning. But what if you have to just grab everything and go? You'd need a bug out plan. This old military term from the 1950s is now almost a brand name for survival gear marketing. Even your loopy great-aunt is now likely to have a "bug out bag" hidden under her pile of cats. The bug out bag (or BOB, for short) is supposed to house all of the necessities of survival, and allow you to live for a period of time under your own power. There's no shortage of people who are ready and eager to speculate on the gear list for the "perfect" BOB, but without a crystal ball, you don't know exactly what you'd need until you actually need it. Different disasters will warrant a few different supplies. Luckily, the basic list is versatile and likely to get you through most emergencies. Stick to basics, such as shelter, water, food, first aid, communications, defense, navigation, clothes, and hygiene supplies. Remember things you'd need to re-boot your life too. Important documents are hard to replace.

PICK A ROLE MODEL Some hardcore preppers have it all wrong: their bug out bags look like they came from the set of a post-apocalyptic movie. You don't need four machetes and three battle axes strapped to your high-tech, camouflaged military backpack. But who has the "right" idea? In my opinion, backpackers do. The thru-hikers that roam the wilderness walking hundreds, or even thousands, of miles (1000+ km) understand what you need to survive. Even though they do it for recreation (mostly), they've got the right recipe for a BOB. Ultra-light tents, sleeping bags, and pads give you a great shelter from the elements. Freeze-dried food and featherweight water filters give you food and drink. These are the folks who really have living out of a backpack down to a science.

GOOD TO KNOW

AVOID OVERLOAD Maybe you were in the military and you survived brutal forced marches with a 100 pound (45-kg) pack on your back, or a scout leader made you hike up a mountain carrying half your body weight. Maybe you never backpacked before in your life. All these scenarios have the same factor: a body can only carry so much weight so far before falling to the ground. We must keep limitations in mind when we start loading up a BOB, for good reason. If you're bugging out, you are in a tough situation. You'll be stressed and maybe underfed or unrested. This diminishes your load bearing abilities. You may also need to run with the pack or swim. The heavy rucksack I first mentioned will stop these activities. Keep the weight as low as you can, while still carrying the essentials. Otherwise, the BOB becomes an anchor.

THE BASIC BUG OUT BAG This life-saving bag is a collection of goods that you would need to survive if you had to flee your home with no guarantee of shelter, food, or water during an emergency. Think of the BOB as your survival insurance policy for any disaster. There may not be one perfect, universally agreed-upon set of equipment, but with a core set of items (similar to those used in backpacking) you can put together a BOB suited for a wide variety of situations.

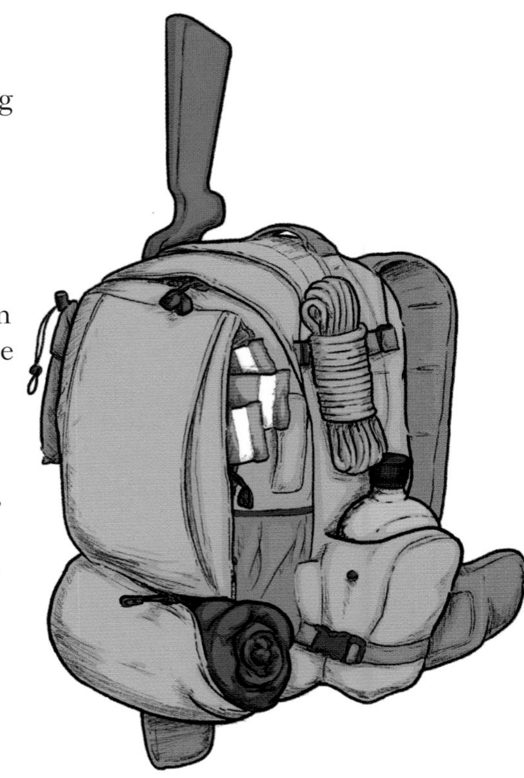

Most people use either a backpack or a duffle bag as the container for their goods, which should include basic survival essentials and a few irreplaceable items. Fill your BOB with a minimum of the following, and seal items inside zip-top bags or dry bags to prevent water damage:

Security Firearms, a large knife, and pepper spray or a stun gun (or both).

Shelter An ultralight tent, pad, sleeping bag, and a space blanket for backup.

Water 2 quarts (1.9 l) of bottled water, two empty canteens, and a water filter for disinfection.

Health First aid, hygiene, and sanitation supplies.

Food Pick ready-to-eat foods that you can eat while walking; carry a LOT.

COMMON MISTAKE

DON'T STAND OUT Let's imagine that a major emergency situation has taken place, and you're trying to get to your OTG grid farm. Whether you are striding down the shoulder of a gridlocked highway, or hiking through the unpaved countryside on a straight line compass bearing, you're eventually going to run into other people out there. If the situation is bad enough to cause you to bug out, then there's a good chance that these other people are likely to be panicking and also very likely to be less prepared than you. If you are carrying a huge rucksack strapped with survival gear, don't you think they'll want it for themselves? For your own safety, your bug out gear shouldn't stand out in a crowd. Don't call attention to yourself by having tools and weapons within view. Choose clothing and backpacks that look sporty rather than "survivally." Dress up like a traveler and wheel your BOB down the side of the road in a large wheeled suitcase. Dress in layers and place your gear in trash bags on a little red wagon like a refugee or homeless person. Find a way to blend in and hide what you've got, and you're likely to make it to your destination in one piece—and with your supplies.

Documents A digital backup of all your important files and pictures. This could be a thumb drive with your bank info, insurance forms, wills, and family photos and videos.

Clothing Walking shoes and seasonally appropriate clothes and outer wear.

Tools Duct tape, trash bags, a head lamp with spare batteries, and a multi tool.

Extras Carry some cash in small bills, waterproof matches, a lighter, hand sanitizer, a compass, a local map, and your mobile phone and a device to charge it.

GOOD TO KNOW

WHEN YOU GOTTA GO In some situations, you don't need a full BOB. You just require enough to get out of Dodge. This kit (aka, your "Get Home Bag") is much leaner and meaner than the average BOB, and its purpose is clear: getting you home. If you are using a Go Bag, then you're planning on camping out at your house, not camping out in the woods. Have one in your car and one at the office. Find ways to modify the bug out bag list to make the kit smaller, lighter, and cheaper (just in case it gets stolen out of your car or at work). Shelter could be just a tarp and fleece blanket or a space blanket if funds or storage room are limited. The water canjust be bottles from a store and disinfection tablets so you can refill your two bottles as you go. Remember, this kit is just to keep you safe until you reach your real gear at home.

NEED TO KNOW

HAVE A LOCATION PLANNED Bugging out without a destination makes you a refugee. If you have an off-the-grid property that you have been developing into a homestead, you already have a great BOL (bug out location). But what if you don't, or if you had to leave that self-sufficient property? Consider a "Site B" as a back-up plan. Your back-up site could be virtually anything and virtually anywhere (as long as you can get to it in a crisis). Site B could be a hunting cabin in the wilds, or the abandoned farm your family once worked in the middle of nowhere. It could be the undeveloped land of a friend or family member or even a spot that you picked on land you don't own. The site needs to have water and natural resources, be off the beaten path and defensible, and it should have a cache of supplies hidden on it.

SURVIVE THE WORST If you want to know what life would be like in a post-disaster, bug-out setting, go live with some homeless folks for a while in a rough part of the world. Living in tents and constantly being victimized by other people is pretty much what that life is all about. You don't dare set up a camp and leave it unattended for long. You could return from a food run to find every last item stolen, or just destroyed out of spite. And you can forget about a good night's sleep: half of the sounds you hear in the middle of the night really are someone creeping around outside. That's why it's so vital to bug out as a group, so you can post watches and take care of each other. And that is also why you should bug out to a remote place where you'll have fewer people to fight on a daily basis.

Don't Go Alone Bugging out alone is a recipe for trouble. You need help, various skills, and more gear than you can possibly carry in a real bug-out situation. It may seem like a badass character type, the lone wolf survivor is a figment of Hollywood's imagination. Lone wolves seldom live very long cut off from all other people. After all, throughout history the worst punishment a community could give was exile, being forced to live out on your own.

Prepare to Start Over How do you put your life back together after a bug-out-worthy disaster? Very few people in modern times have had to bug out and then start their life over again. You

COOL TOOL

SET UP A BUG-OUT VEHICLE If you have to bug out, you're not having a good day. This is not some glorious movie scene where you drive your doomsday wagon down the road bathed in looks of shock and awe from bystanders. Bugging out means fleeing for your life. Now that the fantasy has been dispelled, let's have a real discussion about the things that would help you in an actual bug out vehicle.

Cargo Room Your supplies are your lifeline. They are also bulky and heavy, but they're worth every bit of weight and space. This makes cargo capacity a major factor.

4X4 All-wheel drive or a 4x4 option could mean the difference between getting out and getting stuck.

Ground Clearance You don't need a monster truck, but you don't need a low sports car either.

Passenger Room You should have enough room for your family or group.

Low Profile One more point to consider is blending in. If your vehicle has tools and cargo strapped all over it, others may be interested in the provisions you clearly have. Instead, maybe you should be driving something that looks like a work vehicle or a soccer mom mobile. You could still have all the post-apocalypse supplies you want, but this way you're not advertising it to the panicked masses.

need money, documentation of your identity, and a place to go. If your home was lost in a disaster, then you may be scrambling to find a new place to live. You may also need a new source of income as your money quickly runs out. In localized crisis situations, aid often floods in from other areas—but it's an uncharted territory to rebuild your life in the wake of mass destruction and casualties. Let's just hope we never have to find out how hard it could be to start all over again.

ON THE GRID

BUILD YOUR TEAM You could wait until things get tough to form your survival team. You'll also have no way to judge their competence or suitability to be your team members. Doesn't it make more sense to evaluate and choose your team members before thing go sideways? Make a truthful self-assessment. What are your leadership skills, survival skills, experience, and interpersonal skills? What skills do you have versus what skills are needed? Basic survival? Medical? Tactical? Communications? Food production? Etc? Next, define your intent. Is this a bug-out group, a neighborhood protection team, or something else? After these assessments, make a list of technical skills you want to look for in recruits. Identify and evaluate prospective team members. Once you have all this information, then you can form your team and train as a group.

INTO THE WILD

THE WILDERNESS CAN STILL BE JUST AS DEADLY TO US AS IT WAS TO OUR ANCESTORS. EXPOSURE, DEHYDRATION, INJURY, OR PREDATORS CAN STILL STRIKE IN WILD PLACES. SOMETIMES EMERGENCIES ARE YOUR FAULT; SOMETIMES NOT. BUT IT IS YOUR FAULT IF YOU DON'T PREPARE.

For most of this book, we've been talking about off-the-grid living as a choice—something you plan carefully, execute sensibly, and have the luxury of reevaluating as a choice if it doesn't go as planned. But what about the ultimate off-the-grid experience? The one where you've either been forced into the wilderness by natural disaster or social unrest or you accidentally wander away from your truly remote, OTG plot and can't get back before sundown. What then? Your thoughts and plans for survival should always begin with the survival priorities. This is a list of things you'd need to procure or accomplish during an emergency. This is essentially a "to do" list of all the chores you need to handle and the list starts with the most pressing threat to your survival. For many scenarios, we start with shelter; in a dire situation, you could die within hours without it. You can add in items like first aid and defense to the list as needed, but the basic rundown should almost always go: shelter, water, fire, food, and finally, signaling.

YOU'RE A SURVIVOR Your body is filled with safety systems and protective elements. From our physiology to our immune system, from our psychology to our mentality, we are hardwired for survival. Survivor mentality is made of many different facets. Positive outlook is key to feeling that we'll make it through our troubles. Mental toughness is another survival trait, helping us tolerate our situation and persevere. Our natural creativity and adaptability allow us to change and grow, learning and applying new information in helpful ways. Our motivation may be the most important aspect of the psychology of survival. When we identify the things that mean the most to us, we can hang onto them when situations are at their worst. So, what would motivate you to survive?

NEED TO KNOW

CALORIES ARE SURVIVAL
We constantly work to limit calorie loss during emergencies, while looking for opportunities to collect more calories (food). We can limit calorie loss in many ways. By investing a few hundred calories building a shelter, we stay warm at night and prevent the loss of thousands of calories due to shivering in the cold dark night. The cold can be one of the most ruthless thieves of our body's stored calories. People who become lost on a frigid landscape often suffer a fast and shocking weight loss. Even with warm bedding to sleep in and adequate clothing, your body has to rewarm a lot of tissue with each breath you take. This rewarming happens through your body's efforts to ramp up your metabolism for heat. This burns a lot of calories. Be smart about your calorie expenditures, and you'll live to tell the tale.

SHELTER FROM THE ELEMENTS As we've just noted, the first thing to think about when you realize you're going to be spending a night or more in the great outdoors is shelter, whether from something you've brought or something you need to improvise.

Bring Store-Bought Gear The easiest way to prepare for this critical need is to bring a tent, sleeping pad, and sleeping bag. Few shelters are as effective as these modern versions of tipis and fur blankets. But on the odd chance that your shelter isn't warm enough, add a hot water bottle to the mix. Get a one-liter bottle that doesn't leak, pour in boiling water, screw the lid down tight, and then slide the bottle into a sock. Sleep with this by your feet and you can stay warm all night, even well below the sleeping bag's rating.

BUILD IT YOURSELF A rustic hut made of sticks and leaves can work in a pinch, if you forget your tent and sleeping bag (or if a bear happens to steal them). Start by making a tripod from two forked sticks, each about 1 yard (0.9 m) in length, and another stout pole that's approximately 4 yards (3.6 m) long. Cover the two long sides with sticks, branches, or bark slabs to create ribs. Add insulation such as leaves, grasses, or pine needles (as seen in this illustration) until the walls of vegetation are

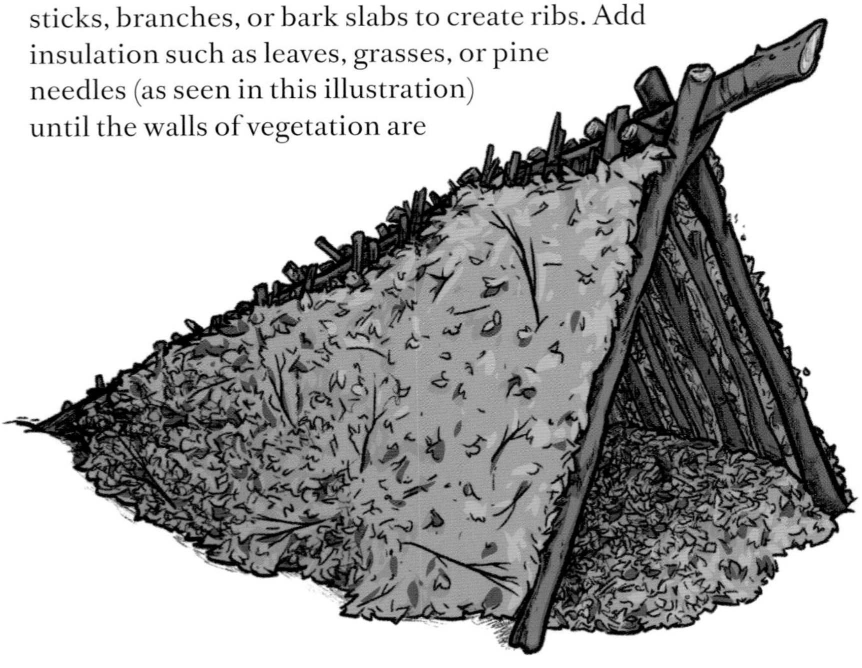

COOL TOOL

PACK A BLANKET Mylar thermal blankets, also known as space blankets, are a survivalist's dream: They're very light, fold down into a tiny package, resistant to rot or mildew and they retain heat incredibly well. They can keep you very warm in a bug-out or wilderness survival situation—and that's just the beginning of their uses. Here are just a few more ideas you can use them for.

Basic Shelter If you don't have a tarp, you can use a mylar blanket for a makeshift covering, or to insulate a shelter.

Heat Reflector That fire you've built can keep you even warmer if you make sure more of its heat gets to you. A space blanket as a nearby backdrop can help with that (just keep it far away enough that the heat doesn't melt it).

Fishing Lure The shiny mylar material definitely attracts the attention of fish; wrap some around the top of your hook or the weights on the line.

Rescue Signal Wrap some of the blanket material around trees or rocks to draw the eyes of rescue personnel, or lay it out on the ground so it can be seen from the air.

almost 1 yard (0.9 m) deep, and well over the top of the frame. Continue building the shelter by covering your insulation with light brush or branches in order to keep wind from stripping it away. Finally—and most critically—fill the inside of the shelter with even more vegetation for bedding, and crawl down inside. Repeat this stuff-and-pack procedure on the shelter's interior at least three or four times, and you're ready to bed down for the night. If you end up having to stay there for awhile, it helps to upgrade your surroundings, as well. Dig out a latrine on a downslope below your shelter's level (well away from any local water sources that you may need) and hang up your supplies high in a nearby tree to keep food and other survival materials away from animals or insects.

A TARP AND A LENGTH OF PARACORD CAN BE USED IN A PINCH TO MAKE A SIMPLE SHELTER. IT'S NOT THE WARMEST, BUT IT'D HELP KEEP YOU DRY AND BLOCK SOME OF THE WIND UNTIL YOU CAN BUILD SOMETHING MORE SUBSTANTIAL.

BARE MINIMUM

STUFF YOUR CLOTHING

You may not want to look like a scarecrow when lost in the middle of nowhere. But if it comes down to looking weird and staying alive, I think you'll take the scarecrow costume. Any kind of debris that makes for a snug, warm survival shelter can also be stuffed in your clothing for insulation. Add grass, leaves, moss, ferns, or other fluffy material to your clothes to increase their insulating value (and a bit of itching). Tuck your pants into your socks and fill your pants on all sides with vegetation. Then tuck your shirt into your pants and fill the front, back, and sleeves. You get bonus points for filling a hat or hood with debris as well. There are plenty of drawbacks to this system. For example, you'll be very uncomfortable, very likely find ticks or other bugs in the vegetation, and you'll no longer move quietly. But I'll bet you're willing to pay the price for survival.

OUT IN THE WILD When the going gets tough, even the tough need to take some extra measures. Here are some ideas for how to stay sheltered in some of the more extreme environments you might find yourself in.

Hide Out Under a Tree You can quickly make an effective snow shelter in a tree well (the depression in snow around a tree trunk formed by the protective canopy of branches above it). First, reinforce the natural enclosure by propping up additional branches around the lowest branches. Next, dig out the snow accumulated around the trunk. Finally, lay evergreen boughs on the floor to make a comfortable sleeping place that can be much warmer than the outside.

Dig a Snow Cave You don't have to spend a cold night in a hollowed-out tauntaun. Where snow has drifted into deep piles and frozen solid, an excellent shelter can be excavated with a shovel, large cooking pot, or even your gloved hands. Add ventilation holes and a "well" to give the colder air a place to fall. Use a backpack or block of snow for a door, and with any of these shelters, pile up a deep mattress of evergreen boughs or other insulating material.

Shelter in a Hammock In hot, wet areas, places filled with snakes and spiders, and in other spots where sleeping on the ground doesn't sound like a good idea, you can pitch a hammock camp. If you're lucky enough to have a manufactured hammock, string it between two strong trees. You can also improvise a hammock by tying up a tarp or some other tough fabric, using a sheet bend knot on each end. (See, knot tying is handy!) Once the hammock is in place—and you've tested it for strength if it's been improvised—string a tarp or some other rain cover over the hammock to keep out the weather and keep out creatures dropping from the trees. If you are concerned about ants, snakes, or spiders climbing down the hammock lines while you slumber, tie a rag around each hammock line, soaked in bug repellent, kerosene, or some other nasty substance that all creatures will shy away from.

Make Like a Caveman If you're in an area that has a cave, you may just be in luck; it's an insulated natural shelter! Just be sure that it's safe for you to be there before you set up your home away from home. A cave might be a home bears, wolves, or other animals. Smaller animals might also be unsafe because of any diseases they carry. A final note: Caves are vulnerable to a cave-in. If you see evidence of instability overhead, fresh rockfalls on the floor, or if there's water flowing through the cave, avoid it.

GOOD TO KNOW

ROCK ON Fighting the cold? Don't underestimate the power of hot rocks! Stones can hold a lot of heat, and radiate that warmth for a long time, if properly insulated. Start with rocks from a high, dry area. Never use rocks from a wet area. They may have trapped moisture which can cause them to explode. Skip glasslike or crystal filled stones and don't use slate or shale, which breaks into flaky slabs. Just use plain old rocks from a dry place. Heat a stone near the edge of a camp fire, so that it is toasty but safe for skin or bedding. It can stay warm for about an hour and you can even walk around with it. For a warm night, heat the stone to about the same temperature as scalding tap water. Wrap it in tough cloth or clothing, put it in your sleeping bag, and drift off to a warm slumber. I've had rocks remain warm as long as seven hours this way.

T/F

HIGH ALTITUDE STREAMS ARE SAFE TO DRINK

FALSE No ground water should ever be considered 100 percent safe. It's not usually all that hard to find water, but you must be sure it's pathogen-free. Except for springs from an underground aquifer, any ground water source can host bacteria, viruses, and protozoa. These organisms can cause symptoms such as diarrhea, vomiting, or dysentery, and even death. Worse still, some organisms such as fluke worms and other parasites can cause liver damage, lung ailments, and a host of odd diseases that are potentially fatal—and very hard to diagnose. Don't take chances or shortcuts with water. Consider all water to be contaminated and in need of disinfection.

STAYING HYDRATED Once shelter is secured, water becomes your next highest next priority, as you could only last a few days without it at the most. Water is always going to be more important than food, even if your empty stomach tries to tell you differently.

Finding Water Looking around the landscape is a great way to get started in survival water collection. Look for natural drainages where the water will flow. For most of the world, you'll simply need to walk downhill until you encounter a waterway. You can also local use vegetation as a water source indicator, looking out for reeds, cattails, sedges, and other aquatic vegetation in the distance. Listen, too, for the sounds of any aquatic animals such as water birds and bull frogs. Remember that rain, snow, sleet, hail, and dew can also be potential water sources. Always melt these (if they are frozen) and then treat them if they could have been contaminated, such as dew on plant surfaces or old snow. The last thing you need is to find a water source only to have waterborne illness strike.

Easy Treatment Store bought water filters are hard to beat for water treatment. Run the water through the unit (or suck it through, in the case of survival straws) and clean water will come out of the other end. Another option is purification tablets. These small pills release iodine or chlorine into water, killing harmful pathogens in the time listed on the product (usually 45 minutes to 4 hours). Boiling has always been a classic method of disinfection. Bring the water to a rolling boil for ten minutes and kiss your worries goodbye. If you happen to have household bleach, add 2 to 4 drops (5.25–6% sodium hypochlorite) per quart (0.9 l) of water. Use 2 drops if it's warm and clear. Try four drops if it is very cold or murky, or use three drops if it's in between. Shake the container for a minute and let a small amount of water flow out to clean the bottle threads and cap. Let it sit for 1 hour in the dark. When opened, it should smell like chlorine. If not, add another drop and wait 30 minutes. (Read your labels. Some bleach is now 8% sodium hypochlorite, so use only 2 to 3 drops.)

RECIPE FOR SUCCESS

MELT SNOW TO MAKE WATER Do you need drinking water, but you have found yourself stuck in a winter wonderland without a single free drop? You can still melt some snow or ice to meet your needs.

Remember that snow is highly expanded in volume compared to solid water (and even ice is expanded by up to about ten percent when water freezes solid) so you will need more snow than you think—you'll need roughly ten liters of snow to yield just one liter of liquid water. If you have it, add a little liquid water to a cooking pot over the fire, and begin adding snow to melt. Let the water warm up between each scoop of snow, and boil the water to disinfect it if it's old snow.

Even if you don't have a pot to melt ice or snow in, you can still get water another way. Begin by propping up a stone slab or a metal sheet over your campfire, and then make a channel of smaller stones at the center of that flat surface to hold the snow in place and direct runoff. Tilt the slab slightly so that, as the chunk of ice or snow melts, the resulting water drains into a container. This method allows you to keep the melting process going as long as needed—just use additional containers to capture more water.

Whatever method you end up using to get that essential water, you should always make sure that you purify it before drinking it. Snow may be white, but that doesn't by any means guarantee that it's going to be clean and safe for you to drink.

GOOD TO KNOW

BOIL WITH HOT STONES Heating water to boiling is easy when you have a campfire and a metal container. But how can you boil water to make it safe without the vessel? By heating rocks in a fire, then adding them to your container. The same rocks we can heat to stay warm can also boil water in odd containers. You can make containers from bark or wooden bowls, and then boil in them without putting them on a fire. For a gallon (3.8 l) of water, place two dozen egg-sized stones in a good campfire. After 30 to 45 minutes, scoop them out with green sticks, blow off the ashes, and drop the first one into your container of water. One at a time, these rocks will impart heat into the water without damaging your flammable, natural vessel. Replace the rock when it stops hissing. This also lets you boil in natural rock cavities, which of course, cannot be moved.

ESSENTIAL SKILL

BUILD A ONE-MATCH FIRE Even if you have a lighter, the techniques for starting a one-match fire will still give you the easiest fire you can make (without gasoline being involved). First, think about protecting your small flame from the wind. Many one match fires fail before the match even gets close to the fire lay. Use your body and hands to shield the infant flame of your match stick from the oncoming breeze. Start burning from the upwind side. This tactic allows air movement to push the heat and flames through your fire lay. Light it close and low. Strike your match very near to the bottom of the fire lay, so that it doesn't have to travel very far. You should be kneeling or sitting right next to your fire lay when the match is struck. Now, just stay still. Don't move that match around at all, until you finally get a spot engulfed in flame.

LIGHT MY FIRE In the wild places, you should always carry at least three methods of fire starting on your person at all times. This may sound like overkill at first, but imagine life without any fire at all! No cooking, no water boiling, no warmth, and no protection from predators in the gloom of night. Not fun.

Ignition Sources This particular group provides the initial flame or spark for you to start your fires. Butane lighters are a great choice. Waterproof or "survival" matches are a nice back-up (although there are many more fires in a lighter than in a matchbox). Ferrocerium rods can be a very good backup fire starter, but while they can light a number of materials on fire, they aren't capable of lighting everything. Smooth or solid tinder sources tend to bounce the spark off, rather than accepting them. This means that crumpled paper or thick dead leaves are difficult to light with a spark rod. Dry, fluffy, soft tinder sources will work much better. Depending on your situation, you'll need different ways of starting your fire.

Dry Fuel Sources These are dry materials, either fibrous or papery, that catch fire quickly. Some great choices are: Cotton balls, dryer lint, shredded inner tree bark, paper towels, and steel wool. Steel wool may sound like an odd choice, but it works amazingly well. It can be lit with sparks from a spark rod, or with electricity. Three volts or more will light up steel wool when you touch the material to the positive and negative terminals of a battery. 9-volt batteries are the best choice, because of the voltage and the close proximity of the negative and positive terminals.

Extended Fuel Sources This group consists of the waxy, oily, or greasy materials that will help your initial fire to become a long-lived flame: Vaseline (or any other similar type of petroleum jelly or oil), fire starting packets (such as Wetfire cubes or grill starter packets), candle wax, and the ancestral favorite found in nature, fatwood—a piece of resin-filled evergreen wood which can burn a long time and will do so even when it is wet.

LIGHT A FLAME IN THE RAIN It's cold, damp, windy, and you're in desperate need of heat and light. But how do you build a fire when it's raining? First, build your fire on a mound to avoid water pooling in a firepit. Gather as much light tinder as possible. Use fuel sources from evergreens, which have more flammable resin than other woods. Peel the bark or outer layers from wood and tinder to find the drier stuff inside. Build your fire upward to take advantage of rising heat, stay away from moisture, and shield the fire with your body by lighting it from the windward side.

MAKE FIRE IN THE SNOW The most challenging time to build a fire is when the ground is wet or covered with snow. Of course, that's when you are most in need of a fire's warmth. Use rocks or branches to isolate the fire's base from snow-covered or damp ground. Build your fire on a platform of stones or green logs laid tightly together so the updraft of warm air doesn't draw dampness from below. The higher and tighter the platform, the better. Get plenty of dry tinder, kindling, and fuel wood before attempting to light the fire. You don't want to scramble to keep the fire burning. Lay damp wood near the fire to dry it. If possible, protect the fire from precipitation by sheltering it from above, but avoid snow-laden or dripping tree limbs.

GOOD TO KNOW

SPLIT YOUR MATCHES

If you are down to your last paper match, there's a neat trick you can do to get two different fires from it: just split the match in half! Tear one free from the matchbook and gently start to peel the paper in half, starting from the torn bottom end of the match. Make sure that the split gives you equal paper on each side, otherwise you might find yourself just tearing off some of the paper before you've managed to truly split the match in half in its entirety. When your split reaches the chemical head, it should then pop into two pieces. Each of these "half-matches" will only have half the burn time of a regular paper match, but if you strike them carefully, each one will work just the same as a normal full sized match, and each should also be more than capable of starting dry, fluffy tinder ablaze and giving you a lifesaving fire.

GOOD TO KNOW

LEARN RESCUE SIGNALS
If you need to convey a message to rescuers, you don't need a radio. An internationally agreed-upon set of emergency ground/air signs can be a perfect way to call for help or let airborne viewers know where you are, where you're headed, or what you need. Here are just a few:

- **I** Require doctor--serious injury
- **II** Require medical supplie
- **X** Unable to proceed
- **☐** Require a map and compass
- **F** Require Food & Water
- **→** Proceeding this way
- **L** Require fuel and oil
- **LL** All well
- **N** No
- **Y** Yes
- **W** Require engineer
- **U** Message received
- **T** Land in this direction (from base to head of T)

GET ME OUT OF HERE! The final item on the survival priority list is signaling. That's because you can't signal for help if you've expired from thirst, cold, or exposure. But once the basic survival needs are handled, it's time to try and get some assistance. Of course this is dependent on just why you are out in the boonies to begin with, but assuming you're not on the run from insurgent forces or the walking dead, here's what to do.

Whistle While You Survive A ridiculously simple item, the signal whistle is an incredibly important piece of emergency equipment. As long as you have breath in your body, you can blow the whistle to catch the attention of search and rescue crews, or maybe a helpful passerby.

Make a Mirror Image If you have a vehicle in your survival situation, you have many mirrors you could use to signal for help. If there is no vehicle, you'd better have brought a mirror with you. Under ideal conditions, the sunlight bounced off a mirror will create a flash of light that can be spotted as far as 10 miles (16 km) away.

Light a Signal Fire A campfire is your best friend in the wild, when it is doing what it is supposed to do. Fire can be used as a very effective signal for help, with many documented successes over the past centuries. Remember that there is a fine line of control when lighting and maintaining big fires. This line is often imaginary, and it is actually controlled by the ambient humidity, the wind, and the amount of dry vegetation downwind of the blaze. Consider these important things about lighting signal fires.

First, the fire should be in a very visible place so that both the smoke and light are visible. Second, the fire should be in a place where it won't get away from you. The middle of the dried grasslands on a breezy day is a very bad place to burn a big fire. Third, don't let the fire get so big that you cannot put it out with the means you have at hand. Finally, think about contrast. Unless you have a ton of birch bark or pitch, every other natural material in the wild will produce a white smoke—hard to spot on a cloudy or foggy day.

REAL FLINT AND STEEL

I know that pop culture has programmed some of you to call a magnesium bar "flint" and to call a ferrocerium striker kit "flint and steel," but listen up! There's only one true "flint & steel" fire starting combo and it's not made out of high-tech material. The real flint and steel set is an early fire making technique that dates back to the first days of iron work in Europe and Asia. This fire starting method creates red-hot sparks by striking a piece of high carbon steel against a sharp, hard stone edge (such as a flake of flint). The high-carbon striker has to be carefully tempered to be soft enough for the stone to scrape off a tiny sliver, yet hard enough to resist denting it with each strike of the stone. To build a fire, these steel sparks are caught in fire charred material, then placed in dry tinder and blown into flame. This charred material can be made from cotton cloth or tinder you found in the woods. It just needs to be charred in a metal can or box for about six minutes, until black, but not burned up.

Smoke 'Em if You Got 'Em Want your signal fire to really stand out? Add plastic or other petroleum based products to the blaze. Throwing some motor oil, brake fluid, chunks of plastic, or pieces of a tire onto the fire will produce thick black smoke, which is much more noticeable.

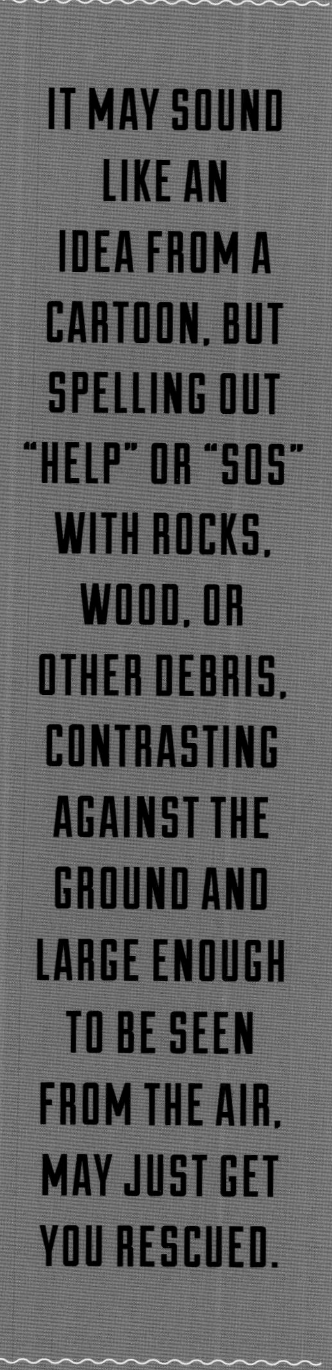

INDEX

U

V

W

Y

Z

ABOUT TIM MACWELCH

From growing his own veggies and raising his own livestock, to being a multiple *New York Times* bestselling author, Tim MacWelch is truly a modern day renaissance man. He is the author of the *Prepare for Anything Survival Manual*, the *Hunting & Gathering Survival Manual*, *How To Survive Anything*, and the *Ultimate Winter Survival Handbook*. He has also been an obsessed practitioner of survival and outdoor skills for over three decades, and he has been teaching the skills he loves for over two of those decades. Tim became interested in survival skills and woodcraft as a result of his experiences backpacking as a teen—while out in remote areas, it seemed like a smart plan to learn some skills. The majority of his training over the years has involved testing survival skills and devising new ones, but the biggest leaps forward came from his experience as a teacher.

Tim's diverse teaching experiences range from spending hundreds of hours volunteering with Boy Scouts, youth groups, summer camps, and more to working with and training adults in all walks of life. Tim and his school have been featured on *Good Morning America*, several *National Geographic* programs, and in many publications including *Conde Nast Traveler*, the *Washington Post*, *Business Insider*, and *American Survival Guide*.

Since late 2010, Tim has written hundreds of pieces for *Outdoor Life* magazine and many other publications. Tim's current and past articles and galleries can be found at outdoorlife.com and you can learn more about the offerings of his survival school on the web at www.advancedsurvivaltraining.com. When he's not teaching survival or writing about it, he lives a self-reliant lifestyle with his family in Virginia.

ABOUT OUTDOOR LIFE

Since it was founded in 1898, *Outdoor Life* has provided survival tips, wilderness skills, gear reports, and other essential information for hands-on outdoor enthusiasts. Each issue delivers the best advice in sportsmanship—as well as thrilling true-life tales, gear reviews, insider hunting, shooting, and fishing hints, and more—to nearly 1 million readers. Its survival-themed web site also covers disaster preparedness and the skills to thrive anywhere from the backcountry to the urban jungles.

ABOUT TIM MCDONAGH

Tim McDonagh spent his younger years growing up in a rural part of West Virginia, surrounded by rattlesnakes and snapping turtles, which in turn led to his fascination with animals. He takes a more traditional approach to illustration using brush and India ink to draw the image and then applying limited color palettes digitally. Tim now lives and works in Brighton, in the United Kingdom. His work has appeared in many publications, including *WIRED* magazine, *Variety*, *Entertainment Weekly*, and *Mojo*.

FROM THE AUTHOR

I'd like to dedicate this book to all of the wonderful people around the world who are taking the leap of faith and living off the grid. These impressive displays of independence proves to me that the human spirit isn't dead, it's just gravely ill—and we can make it well again. For those of you who have chosen a path of toil to live a more meaningful and sustainable lifestyle, I hope that nature rewards you accordingly. Keep walking the talk!

I'd also like to take this opportunity to thank my teammates at *Outdoor Life* magazine, Bonnier Corporation, and of course, Weldon Owen Publishing. To Mariah Bear, my editor, thank you for sharing stories of your off-grid upbringing with me (and your editorial skills). Thanks also to Ian Cannon for all of your help on this book and to Allister Fein for his design expertise and creative ideas. And a round of thanks to our artists, Tim McDonagh and Conor Buckley. You gentlemen have outdone yourselves! Finally, I thank you, our readers. Thanks for buying our books, telling others about them, and putting these skills into practice. Remember, self-sufficient living isn't a step backward—it's a step in the right direction.

CREDITS

ILLUSTRATIONS courtesy of **TIM MCDONAGH** (Cover, 1, 2-3, 4, 5, 6, 14, 16, 19, 21, 22, 24, 28, 30, 34, 37, 41, 42, 45, 46, 51, 56, 61, 64, 66, 71, 72, 81, 86-87, 90, 94, 98, 104, 112,114,117, 118, 122, 126, 127, 130, 132, 134,135, 138, 139, 140, 141, 146,149, 156, 160,168, 169, 173, 174, 179, 183, 187, 188, 190, 193, 202, ,204, 222, and 223) and **CONOR BUCKLEY** (27, 29, 30, 31, 32, 33, 38-39, 43, 48, 49, 52, 55, 59, 74, 77, 79, 82, 83, 84, 89, 93, 95, 97, 103, 106, 108-109, 111, 115, 136, 143, 145,150, 152-153, 155, 155, 158, 164-165, 167, 170-171, 176, 181, 184-185, 196-197, 200, 206, 208, 209, 211, 213, and 215.)

weldon**owen**

PRESIDENT, PUBLISHER Roger Shaw
SVP, SALES & MARKETING Amy Kaneko
FINANCE MANAGER Philip Paulick
ASSOCIATE PUBLISHER Mariah Bear
EDITOR Ian Cannon
CREATIVE DIRECTOR Kelly Booth
ART DIRECTOR Allister Fein
DESIGNER Fortuitous Publishing
PRODUCTION DIRECTOR Chris Hemesath
ASSOCIATE PRODUCTION DIRECTOR Michelle Duggan
DIRECTOR OF ENTERPRISE SYSTEMS Shawn Macey
IMAGING MANAGER Don Hill

Weldon Owen is a division of
Bonnier Publishing USA
1045 Sansome St, Suite 100
San Francisco, CA 94111
weldonowen.com

Weldon Owen would like to thank Bridget Fitzgerald for helping to shape this project in its early days, Brittany Bogan for editorial assistance, and Kevin Broccoli of BIM Creatives for the index.

Library of Congress Control Number on file with the publisher.

ISBN 13: 978-1-68188-152-2
ISBN 10: 1-68188-152-7
10 9 8 7 6 5 4 3
2016 2017 2018 2019
Printed in China by 1010 Printing International

OUTDOOR LIFE

CHIEF EXECUTIVE OFFICER Eric Zinczenko
VP, PUBLISHING DIRECTOR Gregory D. Gatto
EDITORIAL DIRECTOR Anthony Licata
EDITOR-IN-CHIEF Andrew McKean
MANAGING EDITOR Jean McKenna
SENIOR DEPUTY EDITOR John B. Snow
DEPUTY EDITOR Gerry Bethge
ASSISTANT MANAGING EDITOR Margaret M. Nussey
ASSISTANT EDITOR Natalie Krebs
SENIOR ADMINISTRATIVE ASSISTANT Maribel Martin
DESIGN DIRECTOR Sean Johnston
ART DIRECTOR Brian Strubel
ASSOCIATE ART DIRECTORS Russ Smith & James A. Walsh
PHOTOGRAPHY DIRECTOR John Toolan
PHOTO EDITOR Justin Appenzeller
PRODUCTION MANAGER Judith Weber
DIGITAL DIRECTOR Nate Matthews
ONLINE CONTENT EDITOR Alex Robinson

2 Park Avenue
New York, NY 10016
www.outdoorlife.com